International Political Economy Series

Series editor
Timothy M. Shaw
Visiting Professor
University of Massachusetts Boston, USA, and
Emeritus Professor at the University of London, UK

The global political economy is in flux as a series of cumulative crises impacts its organization and governance. The IPE series has tracked its development in both analysis and structure over the last three decades. It has always had a concentration on the global South. Now the South increasingly challenges the North as the centre of development, also reflected in a growing number of submissions and publications on indebted Eurozone economies in Southern Europe. An indispensable resource for scholars and researchers, the series examines a variety of capitalisms and connections by focusing on emerging economies, companies and sectors, debates and policies. It informs diverse policy communities as the established trans-Atlantic North declines and 'the rest', especially the BRICS, rise.

More information about this series at
http://www.springer.com/series/13996

Christopher Wylde

Emerging Markets and the State

Developmentalism in the 21st Century

palgrave
macmillan

Christopher Wylde
School of Communications,
Arts & Social Science
Richmond, the American International
University in London
Richmond, Surrey, UK

International Political Economy Series
ISBN 978-1-137-55654-7 ISBN 978-1-137-55655-4 (eBook)
DOI 10.1057/978-1-137-55655-4

Library of Congress Control Number: 2017939610

Printed on acid-free paper

This Palgrave Macmillan imprint is published by Springer Nature
The registered company is Macmillan Publishers Ltd.
The registered company address is: The Campus, 4 Crinan Street, London, N1 9XW, United Kingdom

For my Nephew and Nieces: Billy, Charlotte, and Isabelita

Contents

1	Emerging Markets and States of Development	1
2	The Role of the State in Development	15
3	Globalisation, the State, and Development	43
4	Developmental Regimes in the 21st Century	71
5	Argentina Under the Kirchner Administrations	97
6	Argentina's Developmental Regime	129
7	Malaysian Development Since Independence	159
8	Malaysia's Developmental Regime	185
9	Developmental Regimes and Emerging Markets	211
Bibliography		223
Index		225

List of Figures

Fig. 5.1 Argentine GDP and GDP per Capita in current US$, 1989–2014. *Source* World Bank (2016) 103
Fig. 5.2 Exports by type of good in Argentina, 1989–2006 (US$bn). *Source* Bezchinsky et al. (2007) 107

List of Tables

Table 1.1 Average annual rates of GDP growth, 1970–2015, select aggregates 2
Table 1.2 Average annual rates of GDP growth, 1970–2015, select countries 3
Table 1.3 Average annual rates of GDP growth 1997–2015, Argentina and Malaysia 9
Table 5.1 Macroeconomic indicators during the crisis period 98
Table 5.2 Individual poverty and indigence (%) in Argentina in selected regions, 2001–2003 99
Table 5.3 Social indicators under the Kirchner administration 114
Table 5.4 Minimum wage compared to the basic basket of goods for a typical family (constant pesos) 115
Table 5.5 Key economic indicators in Argentina 2008–2014 117
Table 6.1 Key economic indicators in Argentina 2003–2014 132
Table 7.1 Select economic indicators for Malaysia, 1975–1997 162
Table 7.2 Structure of Malaysian merchandise exports (percentage), select years 163
Table 7.3 Post-crisis economic indicators in Malaysia 1998–2010 171
Table 7.4 Select economic indicators for contemporary Malaysia 174

CHAPTER 1

Emerging Markets and States of Development

Development theory is about how positive change in society can be shaped and managed. However, one chooses to define development: the processes of development in human societies always involve the organisation, mobilisation, combination, use, and distribution of resources in new ways; it is a historical change process (Kothari 2005). This process is fundamentally political. Because resources are being produced and distributed in different ways, decisions must be made by individuals and different social groups about how such resources are to be used. The presence of power in these (non-)decisions means that development is inescapably political rather than managerial or administrative (Leftwich 2000).

In the context of catch-up development, the single most influential actor, at least in the modern historical period, has been the state. As an entity, it has both the capacity and the autonomy to act in ways that shape positive societal change. However, this influence has not always been beneficial to development, and in all too many instances has actually been inimical to it. The core concern of this book is to further evolve and develop our understanding of the state's role in the development process, more specifically to induce an analytical framework for understanding capitalist states at early stages of development and why they follow certain (non-)developmental trajectories rather than others.

Such a task is important. If measured narrowly as increases in GDP per capita, the record of development from the 1970s onwards can be described as lacklustre at best, and outright disastrous for certain areas

C. Wylde, *Emerging Markets and the State*, International Political Economy Series, DOI 10.1057/978-1-137-55655-4_1

(see Table 1.1). Low-income countries have barely registered any growth at all, averaging just 0.6% between 1970 and 2016. This has often been accompanied by high rates of poverty and sometimes by soaring inequalities. This means that by these conventional measures, most people in low-income countries have registered barely any material improvement in their lives over almost the last 50 years.

Despite the 'third wave' (Huntington 1991; Grugel 2007) of democratisatio, various colour-coded 'revolutions', and the Arab Spring (followed by an Islamic Winter), many political systems have been all too prone to crisis and disorder. Mass atrocities and abuse of human rights have regularly occurred. Simultaneously, pervasive and sometimes spectacular corruption has become embedded in societies. This has spawned a plethora of critical literature and traditions academically, a vast array of non-governmental organisations (NGOs) in (international) civil society and associated 'grey' literature, and millions of column inches in the media, all trying to understand the nature of development, in terms of both means and ends.

It is important to recall in the midst of this avalanche of material that a number of societies in the developing world have achieved and sustained some quite remarkable developmental achievements in the last 50 years. Table 1.2 shows, in the cases of China, Singapore, Korea, or Botswana, for example, that this story of a cycle of torpor and lacklustre economic growth need not necessarily be the case. Although not as ubiquitous as they should be, successful examples of catch-up

Table 1.1 Average annual rates of GDP growth, 1970–2015, select aggregates

Country	*Per capita GDP growth (mean)*
Sub-Saharan Africa (excluding high income)	0.6
Latin America & Caribbean (excluding high income)	1.6
East Asia & Pacific (excluding high income)	6.5
South Asia	3.3
Arab World	1.5
OECD members	1.8
World	1.6
High income	1.9
Middle income	2.9
Low income	0.6

Source Author's elaboration of World Bank (2016) and OECD (2016) data

Table 1.2 Average annual rates of GDP growth, 1970–2015, select countries

Country	*Per capita GDP growth (mean)*
Indonesia	4.1
Malaysia	3.9
China	8.0
Thailand	4.3
Korea, Rep.	6.0
Singapore	5.0
Botswana	5.7
Argentina	1.3
Chile	2.8
Brazil	2.1

Source Author's elaboration of World Bank (2016) and OECD (2016) data

development exist in the historical record. Each of these cases has strong sui generis arguments surrounding our understandings of their success. Some have questionable human and civil rights records. However, they offer up cases of high-growth economies amidst this more general story of stagnation who have pursued (with the notable exception of China)—at different speeds and different directions—democratisation.

These cases represent the starting point of this book. Through appropriate empirical work—both primary and secondary—the cases of Malaysia and Argentina will be used to inductively demonstrate that through the application of a Developmental Regime framework, an appropriate understanding of the form and nature of state-led development in the context of 21st century globalising societies can be reached. In the context of a rapidly changing global political economy, there is clearly a need to maintain and refresh our understandings of societies, how they organise themselves, and the conditions under which they exist. This has significant implications for the discipline of political economy of development specifically and development theory more broadly, implications that this book seeks to explore.

Emerging Markets

The term that has become fashionable, particularly in the world of finance, to collectively understand these cases is 'emerging markets'. This is a long period of gestation, with the term first being used in the 1980s by the World Bank. Emerging markets stand in contrast to developed markets, and it is through this dichotomy that a number of assumptions implicit within the term become apparent. First, the term implies convergence with developed markets; relatively better performance, sustained over time. Second, convergence also implies some of the most egregious aspects of contemporary development theory: that development is essentially a technical problem that must be overcome in order to facilitate every state in the world becoming an advanced capitalist country grounded in an Anglo-Saxon model of capital accumulation. Third, ultimate success is understood in terms of moving from emerging market status to developed market status. Fourth, this 'success' is to be achieved through the pursuit of a liberal market model—preferably democratic—of free-flowing capital and trade. This was not the model pursued by any contemporary developed market in order to achieve their own status.

This term clearly needs to be problematised and nuanced in order to provide any analytical leverage. Emerging markets undergo processes of development in different fashions and according to different sets of priorities. One way of making sense of these is through an application of the framework of governance. Governance is concerned with the 'social and economic, as well as political, processes by which power and influence are put into practice, outcomes are shaped and decisions made and implemented, and broad social, political, and economic trends managed and controlled by a range of actors' (Cerny 2014: 48). Governance can come in a form that academia has collectively termed developmentalism: state involvement in the industrialisation and development process in order to nurture it in ways that will speed that process up. Multiple possibilities exist, grounded in different modes of capital accumulation and different constellations of sociopolitical relationships themselves the result of crosscutting priorities. These social relations can be found in patterns of class, ethnicity, religion, status, gender, or nationalism. Complex webs of power structures and patterns of social domination must be accurately mapped in order to help unlock important and urgent lessons.

This book will argue that a deeper understanding of emerging markets that pursue a developmentalist path can be achieved through the application of a Developmental Regime framework. Such a framework moves beyond the simple dichotomisation of the globe between developed and emerging markets. Instead, it embraces the rich tapestry of different historical trajectories and seeks understanding through application of an induced theoretical framework. The next section will set out specifically and systematically the central claims that this book will make.

The Arguments of the Book

The first core argument of this book is that understanding the state is important in our understanding of development. Reductionist understandings of globalisation meaning the retreat of the state (Ohmae 1995) engage more in the politics of globalisation, rather than the globalisation of politics (Hay and Marsh 2000). It is often all too convenient to make a deductive explanation of (international) politics through a crude application of 'more globalisation must mean less state'. It is true that the hegemony of a neoliberal paradigm in development thinking has led to the dismantling of many state capacities; this does not imply in any way an *analytical* shift in focus from the state. The state acts as a unique site of social cohesion and a coalescing of social forces. The state must therefore be understood as a social relation (see, e.g., Jessop 2016). When combined with a Strategic-Relational Approach (Jessop 2016), this allows us to see the state as a condensation of a changing balance of class forces (Jessop 2002: 195).

It follows that tracing the contours of state capacity and (relative) autonomy involves developing an understanding of the exercise of social power. This is the second core argument of the book: understanding the state requires an understanding of power. When power is seen in terms of social domination expressed through class, ethnic, religious, patriarchal, and other forms, it becomes imperative to map the terrain of these forces in the shaping of any state project, for the purposes of this book a state project of developmentalism and catch-up industrialisation. This again follows a Strategic-Relational Approach, with an essential understanding of structure and agency in the social world to be one characterised by mutual (re)constitution.

A third core argument is that this understanding of power must incorporate an understanding of multilevel governance, in an era characterised by globalisation. The argument moves away from false dichotomies such as state and market, instead embracing the concept of structuration (Hay 2014) to understand the ways in which the state operates within a constellation of levels of governance. Through an application of World Order (Cox 1981), a specific understanding of the stratified social ontology that accompanies this can be reached. This understanding offers a key role for the state: for it is the site of international hegemony and subsequent World Order. In addition, key institutional vehicles for this hegemony—international organisation—can be seen not to dictate, rather shape international development policy through facilitating a 'political economy of the possible' (Santiso 2006) in terms of discrete state projects of a developmentalist nature.

A fourth core argument is that a Developmental Regime approach is best placed to facilitate an analytical framework for understanding capitalist states at early-to-middling stages of development, and why they follow certain development trajectories rather than others. A 'regime tripod' image is developed, the legs of which are socio-economic relations, institutions, and public policy profiles. Socio-economic relations and institutions have a complex relationship that facilitates an understanding of the shaping of state capacity and autonomy—concepts key to the understanding of developmentalism. From this complex interaction emerges a distinct public policy profile: a suite of developmental policies specifically tailored to facilitate catch-up development for emerging markets. That is not to say there is some kind of blueprint for development. Not only can such grand projects be critiqued for assuming a single, reified Archimedean standpoint (see, e.g., Esteva 2010), it is also clear that the owl of Minerva can only spread its wings at the falling of the dusk (Hegel 1820/1952).

Instead, the Developmental Regime offers a framework for understanding states trying to develop in a globalising world characterised by the hegemony of neoliberal World Order. These development paths are inevitably sui generis, because they emerge from the historical structures in which they are grounded. The unique processes of institutionalisation and attendant balance of social forces in any given state can forge a developmental autonomy that is more successful the greater the capacity for doing so. The Developmental Regime approach facilitates a clear understanding of the main forces at play in the process, as well as their interaction.

Empirically, this book argues that Argentina under the Kirchners' pursued a neo-developmentalist agenda that represented a bending and moulding of previous models of capital accumulation. In the Argentine example, this means a forging of a new social contract between the state and the people through a judicious blending of Peronism, neoliberalism, and (neo)developmentalism. This has been labelled 21st century Peronism for a globalising world (Wylde 2011: 449). Analysed in terms of what

Svampa (2014) called the 'four moments', this book will seek to demonstrate that the Kirchner years can best be understood through the application of a Developmental Regime approach.

Malaysia since the Asian Financial Crisis has struggled to recover the levels of growth seen before the crisis, in the context of an increasingly restless civil society that is confronting an increasingly belligerent political class. The ethnic politics that dominates Malaysia is very different to that of Argentina. Nevertheless, through an understanding of social power in broader ontological terms, and subsequent theorisation of the state and attendant institutions at different spatial levels of analysis, the Developmental Regime approach will reveal the interaction of Malaysian capacity and autonomy that has facilitated a developmentalist agenda in this former British colony.

The Methodology of the Book

Theoretically, this book follows an inductive approach. That is, analysis begins with understanding empirical phenomena and then followed with a process of inducing theoretical frameworks from this. This stands in contrast to deductive theoretical reasoning; more closely related to the scientific method and involving hypothesising based on law-like generalisations about how we think the world works. This will lead to somewhat of a theoretical hybridity to understand the complex and empirically rich social world. Throughout the book, the argument will be developed that this is actually an analytical strength: embracing the complexity of social processes and the fundamentally contingent nature of these constellations across both time and space. Theory, or the Developmental Regime approach in terms of this book, becomes a heuristic for understanding Argentina, Malaysia, and emerging markets in general.

In this study of the political economy of development, such heuristic devices must be drawn from the discipline of political economy as a whole. The dominant economic ideology of the early twentieth century sought to restrict both economic reality and economic thinking through a separation of politics from economics. Subsequent critiques of *laissez-faire* capitalism, most notably the birth of Keynesian economics, showed that the free market economy may not be able to achieve an optimal resource allocation at the full employment level of output, thus justifying the practice of active budgetary policy; this required that economics as a discipline (re)acknowledge the role of the state, thereby (re)opening the possibility of the study of *political* economy. In the quarter-century after the Second World War, the so-called Golden Age of Capitalism, interventionist policies were highly successful across the world and firmly established the state as an important and often leading actor in the functioning of the economy. In the advanced capitalist countries, or core, this led to Keynesianism or social democracy; in the developing world, or periphery, to more intervention due to the influence of dependency and structuralism. The collapse of the 'Golden Age' from the late 1960s onwards paved the way for the monetarist critique of Keynesianism and later the rise of neoliberalism. The neoliberal revival represented a partial return to the nineteenth-century *laissez-faire* tradition, supplemented by an emphasis on the limited transferability of knowledge and the role of entrepreneurship.

How should these shifts in the meanings and interpretations of political economy be accounted for? One way to do this is to 'treat this kind of genealogy of development discourse as a deconstruction of development, i.e. as part of a development critique' (Pieterse 2000: 199). Thus, each development theory offers 'a *Gestalt* of development, a total picture from a particular angle, then the array of successive and rival development theories offers a kaleidoscopic view into the collective mirror' (ibid.: 200). The main contours of development thinking can be mapped across different periods, and furthermore can be placed in the context of the pattern of hegemony in international relations and the structures of explanation prevalent at that time.

Development thinking and policy becomes a terrain of hegemony and counter-hegemony (Pieterse 2000: 201). By focusing on the empirical aspects of discrete developmental projects through methods associated with both qualitative and quantitative approaches, this book offers an analysis that seeks to overcome merely reflecting contemporary hegemonic thinking in the political economy of development. Notwithstanding an inevitable Foucauldian backlash associated with a lack of appreciation of the nature of hegemony in knowledge and the mind, a hybrid approach to theory as a result of placing empirical analysis at the start of the process should overcome this temptation.

On Argentina and Malaysia

The choice of Argentina and Malaysia as case studies is for a number of reasons. First, both countries have been represented and understood in the literature through the common lens of developmentalism. In the context of Malaysia this has been from within the Developmental State tradition (see, e.g., Low 2004), even if it has been to characterise the South-East Asian country as a 'paper tiger' (Jomo 2003). In the context of Argentina, this has been historically from the *desarrollismo* tradition associated with ECLA and its 'dependency' critique (see, e.g., Dos Santos 1971), but more recently from a *neodesarrollismo* paradigm (Katz 2006) or Developmental Regime perspective (Wylde 2012, 2014, 2016). This has meant a common history and lexicon of state-driven development, albeit from inevitably different histories and contexts.

From 1997 onwards, these countries have experienced percentage increases in GDP per capita that exceed comparable averages in large parts of the developing world (see Table 1.3). In Argentina's case, this is in spite of severe economic dislocation and crisis in 2001, with a deep, albeit short-lived, recession afterwards. These states are not extremely poor, although there is plenty of extreme poverty in both states. They have undergone historical waves of industrialisation, although both contain strong agrarian and agricultural elements to their economies and societies. They could both be understood as middling-income states, which have at different stages in their history and in different ways attempted to drive the industrialisation process through the state. Argentina and Malaysia have both been buffeted by international economic headwinds emerging from global processes. From the 1980s debt crisis in Latin America to the Asian financial crisis of 1997, through to the global financial crisis of 2007, both states have endured (negative) influences on the nature of their national development projects and their concomitant ability to forge an independent development trajectory.

Table 1.3 Average annual rates of GDP growth 1997–2015, Argentina and Malaysia

Country	*Per capita GDP growth (mean)*
Argentina	3.1
Malaysia	2.7
Latin America & Caribbean (excluding high income)	1.6
Sub-Saharan Africa (excluding high income)	2.0

Source Author's elaboration of World Bank (2016)

Argentina and Malaysia are also embedded in geographical regions that, on the whole, are poorer and less developed. Malaysia has the highest GDP per capital in South-East Asia if the oil-rich micro-state of Brunei is excluded (World Bank 2016). Argentina has the highest HDI in Latin America (UNDP 2015). Whilst there are clearly cases of development success in Latin America and South-East Asia beyond these two countries, they nevertheless represent leading examples of emerging markets in their respective geographical regions.

In these senses, Argentina and Malaysia represent emblematic cases of developmentalism in the Global South. Their selection represents an opportunity to develop a robust understanding of state-led developmentalism in the 21st century. This will be a challenge, as these cases are not 'cherry-picked' based on deductive techniques; rather, they are in many ways fundamentally different societies, with different histories, regional contexts, experiences of (de)colonisation, and contemporary insertion into the international division of labour. This represents first an empirical challenge and second a more analytical challenge, which is to induce robust theoretical understandings of the state and developmentalism in order to further develop and refresh our understanding of these processes in the 21st century.

The Structure of the Book

After this introduction, Chap. 2 seeks to understand the role of the state in development, and how this has changed over time. In so doing, it will develop an understanding of this evolution through distillation into the twin concepts of capacity and autonomy. This will reject a more traditional states-versus-markets approach. The Developmental State literature will be shown to be in need of refreshing in the context of 21st century developmentalism in a number of important ways: first, the need to understand states in a more nuanced and relational sense as a result of a conception of power as social domination; and second, to recognise the theoretical possibility of developmental processes that go beyond a narrow 'embedded autonomy' (Evans 1995). Rather, the *relative* autonomy of a state can be explained as a distillation of a constellation of social forces, which are shaped by different manifestations of social domination: from class, to gender, to ethnicity. This relative autonomy in turn facilitates the political space for state projects grounded in a developmental agenda.

A third point of critique of the original Developmental State literature is the failure to systemically integrate a robust theory of how the state interacts with the forces of globalisation. This task will be completed in Chap. 3. The concept of structuration (Hay 2014) will be introduced. In the context of a stratified social ontology, this will be augmented with Cox's (1981) understanding of World Order in order to show that whilst emerging markets operate within changing confines induced by globalisation, there is scope for the state to forge a relative autonomy not only in the context of domestic societies but also international forces as well. It is within this relatively autonomous space that state projects of developmentalism are forged.

Chapter 4 will draw all of this critique together to produce a framework for understanding 21st century developmentalism: the Developmental Regime. This regime is stabilised through three legs of a tripod: socio-economic relations, institutions, and public policy profiles. This chapter will explore each of these, through a condensation of many of the arguments made in the preceding chapters. Each leg of the tripod will be analysed in turn, with appropriate attention also being paid to their interactions and interrelationships. This will also facilitate, by way of example, the sketching out of common constellations of social relations, institutions, and public policy profiles to be found in analytical labels such as neoliberal states or developmental states/regimes.

Chapter 5 will begin the case study section of the book through an analysis of the Kirchner years (2003–2015) in Argentina. Structured around Svampa's (2014) 'Four Moments', this chapter offers an empirical account of the evolution of Argentine political economy in the post crisis administrations of Nestor Kirchner and Cristina Fernandez de Kirchner (CFK hereafter). It will show an initially successful post-crisis regime that, through a series of internal and external shocks, spirals back into the relative torpor that seems to be the norm in the developing world (see Table 1.1). Chapter 6 will apply the Developmental Regime framework to the case presented in the preceding chapter. It will trace the contours of Argentine political economy and attendant changes in development trajectory through a framework grounded in the regime tripod: socio-economic relations, institutions, and public policy profiles. From this analysis, our understanding of both contemporary Argentine political economy and the nature of 21st century developmentalism will be enhanced.

Chapter 7 will analyse the case of Malaysia. It will demonstrate an understanding of its development trajectory in terms of oscillations between goals of GDP growth and redistribution, in order to maintain both. Split into four sections, each analyses the contemporary development path through exposition of key strategies and policies of the state. It will show that rising ethnic tensions since its independence in 1957 led to a focus on redistribution to ethnic Malays through a series of positive-discrimination policies combined with state-driven industrialisation. After recession in 1985, this turned towards increasing liberalisation in order to reignite GDP growth, and then back to a redistributive emphasis in the context of the aftermath of the Asian financial crisis. The chapter finishes with a final section that analyses current development policy in the context of recent trends, not least the global financial crisis.

Chapter 8 will once again apply the Developmental Regime framework, this time to the case of Malaysia. This will not only shed further analytical light on the previous chapter, but also cement an understanding of Malaysian developmentalism. Simultaneously, when combined with the empirical analysis of Argentina and the theoretical work conducted in the first half of the book, the final conclusions chapter will drive home the overarching argument of this book: that a Developmental Regime framework facilitates deeper understanding of the form and nature of 21st century developmentalism in emerging markets who operate under the aegis of neoliberal globalisation. This understanding reveals greater scope for the development of appropriate capacities and autonomy for successful, state-led catch-up development.

References

Cerny, P. (2014). Neoliberalism: Alive and well? *International Studies Review, 16*(4), 645–646.

Cox, R. (1981). Social forces states, and world orders: Beyond international relations theory. *Millennium: Journal of International Studies, 10*(2), 126–155.

Dos Santos, T. (1971). The structure of dependence. *American Economic Review, 60,* 231–236.

Esteva, G. (2010). Development. In W. Sachs (Ed.), *The development dictionary: A guide to knowledge as power.* London: Zed.

Evans, P. (1995). *Embedded autonomy: States and industrial transformation.* Princeton: Princeton University Press.

Grugel, J. (2007). Latin America after the third wave. *Government and Opposition, 42*(2), 242–249.

Hay, C. (2014). Levels of governance and their interaction. In A. Payne & N. Phillips (Eds.), *The handbook of the international political economy of governance*. Cheltenham: Edward Elgar.

Hay, C., & Marsh, D. (2000). Introduction: Demystifying globalization. In C. Hay & D. Marsh (Eds.), *Demystifying globalisation* (pp. 1–17). Hampshire: Palgrave Macmillan.

Hegel, G. W. F. (1820/1952). *The Philosophy of Right*. London: Clarendon Press.

Huntington, S. P. (1991). Democracy's third wave. *Journal of democracy, 2*(2), 12–34.

Jessop, B. (2002). Globalisation and the national state. In S. Aaronowitz & P. Bratsis (Eds.), *Paradigm lost: State theory reconsidered* (pp. 185–220). Minnesota: University of Minnesota Press.

Jessop, B. (2016). *The state: Past, present, and future*. London: Polity.

Jomo, K. S. (2003). *Southeast Asian paper tigers? From miracle to debacle and beyond*. London: RoutledgeCurzon.

Katz, C. (2006, April 19). Las tendencias de la economia Argentina. *Argenpress*. http://rebelion.org/docs/25473.pdf. Accessed 16 August 2016.

Kothari, U. (2005). A radical history of development studies: Individuals, institutions and ideologies. In U. Kothari (Ed.), *A radical history of development studies*. London: Zed Books.

Leftwich, A. (2000). *States of development: On the primacy of politics in development*. London: Polity.

Low, L. (2004). *Developmental states: Relevancy, redundancy, or reconfiguration?* New York: Nova Science.

OECD. (2016, April 8). *OECD factbook 2015–2016: Economic, environmental and social statistics*. http://dx.doi.org/10.1787/factbook-2015-en. Accessed 25 July 2016.

Ohmae, K. (1995). *The end of the nation state*. New York: Simon and Schuster.

Pieterse, J. N. (2000). Trends in development theory. In R. Palan (Ed.), *Global political economy: Contemporary theories* (pp. 197–214). London: Routledge.

Santiso, J. (2006). *Latin America's political economy of the possible*. Massachusetts: MIT Press.

Svampa, M. (2014). Revisiting Argentina 2001–2013: From *"¡Que se vayan todos!"* to the peronist decade. In C. Levey, D. Ozarow, & C. Wylde (Eds.), *Argentina since the 2001 crisis: Recovering the past, reclaiming the future* (pp. 155–175). New York: Palgrave Macmillan.

UNDP. (2015). *Work for human development*. New York: UNDP.

World Bank. (2016). *World development indicators*. www.worldbank.org. Accessed 5 August 2016.

Wylde, C. (2011). State, society, and markets in Argentina: The political economy of *Neodesarrollismo* under Nestor Kirchner, 2003–2007. *Bulletin of Latin American Research, 30*(4), 436–452.

Wylde, C. (2012). *Latin America after neoliberalism: Developmental regimes in post-crisis states.* Basingstoke: Palgrave Macmillan.

Wylde, C. (2014). The developmental state is dead, long live the developmental regime! Interpreting Nestór Kirchner's Argentina 2003–2007. *Journal of International Relations and Development, 17*(2), 191–219.

Wylde, C. (2016). Post-neoliberal developmental regimes in Latin America: Argentina under Cristina Fernandez de Kirchner. *New Political Economy, 21*(3), 322–341.

CHAPTER 2

The Role of the State in Development

Conventionally, the concept of development has been equated with economic growth. As a result, mainstream literature—both academic and in the media—has viewed development as a fundamentally economic, perhaps even technocratic process. This book argues that development must be understood in much broader terms, as a historical change process (Kothari 2005: 5; see also Wylde 2012). It is the nature of this change that facilitates the marshalling of different resources to enact new ways to promote growth and welfare. After all, to paraphrase a popular analogy, growth on its own is simply about a bigger pie; development is about changing the very contents, make-up, and distribution of that pie—as well as growing its size. How is this intensely complex task to be undertaken, managed, and coordinated? (Neo)liberalism broadly states that this will happen spontaneously, a concept popularised by Adam Smith's 'invisible hand' of the market (Smith 1880/1776: 28). This book will argue that development does not happen *solely* of its own accord, and certainly not with the speed and continuity that is required if a real and sustained improvement in human welfare is to be achieved in the course of a generation. As Adrian Leftwich (2000: 7) noted: '…what is required is a central coordinating intelligence or coordinating capacity which can steer, push, cajole, persuade, entice, coordinate and at times instruct the wide range of economic agents and their groupings to go this way instead of that, to do this and not that, and which itself can act here or when private agents either cannot or will not'.

C. Wylde, *Emerging Markets and the State*, International Political Economy Series, DOI 10.1057/978-1-137-55655-4_2

The only agent capable of achieving these goals on a national scale is the state. This is not to say that there is any a priori relationship between state intervention in the market and an attendant improvement in development. Clearly, this is not the case, especially when development is understood as more than simply economic growth. There are many instances of state involvement in the development process that have been disastrous for those countries: facilitating corruption, incompetence, cronyism, nepotism, patrimonialism, clientelism, and kleptocracy. Also, historically, there have been the kinds of states that Chalmers Johnson (1982) termed 'plan-ideological'. Soviet-type, China, or Cuba are the real-world examples of these states, which used the state to take virtual complete ownership and domination of the market; not simply to guide or manage their economies but to control every aspect of it (and usually their societies as well).

There are clearly a number of different modalities of states, capable of manifesting in non-capitalist as well as capitalist forms, with the latter type further splitting into myriad types of capital accumulation strategies. As well as different forms of state present theoretically and in the historical record, there are a number of different ways of examining the state. Bob Jessop identifies six (Jessop 2016: 7), other contributions more (see, e.g., Hay et al. 2006). However, one chooses to categories a taxonomy of state theory, different viewpoints reveal different facets of the state and state power. Each point has its specific blind spot, which prevents us from seeing what we cannot see from that perspective. So, 'combining *commensurable* perspectives allows a more complex analysis, which may put apparently contradictory statements about the state into a more comprehensive analytical schema that reveals how the truth value of observations and statements depends on the contexts in which they are made' (Jessop 2016: 7) [italics in original].

It is the purpose of this chapter to first outline a theory of the state, and then to sharpen this broad analysis into a theory of the capitalist state in the context of catch-up or latecomer development. Completion of this task also requires a theory of power. Such an exercise will facilitate an understanding of why states follow certain development trajectories rather than others through a framework that has been termed a Developmental Regime—first coined by T.J. Pempel (1999), and subsequently developed in the context of Latin America (Wylde 2012, 2014, 2016). The domestic aspects of the Developmental Regime approach will be dealt with here, with aspects of international political economy and globalisation incorporated in the subsequent chapter. This collectively will provide the theoretical bedrock necessary for a comprehensive analysis of two emblematic cases of state-driven catch-up development strategies: Argentina and Malaysia.

State and Regime in Development Theory

The state is clearly the site of a paradox. On the one hand, it is merely one particular institutional complex among many others within any given social formation; yet on the other hand, it is peculiarly charged with overall responsibility for maintaining the cohesion of the social formation of which it is part. The state thus becomes much more than its associated ensemble of institutions, as whilst its form—or 'strategically selective limits' (Jessop 1990: 353)—is/are constituted through state structures and operating procedures, the outcome of state power also depends on the changing balance of forces engaged in political action both within and beyond the state. The state is everywhere; even where it is not. This suggests a focus on the institutional context of states is necessary, but not sufficient, for analysis of the state. Agent-centred institutionalism becomes an important intellectual tradition for understanding how social forces make history in specific institutional contexts. The focus is on 'complex actors rather than on individuals; on actor's interests, identities, action orientations, and resources in specific actor constellations rather than in generic, context-free terms; and on different forms of interaction' (Jessop 2016: 9). This is clearly important. Examination of the ensemble of 'socially embedded, socially regularised, and strategically selective institutions and organisations' (Jessop 2016: 49)—or *Staatsgewalt*—forms a necessary element of any analysis of the state.

As suggested, this institutional analysis is necessary, but not sufficient, for an understanding of the state. Completion requires an analysis of other substantive aspects of the state: its social bases, state projects, and national-popular objectives. This framework can generate an understanding of all states, albeit fleeting and necessarily temporally specific due to their constantly evolving nature. Bob Jessop has called this *Staatsidee* (Jessop 2016: 49): the policies generated by the particular institutional ensemble of the state, and enacted on the members of a given society, and done in the name of the common interest of general will.

With the core object of interest in this study being the capitalist state, it therefore follows that there is no single logic to capital, unless it is the autopoietic logic of continually reproducing the circuit of capital (Jessop 1990: 354)—regardless of the specific institutionalised forms in which this occurs. The specific type of state that this book is interested in is the one that has the authority, power, and capability to strike a relationship with the market that is not one of domination, but one that is able to 'govern the market' (Wade 1990). The literature has described this kind of formation as a Developmental State, a concept that will be discussed in detail and will form the guiding thread of this book. The literature associated with this area is often concerned over the necessary authority, power, and capability to enact appropriate market governance, which distils into the concepts of *autonomy* and *capacity*. Capacity can be defined as the ability of a state to implement goals, especially over the actual or potential opposition of powerful social groups or in the face of recalcitrant socio-economic circumstances. It follows that in order to have capacity a state must also possess autonomy, defined as when it is able to 'formulate and pursue goals that are not simply reflective of the demands or interests of social groups, classes, or society' (Evans et al. 1985: 9). The government may have to enact unpopular or even harsh policies in the name of development. To effectively guide economic development a state must enjoy the power to direct society and lead it through traumatic changes. Bureaucrats must be able to draft policies that promote national development, not the advancement of private lobbyists.

In order to make sense of these concepts of capacity and autonomy in an era characterised by the dominance of the neoliberal paradigm and its concomitant global institutions this book will argue that the Developmental State literature must be reinvigorated and made fit for purpose in the 21st century. This will involve exploration of the concept of a Developmental Regime: out of which a reformulated regime tripod image is developed; the legs of which are socio-economic alliances and relations, institutions, and public policy profiles. It is the action and interaction, the production and reproduction, of these three areas that facilitate distinct political economies of development and shape the contours of the specific geography of a given state's capacity and autonomy. Although there are complex overlapping tendencies that will be fully explored in later sections, institutions can be understood to represent state capacity, socio-economic relations state autonomy, and public policy profiles the (non-)developmental agenda that emerges from these complex social interactions.

Developmentalism and the Developmental State

In *State-Directed Development*, Atul Kohli (2004: 2) distinguishes between three ideal types of state involvement in the industrialisation (and therefore development) process: neo-patrimonial states, fragmented multiclass states, and cohesive-capitalist states. Neo-patrimonial states are the least effective at state intervention, a classic example for which is Nigeria as well as many other sub-Saharan African states. Fragmented multiclass states are a middling category with various degrees of effectiveness in facilitating latecomer industrialisation; better than neo-patrimonial states, but certainly less effective than cohesive-capitalist states. This last category can be most closely associated with the Developmental State paradigm, which can therefore be seen as the most effective model for effective state intervention in the development process.

The search for understanding the nature of state power and developmental intervention from within the Developmental State paradigm has traditionally sought to ascertain what the specific suite of policies, political organisation, and institutional make-up of the state is necessary in order to facilitate effective catch-up development. Such a scholarly endeavour has been broadly split between two separate schools: the 'political school' and the 'economic school'. The economic school has tended to focus on what policies are necessary for late development: the state is required to accrue economies of scale and scope, coordinate investments within and across sectors, and to harness positive and eliminate negative externalities. The political school, on the other hand, has been concerned with the state itself and whether it has the potential in general, and the independence in particular, to adopt the necessary developmental policies (Fine 2013: 8). This school has suggested that the state must be free of capture by particular interests, and so be able to promote and implement appropriate (developmental) policies. Much scholarly effort has been spent discussing this autonomy, as it has been presented in the literature as the key to effective state intervention. Lack of autonomy leads to state capture by particular interests, such as family members in neo-patrimonial states, whose interests are not a priori appropriate for effective national developmental goals.

The two schools have traditionally understood the Developmental State concept in terms of a state-market dichotomy; the economics school seeing the state overruling the market and improving upon it, whilst the political school visualising the state as standing aloof from the market and the economic interests found within it. This approach can be significantly critiqued and found to be problematic. From the economics school perspective, this view assumes that market actors would like to extend market forces at all opportunities, whereas states would ideally like to infringe upon the market. In other words, states and markets are viewed as two different if not incompatible sources of resource allocation (Palan and Abbott 1999: 32). The problem with this view is that states and markets do not comprise two sets of actors and dynamics that are profoundly different. For example, Trans-National Corporation (TNC) activity—a quintessential market agent—has been shown to actively seek and promote state bureaucratisation (Galbraith 2007/1967), whilst mainstream global governance such as the Bretton Woods Institutions—by definition constituted and run by states—actively promote markets. From the political school perspective, this suggests a theoretically very narrow perception of the state, one that views society as constituted in narrow market terms as well as potentially underplaying the role of class relations through seeing different class interests more in terms of social groups (Chang 2013: 90). Alternatively expressed in the words of Ben Fine, '[the state-market dichotomy] conceals the simple fact that economic development is a complex amalgam of processes and outcomes derived from capital accumulation, where state and market—and their interaction—are themselves attached to the economic and political relations and interests which act upon them' (Fine 2013: 25).

In order to overcome this restrictive analysis, the lexicon of state-market complexes should be ejected and replaced with a more nuanced understanding of agency and structure that distils into the regime tripod concept. Public policy profiles capture the essence of this redundant dichotomy best perhaps and can be seen as emerging from the complex interactions of socio-economic alliances and relations, institutions and institutionalisation, and the overarching impact of globalisation on all three legs of the tripod. This all crystallises into a Developmental Regime concept that helps understanding of developmentalism in the 21st century, and simultaneously overcoming a number of shortfalls in the Developmental State literature.

The concept of the Developmental State emerged from an analysis of late development tactics of specific states in East Asia. When attempting to explain why these states adopted this specific political economy many of these analyses concentrate on specific geopolitical factors such as the

US confrontation with Communist China (Doner et al. 2005: 329), or to specific sociopolitical factors within the Developmental States themselves, such as the colonial legacies present at the beginning of the industrialising process in South Korea (Kohli 1994: 1270–1271). Certainly a strong and persuasive body of literature exists that suggests this East Asian development experience was unique as a result of specific colonial legacies and a specific geopolitical context in the second half of the twentieth century (Stubbs 2005; Doner et al. 2005; Cumings 1987: 44–83; Koo 1987). Alternative analyses steer away from *sui generis* arguments and instead ground understandings of developmental success in specific institutional formats, such as Johnson and his analysis of MITI in Japan. From these alternatives, two core principles can be identified: the role of industrial policy, and business–state relationships.

Industrial Policy

Ha-Joon Chang (see, e.g., 1993, 1995, 1999) has contributed more than most to the role of industrial policy and economic policies more widely within the Developmental State concept. His work has facilitated the argument that 'a fundamental characteristic of the Developmental State is having a strategic industrial policy organised around government directives that are broad-based in scope and leave the operational detail to the individual firms' (Madjd-Sadjadi and Karagiannis 2007: 244). Chang points out that both national and transnational bourgeoisie in developing countries tend not to invest in new industries because they do not know whether other, complementary investments will come along; hence, there needs to be a centralised coordination of investment plans (Chang 1999: 192). State intervention can therefore reduce transaction costs, for example through 'indicative planning' (Chang 1993: 53). Furthermore, infant industry arguments can be deployed. First, to raise an industry from the ground requires sums of capital beyond the reach of the private financial sector. The state, therefore, has a role to play, since through its actions it can raise the capital through borrowing, taxation, and the direction of export earnings (Rapley 2008: 141). There is also a role to play in the accumulation of human capital. State investment in education, for example, allows for its population to develop the skills necessary to compete in a global marketplace. Second, to acquire, adapt, and alter production technologies imported from the developed world, firms must be given a learning period during which the state protects them from foreign competition. To make it possible for firms to move into a market in which barriers to entry and brand loyalty favour established producers, the state may need to reserve its domestic market for local producers for a set period of time (Gerschenkron 1962; Rapley 2008: 143).

Whilst the infant industry argument was deployed by the structuralists during the 1970s and therefore associated with Import Substituting Industrialisation (ISI), the Developmental State concept used it with important differences. First, rather than building an industrial base to satisfy local demand (the very *raison d'être* of ISI), it focused on building export industries in order to foster new comparative advantages based upon dynamic rather than static efficiency. Second, rather than provide local industry with indiscriminate protection, governments choose winners, strategically selecting a few companies in key industries which they will help raise to maturity, leaving the others to die (Amsden 1989; Rapley 2008: 143). A final point concerns the nature of industrial and agricultural development. Neoclassical theory has criticised traditional ISI for its urban bias (Rapley 2008), for transferring resources from the rural sector to the urban industry when their best comparative advantages lay in that rural economy. However, the early Developmental States of East Asia did not necessarily follow these practices, as they nurtured both agriculture and industry, with protection for agricultural markets also offered (Jenkins 1991). For example, the principle adopted by South Korea was to initially focus on the primary sector and use these surpluses to fund manufacturing industry.

Embedded Autonomy

Scholars draw attention to the strength, capacity, and autonomy required for successful Developmental States (Rapley 2008: 155; Evans et al. 1985: 9). As introduced earlier, capacity can be defined as the ability of a state to implement goals, especially over the actual or potential opposition of powerful social groups or in the face of recalcitrant socio-economic circumstances. In the Developmental State literature, this capacity should arise less from crude power and more from a marriage between a technocratic state and a well organised indigenous capitalist class. It follows that in order to have capacity a state must also possess autonomy, defined as when it is able to 'formulate and pursue goals that are not simply reflective of the demands or interests of social groups, classes, or society' (Evans et al. 1985: 9). The government may have to enact unpopular or even harsh policies in the name of development.

To effectively guide economic development a state must enjoy the power to direct society and lead it through traumatic changes. Bureaucrats must be able to draft policies that promote national development, not the advancement of private lobbyists. This idea is key. The failure of industrial policy to promote successful catch-up development in different parts of the world (large swathes of sub-Saharan Africa, for example) can be understood in terms of an inappropriate mix of capacity and autonomy.

Research on capacity has centred on the nature of the business–state relationship in a Developmental State and the presence of a domestic capitalist class who articulate their interests and concerns via interest groups and chambers of commerce, so the state does not to reduce itself to crony capitalism (Wu 2008) and (neo)patrimonial politics (Rapley 2008). Furthermore, capitalists make up for their shortcomings, which in a developing country centre on the fact that they do not yet contribute large amounts to the national economy, by linking their businesses to entry points in the state. This produces a two-way information flow as not only can the capitalists express their concerns to policymakers, but policymakers can communicate more effectively with chief players in the economy (Rapley 2008). With Japan, for example, this manifested itself at one end in the form of a competent state bureaucracy, with a pilot agency with overall strategic responsibility for industrialisation: the Ministry of International Trade and Industry (MITI). Furthermore, MITI had organisational and institutional links at the other end with major private sector firms and capitalists.

Somewhat paradoxically, the linkages between state and society (or bureaucracy and domestic bourgeoisie more specifically) must be complemented with state autonomy. Early Developmental State theory views the state to be necessarily separate from society in order to insulate it from competing interests (a classic authoritarian state), and those who may bear the costs of economic development incurred due to the lack of perfect mobility of factors of production. Johnson (1987) has argued that whilst there is no necessary connection between the Developmental State and authoritarianism there is an 'elective affinity' between the two, echoing the work of O'Donnell (1973) and his analysis of the connection between bureaucratic-authoritarian regimes in Latin America and their emphasis on heavy industrialisation. However, this link between authoritarianism and the Developmental State has been questioned by a number of scholars, with a whole literature on democracy and the Developmental State emerging (see, e.g., Robinson and White 2002).

With regard to this link Bruce Cumings (1999: 69) argues that 'theoretically speaking… there is no reason why this [the link between the developmental state and authoritarianism] has to be'. The traditional reason has of course been because of autonomy, but Bruce Cumings reminds us that—at least on the level of theory as this is what we are currently concerned with—there are other ways of achieving autonomy that are different from an authoritarian government.

Peter Evans (1995) coined the term *embedded autonomy* to better characterise state autonomy within a Developmental State beyond simple separation of the state from society through authoritarianism. Drawing together the work on capacity and state bureaucracies with the concept of state autonomy his argument suggests that a Weberian-style bureaucracy in the sense of selective, meritocratic entrance requirements and independent long-term career rewards gives them autonomy. However, here he departs from Weber and suggests that far from being insulated from society, 'they are embedded in a concrete set of social ties that binds the state to society and provides institutionalised channels for the continual negotiation and renegotiation of goals and policies' (Evans 1995: 12). These ties are predominantly with captains of industry—or domestic bourgeoisie—and it is this embedded autonomy that best facilitates the state's role in industrial transformation.

It is this embedded autonomy that facilitates the kind of strategic industrial policy witnessed in the East Asian Newly Industrialised Countries (NICs), rather than that seen during the Latin American ISI period. Contributions by Koo and Johnson in Deyo (1987) highlight a key distinction between the political basis for strong, autonomous developmentalist states and the institutional basis for state intervention and effective industrial policy implementation. Analysis suggests that not only did this political basis exist in certain East Asian countries in the form of a specific sociopolitical context that facilitated strategy formulation conducive to rapid industrialisation and economic development, but that this basis, although separate from the institutions and structures through which policies are implemented, represented a fundamental aspect of development capacity (Öniş 1991: 114). Therefore, the strategic power of the East Asian Developmental State depended on the formation of political coalitions with domestic industry; whilst successful state intervention relied on organisational and institutional links between politically insulated state agencies and major private sector firms.

Underlying these Developmental State imperatives were the two central features of unusual degrees of both bureaucratic autonomy and public-private cooperation. This facilitated the formulation of independent national goals by the state and its bureaucracy, as well as translating these broad national goals into effective policy action. Therefore, the coexistence of these two features was essential. For example, in the absence of bureaucratic autonomy public-private cooperation could easily degenerate into situations in which state goals are directly reducible to private interests. Argentina and Brazil during their bureaucratic-authoritarian periods could be examples of such a political economy, where close government–business cooperation materialised in the context of a weak state, in the sense that it lacked autonomy from powerful groups in society. The logic of the Developmental State therefore rests precisely on the combination of bureaucratic autonomy and public-private cooperation; the central insight of which is that the degree of government–business cooperation and consensus on national goals is not purely the product of a given cultural environment but has been largely engineered by the state elites themselves through the creation of a special set of institutions (Öniş 1991: 115).

This thought was further developed as Evans and his concept of embedded autonomy was critiqued for having an inadequate or incomplete understanding of state–society relationships; it was not a sufficient explanation of successful development experience as *both* strong states and strong economic groups in society are needed to create 'governed interdependence' (Weiss 1998: 38). Pempel's (1999: 157) analysis captures this well when he critiques the Developmental State literature for privileging the political and economic role played by state bureaucrats. This is because they are treated as totally depoliticised, socially disembodied, and in rational pursuit of a self-evident national interest (ibid.: 144). In the words of Chalmers Johnson (1982: 356) 'politicians merely reign, whereas the bureaucrats actually rule'. This led Bruce Cumings (1999: 61) to suggest that the state then emerges as a 'web without a spider'. This critique makes the observation that 'if not from the politicians from whom do bureaucrats get their sense of direction?' (ibid.: 145). Bureaucracies may well be rational, but in whose interests are they rational? One answer could be the national interest, derived from the possible interests of the politicians or at least of those in power. This opens the door to the possibility of multiple capitalisms and many varied versions of economic development; or many different capitalisms or forms of development, each promoting the interests of different specific socio-economic groups (Pempel 1999: 145). As a result, different 'Developmental Regimes' (see Pempel 1999; Wylde 2012, 2014) are possible, based on different constellations of socio-economic interests rooted in state–society relationships that go beyond the narrow confines of embedded autonomy, authoritarianism, and the Developmental State concept.

It is this critique that the concept of the democratic Developmental State is grounded in. In the early Developmental State literature, democracy was perceived to be a luxury that was feasible only in countries that had achieved developmental success. Democratic politics were considered to be a barrier to sustained development since unbridled political competition could generate pressures that led to deviation from the appropriate path necessary for sustained economic development (Robinson and White 2002: 1). Whilst developmental democracy is not an assured outcome of a simultaneous process of economic and political liberalisation, it should not be totally discarded. The political and institutional basis for a number of states that have demonstrated broad-based sustainable development combined with a legitimate and inclusive democracy lies in the form of the democratic Developmental State (Robinson and White 2002: 1; White 2002). An effective Developmental State requires a particular mix of politics and institutions that can create, maintain, and deepen democratic structures and shape developmental outcomes in both productive and equitable ways. This mix can move beyond state–society relations characterised by embedded autonomy, achieving the same developmental results—i.e. sustained economic growth and industrialisation—yet grounded in a social contract characterised by democratic institutions. This opens the (theoretical) door to the possibility of different constellations of state–society relationships beyond embedded autonomy that can lead to effective development.

The Developmental State's preoccupation with the insulation of state bureaucrats as key to economic development can therefore be (re) interpreted as theoretically constricting. Evans emphasis on the role and character of the state's bureaucracy at the expense of other explanatory factors reduces the basis of legitimacy for state-led developmental intervention to bureaucratic links with industrial capital (Woo-Cumings 1999: 31; Pempel 1999: 144). The possibility of legitimacy based on other forms of state–society relationship, or indeed multiples and combinations of different relationships, is not considered. As Pempel (1999: 147) suggests, 'bureaucratic autonomy and mandarinate competence in the absence of numerous other conditions are thin reeds on which to rest a strategy of economic development'. In a critique of the Developmental State literature in terms of its analysis of bureaucracies, Woo-Cumings (1999: 31) contends that 'trimming some bureaucratic fat off the Developmental State does not mean the end of the Developmental State; rather, it is a requirement for survival'.

Towards a 21st Century Developmental State?

The ontological theorisation of state–society relationships in classic Developmental State thought, as outlined in the previous section, can be brought into question. Developmental State theory, and indeed the Developmental Regime (at least in its original form as understood by Pempel), conceptualises society as a set of social groups with different economic functions. Therefore, the actions of states (including those of a developmental persuasion) can be explained through the 'organisational features' of a given state. Organisational features can be defined as a set of organisations through which collectives of officials may be able to formulate and implement distinctive strategies of policies (Evans et al. 1985: 20–21). In terms of a Developmental State, this led to focus on bureaucratic strength and coherence; what matters is the relation between the state and other groups of collective individuals. In terms of Pempel's Developmental Regime, this led to a focus on socio-economic alliances as one of the legs of the tripod. This was achieved by interpreting the state as an independent agent that develops and institutionalises relationships with different groups—for the Developmental State with business sectors and for the Developmental Regime a wider constellation of different social groups dependent upon the specific case under consideration. States pursue a distinct 'national interest', independent of discrete social and political interests. Economic competition can be understood as an extension of the national interest, and traditional Developmental State/Regime theory accommodates this in a traditional states-and-markets, neo-Weberian fashion.

What is needed to solve this problem is an explanatory framework that instantiates the limits placed by capitalist relations of production on the variation in the scope of state action (Radice 2008: 1161–1162). The liberal political hegemony that dominates the intellectual understanding and conceptualisation of the state as a congruence of ideas, interests, and institutions obscures this task as it marginalises the role of class and social relations (ibid.: 1168). The classic example of such a conceptualisation is Evan's embedded autonomy: where the key aspects of a (developmental) state are reduced to state bureaucratic links with domestic capital (Evans 1995). Class according to this theory are not classes in any relational sense, rather a series of 'social groups' with different economic functions (Chang 2013: 90). Evans et al. (1985) achieved this by putting the state as an independent agent at the centre of analysis, autonomous from classes and class relations. This downplayed the dependence of the state upon capital (or other class) relations (Chang 2013: 91). Instead, understanding of difference in terms of developmental outcomes of state intervention was grounded in different organisational features of a state. This led to a focus on bureaucratic strength—and hence embedded autonomy—and therefore what matters is not the relation between the state and class relations, but the relations between the state and other groups of collective individuals (Chang 2013: 92). Although Pempel's Developmental Regime offers a wider set of theoretical constellations of social groups and their relationship with the state that can achieve successful developmental outcomes beyond embedded autonomy, these relationships remain the same at an ontological level.

Such a view of the state has been critiqued by neo-Marxists (see, e.g., Jessop 2016) as for this theory of the state to work politics must be viewed as analytically separate from economics—or the state as autonomous from classes. 'Class' in Developmental State theories are therefore not actually classes in any relational sense, but closer to 'social groups' with different economic functions. Such a view misrepresents or downplays the dependence of the state upon capital (or other class) relations (Chang 2013: 90–91). The logical climax of this argument is a concept of the state that stands above class relations without any regard of its relationship to the (re)production of class relations. As Poulantzas (1973) has argued, policies are shaped primarily by the constellation of interests *and* the struggle between them. Without this understanding, states are seen as pursuing a 'national interest' independent of social and political interests. As highlighted earlier, this results in such a 'national interest' being defined in abstraction from societal interests—or the state becomes a web with no spider (Cumings 1999).

To untie this particular Gordian knot requires not a simplistic Alexandrian solution; rather, what is needed is an analytical framework that can generate leverage towards a reinvigorated understanding of the concepts of capacity and autonomy. An understanding that is sensitive to the relational role of class as well as other aspects of social contracts, that understands at a much deeper level the role of power in these processes, and that understands the role of multilevel governance and the interaction of different levels of analysis in an era characterised by globalisation. In other words, what is needed is an appropriate theory of the state, a more nuanced theory of power, and a theory of global governance. This is in order to get leverage on the overarching problem of how a 'national interest' of developmentalism and industrialisation emerges, or more specifically in the empirical context of this book, what constitutes different kinds of Developmental Regime in the developing world. The rest of this chapter will complete the first two of these tasks through suggesting an understanding of the state as a social relation(ship), and through an exploration of the concept of (relative) autonomy. The third will be achieved in the following chapter through integrating a sound understanding of the role of international political economy in an era characterised by (neoliberal) globalisation.

The State as a Social Relation(ship)

An understanding of class in relational terms facilitates an understanding of the state itself as a social relation (Poulantzas 1969, 1973). Whilst lengthy, Bob Jessop's definition of the state from this perspective sums up this complex idea best:

> ...the exercise of state power as an institutionally and discursively mediated condensation (a reflection and a refraction) of a changing balance of forces, which seek to influence the forms, purposes, and content of the polity, politics, and policy in specific conjectures, marked by a variable mix of opportunities and constraints, themselves linked to the wider natural and social environment. (Jessop 2016: 53)

Somewhat more pithily, the state can be understood as '...a strategically selective terrain which can never be neutral among all social forces and political projects; but any bias is always tendential and can be undermined or reinforced by appropriate strategies' (Jessop 1990: 354); or, a 'condensation of a changing balance of class forces' (Jessop 2002: 195).

This concept has a clear concern for the class character of the state, and is therefore associated with (neo-)Marxist analysis (see, e.g., Bonefeld 2012; Jessop 2016). It postulates that the state has inbuilt biases that privilege some agents and interests over others, but how these biases are actualised depends on the changing balance of forces and their strategies and tactics. It therefore tries to capture the effects of state power as a contingent expression of a changing balance of forces that seek to advance their respective interests inside, through and against the state system (Jessop 2016: 54). This changing balance of forces is clearly mediated institutionally and discursively—hence the need to seriously and systematically consider the role of the institutions of the state. As Jessop notes (2016: 54) '[the changing balance of forces] is conditioned by the specific institutional structures and procedures of the state apparatus as embedded in the wider political system and environing societal relations'. The mixing of these two approaches—agent-centred institutionalism and (neo-)Marxism—is a core postulate of this book and will be expanded upon considerably throughout this chapter.

The state must be treated as a specific structural ensemble with its own effects on the reproduction of a society divided into classes. Furthermore, classes have no abstract, unifying consciousness but are constituted as political forces through the state itself (Jessop 2016). This expands understanding of state capacity beyond narrow and perhaps ephemeral links between business groups and the state—understood in abstraction from their relational terms. Actors act not only because of, and through their particular relationship with the state but also in a more immediate relational sense—due to the nature of structure and agency. Bob Jessop's 'Strategic-Relational Approach' that underpins the concept of the state as a social relation reveals that structure consists in differential constraints and opportunities that vary by agent; and that agency in turn depends on strategic capacities that vary by the structure as well as according to the actors involved. This further reveals a dialectic between acting routinely or habitually, and 'evaluating the current situation in terms of the changing "art of the possible" over different spatiotemporal horizons of action' (Jessop 2016: 55). Structures are only strategically selective, rather than absolutely constraining. As a result, scope exists for actions to overwhelm structural constraints; subjects are unlikely to absolutely know their own strategic action(s); and '…calculating subjects that operate on the strategic terrain constituted by the state are in part constituted by the current strategic selectivity of the state system as well as by past state interventions' (Jessop 2016: 56).

Through this use of neo-Marxist tools, the state becomes 'the instance that maintains the cohesion of a social formation and which reproduces the conditions of production of a social system by maintaining class domination' (Poulantzas 1969: 77). The modern state therefore possesses two fundamental roles: an 'accumulation imperative' and a 'legitimation imperative' (Poulantzas 1969: 76). The accumulation imperative is the repressive apparatus of the state—the government, army, police, tribunals, and administration—and deal with factors such as infrastructure, the rule of law to ensure growth (especially private property), and defence. The legitimation imperative is there to make the whole system legitimate to workers both institutionally—through the welfare state for example—and ideologically—through concepts such as developmentalism and/or redistribution. Following Gramsci (1971), the ideological apparatus of the state are institutions such as the Church, political parties, schools, mass media, and in certain instances the family.

The historical emergence of society and associated social entities cannot be separated from the evolution of the state. The state is no longer simply defined as a 'black box' where competing social interests form, rather it centralises and concentrates social power so that it can be exercised, executed, and directed. (Developmental) policy that emerges from this becomes the application of this social power, grounded in material conditions. Ideology is reduced to the facade (or 'hegemonic project' for Poulantzas) of coherence in policy, with its presence helping maintain consistency through the articulation of a worldview. The state is therefore a dynamic and constantly unfolding system. Its specific form at a given moment in time in a particular national setting represents a 'crystallisation of past strategies' which privileges certain strategies and actors over others. As such, 'the state is located within a complex dialectic of structures and strategies' (Hay 2006: 129). It thus becomes 'a strategic site traversed by class struggles and as a specific institutional ensemble with multiple boundaries, no institutional fixity and no pre-given formal or substantive unity' (Jessop 1990: 267). The era of the neoliberal state witnessed the separation of the state from the economy. This separation 'maps out new spaces for the state and the economy by transforming their very elements' (Poulantzas 1978: 18). The problem lies in understanding how the shape of these 'new spaces' and their interrelations are transformed through the historical development of capitalism.

Viewed in these terms the state is neither a neutral instrument nor a rational calculating subject (Jessop 1999: 11). For the purposes of this discussion, the critique of underplaying class through treating the state as equally accessible to all forces and useful for any purpose is overcome.

This plugs a key gap in mainstream understandings of the state—pluralism and elite theory—which view class as social groups. A further shortcoming that is overcome is that of seeing the state as possessing a pre-given unity and clear purpose, in the context of the Developmental State literature an a priori national interest in favour of developmentalism. Instead, the state is the crystallisation and ongoing metamorphosis of the continuing interaction between 'the structurally-inscribed strategic selectivities of the state as an institutional ensemble and the changing balance of forces operating within, and at a distance from, the state and perhaps, also trying to transform it' (Jessop 1999: 11).

A number of important observations emerge from this understanding of the state as a social relation. The first is the analysis of unequal access to the state for different agents. A strategic-relational approach combines nicely with (neo)pluralism given the shared concern with the changing balance of diverse forces, shared sensitivity to crosscutting and intersecting groups and social forces, and a shared focus on conflict, competition, and coalition building. However, the introduction of a consideration of the more relational aspects of class—as opposed to simply treating classes as social groups whose relationship with the state is the only ontologically relevant force—further improves our understanding of the strategic selectivity of the state itself. (Neo)Pluralist analysis gives equal weight, analytically, to the structurally inscribed, strategic, selective asymmetries involved in institutions, institutional orders, and societal configurations. Also, it is less attuned to the specificities of the capital relation—especially its inherent structural contradictions, strategic dilemmas, and social antagonisms; less attuned to the relative primacy of profit-orientated, market-mediated accumulation as a principle of societal organisation; and less attuned to the ways in which these shape the overall pattern of constraints and opportunities in contemporary societies (Jessop 2016: 70).

The second is a better understanding of the mechanisms and modes of state intervention. Combining strategic-relational concerns with (neo) pluralism introduces very important relational aspects to the concept of state capacity. It facilitates a framework for understanding the differentiation between what Michael Mann (1984: 185) called 'despotic power' and 'infrastructural power'. Infrastructural power gives the state the capacity 'to penetrate [Sic.] society and organise social relations throughout its territory on the basis of its political decisions' (Jessop 2016: 70). This is opposed to despotic power, which 'can be "measured" most vividly in the ability of… Red Queens to shout "off with his head" and have their whim gratified without further ado' (Mann 1984: 189). What strategic-relational concerns provide is an understanding that these capacities are relational. For, even when they meet no resistance, states are not omnicompetent—because every mode of intervention has its strengths and weaknesses.

The third and final contribution for understanding the state concerns the unequal capacity of agents to shape, make, and implement decisions. The structural dominance that facilitates unequal access to the state must be combined with a widely accepted 'hegemonic project' if the structurally privileged class (fraction) is to become truly hegemonic. In the absence of this condition, state structures can undermine the pursuit of a project favourable to a class (fraction) other than the structurally privileged. In turn, this indicates that a long-term shift in hegemony requires not only a new hegemonic project but also the reorganisation of the state system towards underwriting a more durable shift in the balance of forces (Jessop 2016: 69).

On (State) Power

Understanding the state as a social relation draws attention to the configuration of the social bases of state power and the inherently unstable equilibrium of compromise that it is refracted through. In other words, to draw out all the implications of understanding the state as a social relation for the concepts of capacity and autonomy in the context of developmentalism requires a more complete understanding of power. For Gramsci (1971: 257–264), state power was shaped by the relation between the state and the institutions and forces in the broader political system and in society as a whole. Some Gramscian analytical categories are useful here: the 'power bloc', a durable alliance among dominant classes that define the 'art of the possible' (Jessop 2016: 73); the 'hegemonic bloc', a broader ensemble of national-popular forces mobilised behind a specific hegemonic project; and a 'historic bloc', a mutually supportive relation among the economic base, juridico-political organisations, and the moral and intellectual field (ibid.). These are the building blocks of durable state projects, or hegemonic visions. In the context of latecomer development: a coherent and cohesive national interest rigorously pursued and defined in terms of developmentalism.

Whilst the Marxist debates of the late 1970s imploded 'under the weight of a multitude of competing theoretical starting points and an over-emphasis on highly abstract theorising that blithely disregarded the historical variability of political regimes and the different forms taken by capitalism' (Jessop 2001: 150), the concepts of the state as a social relation and 'relative autonomy' can be retrieved from the wreckage and help facilitate an understanding of the relational aspects of power and its exercise by the state. Having analysed the state as a social relation and its consequences for an understanding of capacity, the rest of this section will now analyse the concept of relative autonomy and the attendant understanding of power relations that result in order to generate more sophisticated understandings of autonomy that can complement the work on capacity. Combined with an analysis of multilevel governance (see next chapter), a more robust understanding and conceptualisation of the related concepts of capacity and autonomy can be generated—unlocking a framework for understanding 21st century developmentalism in the process. This is to ultimately generate a reinvigorated Developmental Regime concept capable of dealing with the issue of how and why states at early stages of development follow certain trajectories rather than others.

The state as a social relation(ship) should not be seen as a mere reflection of class interests—the 'economic committee of the bourgeoisie'; rather, the state should be seen as possessing 'relative autonomy' from different class interests as it advocates the interests of capitalism rather than capitalists. Such an understanding facilitates a firmer grip on the necessary ensemble of social relations of production and associated institutions that link society with the state that best facilitates latecomer industrialisation. This view allows for a holistic understanding of the state and its forms. Classic state theory (the debate between Elite theory and Pluralism) views the state as an adjudicator between conflicting interests and groups. Marx saw the state as controlling and suppressing the lower classes. The discipline of public policy looks to how the state achieves targeted goals. But really the state is all of these things (Palan and Abbott 1999: 45). Given these functions, the key question becomes how to maintain loyalty to the state by its members? The liberal tradition answered this in one particular way. Starting with Hobbes the solution was the sovereign (or 'might is right'), through to Locke with the guarantee of life, liberty, and property, and then to Rousseau with the concept of the social contract underpinned by the General Will. However, a social contract must pre-suppose the state because people must already have a strong consciousness of their membership of a social community (Palan and Abbott 1999: 46). In other words

(Löwith 1964: 242) '...the individual member of bourgeois society is educated behind his back to the generality of his personal interests. Bourgeois society... is forced against his will to become the true state of an absolute community'. This Hegelian conceptualisation was critiqued by Marx (2000 [1843]: 33) when he highlighted the fact that the state wasn't a separate social body, but the encapsulation of the entire civil society. Furthermore, it was a material entity, a form of class organisation—rather than a Hegelian spiritual one.

Poulantzas extended this analysis through the observation that the gap between 'citizenship' and 'individuality' are not problems that can be surmounted, but profound reflections of changing material conditions. This led to the conclusion that the state must simultaneously be autonomous from and embedded within civil society: or, in other words, it must possess 'relative autonomy'. It must be autonomous because the government needs to pursue the true interests of the people, and embedded because the government needs to be implanted in the social. The state enjoys a degree of independence from the economy because of its location in the autonomous sphere of politics, but this does not render the state independent of classes which influence the economy through the state. The state thus fulfils its adjudicatory role between contradictory interests, and development stalls where a state is no longer able to do this—it no longer has (or perhaps never had in the first place) relative autonomy.

Class domination of the state does not simply mean that its form—the institutionalisation of a suite of policies in the form of a public policy profile and the ideological justification underpinning that profile—is a simple reflection of the interests of the dominant class. Rather, the very existence of this domination is made possible by the relative autonomy of the state. That is, state power must be seen in relational terms, i.e. as founded on an unstable equilibrium of compromise among class forces rather than as a monopoly of one class (fraction) (Poulantzas 1973: 191–193). This power is conceptualised, following Gramsci, as hegemonic leadership, in which prominence is given to the organisation of an ideological and political unity among the classes and fractions of the power bloc, and to the securing of 'active consent' on the part of the dominated classes (Benton 1984: 149). An essential condition of hegemonic domination over the dominated classes is that they, in turn, have ideological apparatuses—for example, trade unions and political parties—which pursue their interests and thereby achieve concessions (ibid.).

The concept of relative autonomy helps overcome this reductionist and constricting approach by 'bringing class back in'. The state fulfils an adjudicatory role between contradictory interests and is therefore simultaneously autonomous from and embedded in social relations. It is autonomous because the state needs to pursue the 'true' interests of the people as a whole, rather than any distinct class (fraction), and it is embedded as it is itself part of the social formation of society. Therefore, the historical emergence of society and associate social entities cannot be separated from the evolution of the state. For example, development often stalls where a state has no relative autonomy from society—with sub-Saharan Africa being a clear example of this as states have often been captured by discrete interests. The state centralises and concentrates social power so that it can be exercised, executed, and directed. Policy is therefore the application of social power, and the policies of the state must be understood in the context of this application.

Relative autonomy represents an excellent tonic to the limited ontology associated with either Evans' embedded autonomy or structural Marxism; it distinguishes between either overly deterministic or overly agent-driven understandings of power. But it isn't in itself a theory of power: it is an explanandum, not an explanans (Jessop 2016: 93). In other words, in the context of empirical analysis it becomes descriptive rather than analytical. Instead, it must be recognised that relative autonomy arises from relationships between economic region, civil society, institutional structures, social bases of support and resistance, and effectiveness of policies. As a result, a theory of power needs to be articulated that encapsulates an understanding of how power comes to be realised and exercised in the context of the hegemony of different constellations of class (fractions). Or, how a general will is realised and, in the specific context of the research agenda of this book, how a national interest in favour of rapid development comes to be hegemonic within the state.

The elaboration of a state project clearly emerges from the historic record: both in terms of institutions and social relations. This state project—or specific accumulation strategy—can be seen as the product of the hegemony of one class fraction. Although, and crucially, a class fraction that is seen to represent at least some of the interests of different fractions of capital (finance capital, commercial capital, national capital, etc.). This state project must be relevant to the interests of the hegemonic fraction, but also to a critical mass of different fractions of capital. Furthermore, and once again following Gramsci (1971), this hegemony is (re)produced through elements of civil society—which are themselves part of the state; and hegemony is only truly achieved through the consent of both subordinate classes and the non-hegemonic fractions of capital.

The overall implications of this are a hegemonic accumulation strategy that is linked to the changing balance of forces between capital and labour as modified from time to time by the influence of other class or non-class forces (Jessop 2016: 114). Therefore, hegemonic politics and policies acquire a particular content as a result of the exercise of power. In other words, hegemony of a particular accumulation strategy can be seen as the product of domination. For (neo-)Marxists, this is expressed through class domination, with class understood very much in a *relational* sense and therefore it is social relations that acquire ontological primacy. For (neo-)Weberians, this domination is expressed through political party, status, *and* class domination—although class here is understood more in terms of social groups and therefore relational aspects are not analysed. For Feminists, it is patriarchal domination that is of utmost importance. For (neo)pluralists, it is a vast array of resources, identities, and interests across an array of governance levels that form domination. What all these approaches can have in common is a rejection of state power being above society, and class power being anchored wholly in the economy or in civil society. Therefore, state power is in fact a mediated effect of the changing balance of all forces—class, party, status, gender, identities, and interests—in any given scenario. It therefore follows that state power itself is an explanandum (Jessop 1990: 117), and the explanans is the strategic-relational terrain that reflects and refracts mediated power grounded in a constantly changing balance of different forces: a state's relative autonomy.

Conclusions: Whither the State?

The levels of coordination and capital required to facilitate successful catch-up development in the form of rapid industrialisation require more than just markets. It requires markets to be harnessed in order to act in a long-term national interest, rather than short-term individual interests. The only viable contemporary institution that is capable of such coordination is the state. The pre-requisites of successful state-led interventions to facilitate catch-up industrialisation have been investigated through the vehicle of Developmental State theory. This chapter has attempted to show that whilst this has represented a good start, in order for these theories to remain relevant in the 21st century further analysis is required.

This analysis involves two fundamental reformulations of traditional Developmental State theory: the first concerns better understanding of state–society relations, the second integration of national–international concerns in an era of accelerated (neoliberal) globalisation. This chapter has completed the first task, with the next chapter examining the second. In terms of the first task, the state and its associated capacity must be understood as a social relation(ship)—an entity that is the product of a changing balance of social forces. The constitution of those social forces is best conceptualised through the lens of relative autonomy. State power is not therefore a simple reflection of dominant class interests or the monopoly of one class, but rather a complex amalgam and unstable equilibrium of compromise among class, and other social forces. The state provides a context within which political actors are seen to be embedded, and with respect to which they must be situated analytically (Hay 2006: 10). The state therefore is the institutional landscape which political actors must negotiate. For Bob Jessop this landscape is 'strategically selective'—i.e. it is more conducive to certain strategies, and therefore certain actors, than to others (Jessop 1990: 9–10). The state therefore becomes a 'factor of cohesion' (Hay 2006: 62); or, '...the state is understood in terms of its effects and is defined in terms of its role in maintaining the unity and cohesion of a social formation by concentrating and sanctioning class domination' (Poulantzas 1978: 24–25; see also Jessop 1985: 61, 177). In being strategically selective, the state presents an uneven playing field whose complex contours favour certain strategies (and hence certain actors) over others. As a result, '...there can be no general or fully determined theory of the capitalist state, only theoretically informed accounts of capitalist states in their institutional, historical, and strategic specificity' (Hay 2006: 76).

It must never be forgotten that this relative autonomy not only functions in the context of competing and conflicting domestic social interests, but also (real and perceived) external environmental interests: i.e. those of (neoliberal) globalisation and the forces of international capital. In other words, amidst this theorisation and conceptualisation of the state is globalisation. Integration of social relations and relative autonomy into a robust theory of the state requires an appreciation of the fact that 'long-term, structurally consolidated, class or class-fraction alliances are no longer located purely on the national level' (Jessop 2002: 190). However, this does not mean that foreign capitals directly participate as autonomous forces in power blocs: 'instead they are represented by certain fractions of the interior bourgeoisie within the power bloc and also have access, through various channels, to the state apparatus' (ibid.). Therefore, the state does not have its own independent power which can either be fused with that of capital or eliminated due to the growing counter power of capital. Instead, state power must be seen in terms of class power; that is, the actions of the state can only be understood as a product of the interaction of social relations of production constituted at a domestic level. Different class fractions that constitute the building blocks of those social relations of production are the product of complex interactions of domestic and international pressures must not be forgotten in the analysis, and through such an approach the role of contemporary neoliberal globalisation can be integrated into a framework for understanding the contemporary (capitalist) state. This task will be undertaken in the following chapter. This will allow the generation of a robust, 21st century theory of state-led developmentalism, paving the way for the empirical analysis of the second half of the book which will apply this framework to two contemporary emerging markets in the form of Argentina and Malaysia.

References

Amsden, A. H. (1989). *Asia's next giant: South Korea and late industrialisation.* New York: Oxford University Press.

Benton, T. (1984). *The rise and fall of structural Marxism: Althusser and his influences.* London: MacMillan Press.

Bonefeld, W. (2012). Freedom and the strong state: On German ordoliberalism. *New Political Economy, 17*(5), 633–656.

Chang, H.-J. (1993). The political economy of industrial policy in Korea. *Cambridge Journal of Economics, 16*(2), 131–157.

Chang, H.-J. (1995). *The role of the state in economic change.* Oxford: Clarendon Press.

Chang, H.-J. (1999). The economic theory of the developmental state. In M. Woo-Cummings (Ed.), *The developmental state* (pp. 182–199). New York: Cornell University Press.

Chang, D. (2013). Labour and the 'developmental state': A critique of the developmental state theory of labour. In B. Fine, J. Saraswati, & D. Tavasci (Eds.), *Beyond the developmental state: Industrial policy into the twenty-first century* (pp. 85–109). London: Pluto Press.

Cumings, B. (1987). The origins and development of the North-East Asian economy: Industrial sectors, product cycles, and political consequences. In F. C. Deyo (Ed.), *The political economy of new Asian industrialism* (pp. 44–83). Ithaca: Cornell University Press.
Cumings, B. (1999). Webs with no spiders, spiders with no webs: The genealogy of the developmental state. In M. Woo-Cumings (Ed.), *The developmental state* (pp. 61–93). New York: Cornell University Press.
Doner, R. F., Ritchie, B. K., & Slater, D. (2005). Systemic vulnerability and the origins of developmental states: Northeast and Southeast Asia in comparative perspective. *International Organisation, 59,* 327–361.
Evans, P. (1995). *Embedded autonomy: States and industrial transformation.* Princeton: Princeton University Press.
Evans, P. B., Rueschemeyer, D., & Skocpol, T. (Eds.). (1985). *Bringing the state back in.* Cambridge: Cambridge University Press.
Fine, B. (2013). Beyond the developmental state: An introduction. In B. Fine, J. Saraswati, & D. Tavasci (Eds.), *Beyond the developmental state: Industrial policy into the twenty-first century* (pp. 1–32). London: Pluto Press.
Galbraith, J. K. (2007/1967). *The new industrial state.* Princeton: Princeton University Press.
Gerschenkron, A. (1962). *Economic backwardness in historical perspective: a book of essays.* Cambridge, MA: Belknap Press of Harvard University Press.
Gramsci, A. (1971). *Selections from the prison notebooks of Antonio Gramsci* (Q. Hoare & G. Nowell-Smith, Ed. and Trans.). London: Lawrence and Wishart.
Hay, C. (2006). (What's Marxist about) Marxist state theory. In C. Hay, M. Lister, & D. Marsh (Eds.), *The state: Theories and issues.* Basingstoke: Palgrave.
Hay, C., Lister, M., & Marsh, D. (2006). *The state: Theories and issues.* Basingstoke: Palgrave.
Jenkins, R. (1991). The political economy of industrialisation: A comparison of Latin American and East Asian industrialising countries. *Development and Change, 22,* 197–231.
Jessop, B. (1985). *Nicos Poulantzas: Marxist theory and political strategy.* Hampshire: Palgrave Macmillan.
Jessop, B. (1990). *State theory: Putting capitalist states in their place.* Cambridge: Polity Press.
Jessop, B. (1999). The strategic selectivity of the state: Reflections on a theme of Poulantzas. *Journal of Hellenic Diaspora, 25*(1–2), 1–37.
Jessop, B. (2001). Bringing the state back in (yet again): Reviews, revisions, rejections, and redirections. *International Review of Sociology, 11*(2), 149–173.
Jessop, B. (2002). Globalisation and the national state. In S. Aaronowitz & P. Bratsis (Eds.), *Paradigm lost: State theory reconsidered* (pp. 185–220). Minnesota: University of Minnesota Press.
Jessop, B. (2016). *The state: Past, present, and future.* London: Polity.

Johnson, C. (1982). *MITI and the Japanese miracle*. Stanford: Stanford University Press.

Johnson, C. (1987). Political institutions and economic performance: The government-business relationship in Japan, South Korea, and Taiwan. In F. C. Deyo (Ed.), *The political economy of new Asian industrialism*, (pp. 165–179). Ithaca: Cornell University Press.

Koo, H. (1987). The interplay of state, social class, and world system in East Asian development: The cases of South Korea and Taiwan. In F. C. Deyo (Ed.), *The political economy of new Asian industrialism* (pp. 165–179). Ithaca: Cornell University Press.

Kohli, A. (1994). Where do high growth political economies come from? The Japanese lineage of Korea's "developmental state". *World Development, 22*(9), 1269–1293.

Kohli, A. (2004). *State directed development*. Cambridge: Cambridge University Press.

Kothari, U. (2005). A radical history of development studies: Individuals, institutions and ideologies. In U. Kothari (Ed.), *A radical history of development studies*. London: Zed Books.

Leftwich, A. (2000). *States of development: On the primacy of politics in development*. London: Polity.

Löwith, K. (1964). *From Hegel to Nietzsche* (D. Green, Trans.). Garden City: Columbia University Press.

Madjd-Sadjadi, Z., & Karagiannis, N. (2007). *Modern state intervention in the era of globalisation*. Cheltenham: Elgar.

Mann, M. (1984). The autonomous power of the state, its origins, mechanisms and results. *European Journal of Sociology, 25*(2), 185–213.

Marx, K. (2000 [1843]). Critique of Hegel's 'philosophy of right'. In D. McLellan (Ed.), *Karl Marx: Selected writings*. Oxford: Oxford University Press.

O'Donnell, G. (1973). *Modernisation and bureaucratic authoritarianism*. Berkeley: Institute of International Studies.

Önis, Z. (1991). Review: The logic of the developmental state. *Comparative Politics, 24*(1), 109–126.

Palan, R., & Abbott, J. (1999). The state in the global political economy. In R. Palan & J. Abbott (Eds.), *State strategies in the global political economy* (pp. 32–54). London: Pinter.

Pempel, T. J. (1999). The developmental regime in a changing world economy. In M. Woo-Cumings (Ed.), *The developmental state* (pp. 137–181). New York: Cornell University Press.

Poulantzas, N. (1969). The problem of the capitalist state. *New Left Review, 58*, 67–78.

Poulantzas, N. (1973). *Political power and social classes*. London: Verso.

Poulantzas, N. (1978). *State, power, socialism*. London: New Left Books.
Radice, H. (2008) The developmental state under global neoliberalism. *Third World Quarterly, 29*(6), 1153–1174.
Rapley, J. (2008). *Understanding development: Theory and practice in the third world*. London: Lynne Rienner.
Robinson, M., & White, G. (2002). *The democratic developmental state*. Oxford: Oxford University Press.
Smith, A. (1880/1776). *The wealth of nations—Book IV*. London: G. Bell & Sons.
Stubbs, R. (2005). *Rethinking Asia's economic miracle: The political economy of war, prosperity, and crisis*. Basingstoke: Houndmills.
Wade, R. H. (1990). *Governing the market: Economic theory and the role of government in East Asian industrialization*. Princeton: Princeton University Press.
Weiss, L. (1998). *The myth of the powerless state*. Cambridge: Polity.
Woo-Cumings, M. (1999). *The developmental state*. Cornell: Cornell University Press.
Wu, Y. (2008). *The role of institutional quality in a currency crisis model* (IMF Working Paper, WP/08/5).
Wylde, C. (2012). *Latin America after Neoliberalism: Developmental regimes in post-crisis states*. Basingstoke: Palgrave Macmillan.
Wylde, C. (2014). The developmental state is dead, long live the developmental regime! Interpreting Nestór Kirchner's Argentina 2003–2007. *Journal of International Relations and Development, 17*(2), 191–219.
Wylde, C. (2016). Post-neoliberal developmental regimes in Latin America: Argentina under Cristina Fernandez de Kirchner. *New Political Economy, 21*(3), 322–341.

CHAPTER 3

Globalisation, the State, and Development

Globalisation is the structural condition that dominates the current study of the political economy of development. It is not though a new phenomenon; rather, it is the 'intensification of an old process, the continuing internationalisation of commodity production and capital accumulation' (Soloman and Rupert 2002: 284). Whilst it clearly has many other facets—social, cultural, technological—the consequences of its processes on broader structures of (global) political economy and attendant development trajectories of emerging markets are the subject of this book.

The changing nature of capital accumulation has significant and long-lasting implications for development in the 21st century, this much is certain. However, tracing the contours of power relations in this ever-changing landscape represents an empirical challenge, along with associated theoretically induced confrontations. How do states carve out new development spaces in a world dominated by the hegemony of neoliberal capitalism? What is the exact nature of the relationship between states and broader structures of global political economy? Can development move beyond simple economic growth and enter some form of post-hegemonic era?

It is the purpose of this chapter to answer these rhetorical questions, and to do so in a manner that integrates their understanding into the work of the previous chapter on the role of the state in development. In other words, it is time to consider the national–international relationship and develop an understanding of the nature of its influence on

C. Wylde, *Emerging Markets and the State*, International Political Economy Series, DOI 10.1057/978-1-137-55655-4_3

state-led development processes in the 21st century. In order to achieve such a project, the chapter will first consider the nature of global political economy and its related structures of governance, and how they have changed over time. Starting with the end of the Second World War, the chapter will map the terrain of hegemony and counter-hegemony, culminating in a consideration of 21st-century global political economy. Once complete, the chapter will consider the integration of the role and power that these global forces exercise in order to influence national development trajectories over time. This will be achieved through an analysis of the impact of the forces of globalisation on the state. Whilst ubiquitous forces associated with neoliberalism permeate and shape state capacities and autonomy, they do not merely condemn them to be a reflection of contemporary World Order. Instead, the state acts as a site of congruence, where social relations and institutions shape and are shaped by both domestic (i.e. 'below' the state) and international forces (i.e. 'above' the state). To make sense of these complex relationships the concept of structuration (Hay 2014; see also Cerny 2010) is required. After this, an examination of the specific ontology of these relationships requires an understanding of the difference between government and governance, with this chapter proposing a synthesis of (Transnational neo) Pluralist and Gramscian literatures. Developing a framework for integrating an understanding of these forces into the Developmental Regime concept will complete the construction of a robust theoretical model that facilitates consideration of 21st-century developmentalism. This paves the way for an application of this concept in the second part of the book to two emblematic case studies of emerging markets in the 21st-century global political economy: Argentina and Malaysia.

The Construction of the Modern Global Political Economy

The post-Second World War political settlement in the West in the form of NATO and a nascent EU was complemented economically by the establishment of the Bretton Woods institutions (IMF, GATT—later WTO—and the World Bank) and the building of an 'embedded liberalism' internationally (Ruggie 1983). Ruggie's concept of embedded liberalism, part of a wider literature on International Regimes (see especially, Krasner 1983), is a key starting point to understanding not only the nature of post-War global political economy, but also its subsequent evolution.

Ruggie draws heavily on the canonical work of Polanyi's *The Great Transformation* (1944), which develops an understanding of domestic models of capital accumulation as products of hegemonic social orders. In Polanyi's words, 'the economic order is merely a function of the social, in which it is contained' (Polanyi 1944: 171). Or, more pithily, 'laissez-faire was planned' (Polanyi 1944: 51). Embedded liberalism is the concept that transposes Polanyi's analysis onto international regimes—suggesting in the process that to say anything about the content of international economic orders and about the regimes that serve them, it is necessary to look at how power and legitimate social purpose become fused to project political authority into the international system (Ruggie 1983: 198).

The international regime that emerged from the ashes of two World Wars and an interregnum that consisted of economic depression and dislocation must be understood in this Polanyian sense. That is, the task of post-war institutional reconstruction was to manoeuvre between the old, discredited liberal internationalist orthodoxy and the rejection of unimpeded multilateralism that accompanied the rise of nationalist economic objectives (most clearly those associated with Germany—both in its Imperialist and Nazi forms). The challenge became to devise a framework which would safeguard and even aid the quest for domestic stability without, at the same time, triggering the mutually destructive external consequences that had plagued the interwar period (Ruggie 1983: 209). This indeed was the essence of the embedded liberalism compromise: unlike the economic nationalism of the thirties, it would be multilateral in character; unlike the liberalism of the gold standard and free trade, its multilateralism would be predicated upon domestic interventionism (Ruggie 1983: 209). In other words, multilateralism and domestic stability were linked to and conditioned by one another. Movement towards greater openness in the international economy was to be coupled with measures designed to cushion the domestic economy from external disruptions; with those measures adopted being commensurate with the degree of external disturbance and compatible with the long-term expansion of international transactions.

This embedded liberalism can be (re)interpreted as a reinvigorated class compromise between capital and labour in the aftermath of the Great Depression and two world wars of the first half of the twentieth century. Thus, social *relations* are key to understanding the form and nature of the post-war international macroeconomic architecture.

This immediate post-war class compromise involved states actively intervening in industrial policy and moving to set standards for the social wage by constructing a variety of welfare systems (Harvey 2005: 10). In the developed world this facilitated 'redistributive politics (including some degree of political integration of working-class trade union power and support for collective bargaining), controls over free mobility of capital (some degree of financial repression through capital controls in particular), expanded public expenditures and welfare state-building, active state interventions in the economy, and some degree of planning and development' (Harvey 2005: 11). The state therefore became a 'force field' that internalised class relations, where working-class institutions such as labour unions and leftist political parties had very real influence in the exercise of state power (Harvey 2005: 12).

The international institutional framework that embodied and facilitated this embedded liberalism was the Bretton Woods system. In the words of Gerard Strange (2014: 15): '[t]he core *embedded* component of Bretton Woods was its commitment to the accommodation of *national*-level macroeconomic adjustment, economic reconstruction and industrial and state as well as market-driven capacity building (development)'[italics in original]. So, the IMF provided finance to states with short-term balance of payments problems associated with open international trade. Unlike the previous gold standard, 'adjustment' to new external economic realities would not be borne by domestic constituencies through unemployment and wage repression to suppress aggregate demand at the domestic level. Instead, the IMF policed a new regime where global currencies would be pegged to the US dollar, which in turn would be pegged to gold. Domestic currency depreciation and subsequent price inflation was the solution, rather than deflation through unemployment and wage repression. Therefore, development at the national level was prioritised over the ideological purity of the international liberal trading system. The other Bretton Woods institutions complemented this embedded liberalism of the IMF. The World Bank provided long-term investment financing alongside private investment flows to help foster industrial capacity building for development at the level of the state. The GATT/WTO system helped to cement the foundations of a Fordist international production regime through the consolidation and exploitation of national comparative advantages. Multilateralism was thus assured through the non-discrimination and most favoured nation principles of GATT/WTO negotiations.

Agriculture was largely excluded from this new regime, as part of the embedded liberalism's compromise with national-level adjustment and development. This facilitated an international economic regime where high-value-added production chains were (initially) confined to Western Europe and the USA (the core), who were supplied with raw materials for manufacture by the primary producers (the periphery).

Embedded liberalism was not felt in large swathes of the developing world. High income flows from international trade going to the core enabled core states to sustain high-wage and Keynesian modes of regulation, but also presupposed relatively low wages in and income flows to the periphery (Strange 2014: 17). The perpetuation of this external dependency condition must be understood in terms of internal power relations within the developing world. Capitalist and landowning elites dominated the states of the developing world, who benefited from an international trade regime that facilitated free trade in the primary products these elites produced (Sunkel 1973). Public policy—continued engagement with the international liberal trading and monetary regimes in this case—therefore remained sympathetic to these goals as domestic class relations reflected these priorities. This international Fordist production chain and associated Bretton Woods system was also supported through US largesse to many developing states through further financial and military assistance—often to authoritarian military dictatorships. Embedded liberalism in the core, and exploitation of the periphery were thus two sides of the same coin.

The concept of exploitation of the periphery formed the basis of a new attempt to understand the nature and influence of the contemporary, and constantly evolving, global political economy. The dependency school of thought arose in Latin America as a result of the failure of the ECLA programme of the 1960s. The ECLA development strategy of protectionism and industrialisation through import substitution in the 1950s was widespread among populist regimes throughout Latin America. Under this 'ECLA Manifesto', Prebisch (1950) contended that reliance on exports of food and raw materials would inevitably lead to a deterioration of Latin America's terms of trade, which in turn would adversely affect its domestic capital accumulation. Therefore, industrialisation should be speeded up through substitution of current imports with domestic production, income from exported raw materials would be used to import capital goods and thus increase the rate of growth, and governments would actively participate as coordinators of the industrialisation programme (So 1990: 94).

Dos Santos provides the classic definition of dependency, arguing that the character of the relationship between two or more countries 'assumes the form of dependence when some countries (the dominant ones) can expand and can be self-starting, while other countries (the dependent ones) can do this only as a reflection of that expansion' (1971: 226). Therefore, the main observation of the dependency school is that dependency is an external condition and that the main obstacle to development lays outside of the national economy (Gwynne and Kay 1999: 112). This observation represented a fundamental critique of the modernisation school, which assumed that there were internal problems associated with traditional culture, overpopulation, low investment, or lack of entrepreneurial ability (Frank 1960). As Sunkel (1973) observed, modernisation theory saw the world as uniformly progressing towards an 'end point' of development. In reality, underdevelopment is part of the structure of the economy and the result of 'structural elements'. Therefore, the structure of the system changes as a consequence of exogenous factors, which are a product of the evolution of the hegemon in the international system.

These 'structural elements' are the result of the legacy of colonialism. This historical legacy has resulted in emerging markets being totally restructured, and therefore altering their paths to development. There has been a 'development of underdevelopment' through a 'metropolis-satellite' relationship (Frank 1960). Colonialism meant the structuring of LDC economies with the aim of facilitating the transfer of economic surplus to the West, which has produced the underdevelopment of LDCs, and development in the 'West' or the 'core'. In other words, '...the historical process that generates development in the Western metropolises also simultaneously generates underdevelopment in Third World satellites' (So 1990: 97).

By the end of the 1960s, embedded liberalism began to break down, both internationally and within domestic economies. There was significant monetary change with the end of US dollar convertibility into gold and the adoption of a fully floating rate of exchange. Floating regimes were widely perceived to provide a greater cushion for domestic macroeconomic policy, given attendant impacts on the balance of payments to any form of currency depreciation or appreciation. There was also a significant trade change with the rise of a 'new protectionism' (Ruggie 1983: 221). This entailed a proliferation of non-tariff barriers (in the context of several successful GATT rounds that had been successful in reducing tariff barriers) in the form of domestic interventions (subsidies, bailouts, etc.) as well as internationally negotiated export constraints.

The elections of Mrs Thatcher in the UK in 1979 and Ronald Reagan in the USA in 1980 can be viewed as inaugurating the formal period of neoliberal economic policy dominance. Such principles were then adopted by large parts of the developing world through Structural Adjustment Programmes (SAPs). The 30 years since have seen an application of neoliberal policy ideas within the economies of both industrialised and developing countries (Palley 2005: 24). In the industrialised world this took the form of the 'US model' (Palley 2005: 25), which, whilst far from implemented uniformly, broadly involved the deregulation of financial markets, privatisation, weakening the institutions of social protection, shrinking government, cutting top rates of tax, opening international goods and capital markets, and abandoning the goal of full employment in favour of the natural rate.

The demise of the Keynesian era in the form of the Post-War Consensus, and the declining faith in ISI policies as a result of the debt crisis in the 1980s (Grugel et al. 2008: 500; Colás 2005: 75; Lapavitsas 2005: 37), as well as the role of externally imposed SAPs, all paved the way for the resurgence of this neoclassical orthodoxy in the developing world, which would later converge in what was called the 'Washington Consensus' (Chudnovsky 2007: 5). The term 'Washington Consensus' was first coined by John Williamson (1990: 1) to describe a set of technocratic prescriptions that emerged from 'Washington', a phrase that for Williamson includes the IFIs, the US Treasury, the Federal Reserve Board, senior members of the US administration and Congress, and think tanks (such as the Institute for International Economics).

Whilst responses to the crises in the 1980s were far from uniform, enough sites of convergence were identified to justify the use of the term 'Washington Consensus'; although Williamson himself suggests that the use of the word 'consensus' may be too strong and perhaps a more 'accurate, if less memorable' phrase would be 'universal convergence' (Williamson 1990: 2). Therefore, whilst individual developing nations often engaged in neoliberal reform, they did so with key idiosyncrasies due to the specific and individual nature of the economies and societies in which the reforms were taking place. However, despite this qualification by Williamson, he suggests that there are ten specific policy areas that collectively shape the nature of the Washington Consensus. These policies can be summarised as 'macroeconomic prudence, outward orientation, and domestic liberalisation' (Williamson 1990: 1), but more specifically the ten areas are: fiscal deficits, public expenditure priorities, tax reform, interest rates, exchange rate policy, trade policy, FDI, privatisation, deregulation, and property rights (Williamson 1990: 8–17). Therefore, the Washington Consensus was a set of neoliberal ideas, demanding of developing countries that they should achieve macroeconomic stability (typically by cutting government spending including subsidies to the poor), deregulating domestic markets, privatisation of state enterprises, and the opening of the economy to foreign trade and finance (Lapavitsas 2005: 37–38).

In many instances, such policy prescriptions were achieved through 'conditionality'. This was where the IMF or World Bank would withhold loans (in a context of a debt crisis in the developing world) unless the country receiving IFI money agreed on a series of structural reforms, collectively known as SAPs (Cornia et al. 1987). Therefore, Munck (2005: 77) concludes that 'for the weaker states and economies in the international system, neoliberalism arrived as an external force, principally in the shape of IFIs and through the mechanisms of SAPs in the 1980s'. However, '...developing countries [were] not simply hapless victims or passive objects of global neoliberalism: they [were], like other states, populated by classes and social forces with their own interests and strategies, many of which [were] consonant with the ruling ideology of neoliberalism' (Munck 2005: 78). Therefore, as Grugel et al. (2008: 502) conclude: 'while popular images of the Washington Consensus as a set of imperial policies forced on passive developing countries by the self-interested western powers are plainly a gross over-simplification, neoliberalism came to set the agenda for political economy globally in ways that narrowed the sphere of the possible and concentrated debate around questions about free markets to the apparent exclusion of other possibilities'.

As a result of these criticisms, and through the work of academics such as Joseph Stiglitz, the IFIs changed the prescriptions of the Washington Consensus—repackaging the policies as the 'post-Washington Consensus', and using the vehicle of Poverty Reduction Strategy Papers (PRSPs) rather than SAPs. The New Institutional Economics (NIE) critique by first North (1981) and subsequently used, for example, in the work of Stiglitz (2002) drew attention to the implications of market failure, as well as the institutional setting of economic activity, which can affect economic outcomes due to changes in these.

Therefore, the 'post-Washington Consensus' was supposed to reconcile open market policies with a commitment to democratic politics and poverty reduction (Grugel et al. 2008: 503). This manifested in increases in international aid flows, a renewed concern and drive to combat climate change, and social investment to boost human capital and investment. This partially reflected a shifting in the balance of power in the global political economy with the rise of the BRIC(S) economies. However, such an approach shared the same methodological foundations as the Washington Consensus. The market is seen as natural and not a socially created institution, and the policy prescriptions that emerged from such considerations were broadly the same as those of the original Washington Consensus (Munck 2005; Saad-Filho 2005: 117).

The impact of the (post-)Washington Consensus on the developing world cannot be overestimated. Whilst Williamson aimed to emphasise the technical, externally orientated, macroeconomic aspects of the 'counter-revolution' in development economics, the Washington Consensus went beyond deflationary adjustment, the need to counterbalance of payments deficits, or controlling inflation and balanced budgets. Indeed, privatisation, liberalisation, and an attack on corporatism, labour organisation, and welfare regimes constituted a radical change in the basis of domestic legitimacy and state–society relationships (Grugel et al. 2008: 501).

The global financial crisis of 2007 is an interesting final reference point for bringing the discussion up to date. Here is not the place for a comprehensive account of the crisis—such a task has already been completed (see, e.g., Gamble 2009; Harvey 2011). Rather than repeating and summarising a well-mapped debate that essentially falls between explanations of policy inevitability and understandings of structural inevitability, the arguments pertaining to the (non-)transformation of global political economy are most pertinent for this book. Gerard Strange (2014) suggests that the global financial crisis was one manifestation of a complex transition in which structural and agential power has become increasingly diffused: structural power as a result of increasing multipolarity and the attendant decline in 'global new constitutionalism' (Gill 2008); and agential power as a result of the re-politicisation of the economy through state-led developmentalism (Strange 2014: 3).

In terms of structural power, during the neoliberal period as analysed earlier policy prescriptions emerged from the institutions of the World Order—international organisation—that facilitated the increasing marketisation of activities previously outside of its purview: decreasing barriers to trade, and the privatisation of state assets. This was all designed to increasingly integrate peripheral states and classes into a more prosperous society (or societies) grounded in market-based social structures. For Colin Crouch (2008), this was facilitated through sustained global economic growth that was based on the expansion of private credit alongside consumer price deflation and asset price inflation.

In terms of agential power, Strange concludes that the post-global financial crisis world has led to a further diffusion of agential power as 'state autonomy becomes increasingly passive, existing de-jure, in different configurations of formal sovereignty, but losing its de-facto potency in terms of the capacity to act with operational independence, as it becomes subject to the play of external global forces and power actors' (Strange 2014: 6; see also Cohen 2006: 46). This is the result of agency—or agential power. Grounded in the market mechanism but not overdetermined by it: '[u]ltimately, this points to a developmentalist transformation of globalisation, rather than resistance to it and globalisation's deconstruction' (Strange 2014: 5).

This understanding points to a central feature of the relationship between the state and the global political economy. States clearly possess some autonomy from the principles of World Order that shape the limits of the possible for emerging markets; autonomy that for Strange at least is decreasing. However, understanding autonomy in this zero-sum way does not allow us to get to grips with the complete nature of the (re)constitution of state (relative) autonomy. Application of relative autonomy principles, as analysed in the previous chapter, to this overarching issue of the relationship between agency and structure in the global political economy will inform the discussion of the rest of this chapter.

The State and the Rise of Governance

The stylised account of post-war IPE and the attendant construction of the modern global political economy in the above section is essentially one of the rise of multilevel governance. The issue of governance is not a dry technical question, but goes to the heart of how order is established and sustained in human societies and, therefore, what a good society is (Gamble 2014: 13). Whilst 'government' is about institutions, 'governance' is about the 'social and economic, as well as political, processes by which power and influence are put into practice, outcomes are shaped and decisions made and implemented, and broad social, political, and economic trends managed and controlled by a range of actors' (Cerny 2014: 48). This clearly challenges our understanding of the state and state power. Whereas statehood presupposes an apparatus or bureaucracy, governance lacks this fixed institutional reference point. In addition, the concept of the state signifies a direct relationship to a polity, and governance is more related to policy. Governance is broader in scope and 'advocated as a means to avoid the iron fist (even when concealed in a velvet glove) of state power' (Jessop 2016: 166).

In broad terms, governance refers to the mechanisms and strategies of coordination in the face of complex reciprocal interdependence among operationally autonomous actors (Jessop 2016: 50). These actors can come from 'above' the state in the form of regional or global institutions, (transnational) corporations, or global markets and their attendant social relations that produce World Order (Cox 1996: 98); or 'below' the state with more national or local actors and, at least for Foucauldians, the governance of minds and bodies through the concept of 'governmentality' (Foucault 2008/2004) . Governance then can be said to operate at different spatial levels of analysis, with complex mutually reconstitutive interactions between them. Yet, the previous section showed empirically that these different spatial levels of analysis interact with each other differently across those very spatial contexts, as well as changing over time. In other words, '... interdependence is hardly likely to prove politically neutral' (Hay 2014: 33). Relationships between actors at different spatial levels of analysis can be characterised by either interdependence or dependence, with the latter being far more biddable than the former.

One analytical solution to the problem of differentiated power across spatial levels is called structuration. This is a complex process that would benefit from extended definition:

> '...a dynamic system in which the conduct of actors and the context in which they find themselves are intimately and iteratively interlinked... we conceive of political-economic processes as operative at distinct spatial levels within each of which actors orient themselves strategically to the context in which they perceive themselves to be located and seek to realise specific goals and intentions'. (Hay 2014: 38)

By introducing the concept of power into this analysis, it follows that there are deeper levels of structuration present—a stratified social ontology.

Structural constraints can be imposed by the agency of the more powerful, setting the context for the less powerful (or powerless). In other words, 'they [powerful agents] condition the possible range of strategies and actions within a specified social and political context, but are not immediately accessible to transformation by the agents that they embed within such a context' (Hay 2014: 39). If follows that power in this context becomes the ability to transform aspects of the context in which other less powerful groups and individuals are constrained to formulate their strategies. Also, it follows that higher levels of structuration are not immediately accessible to direct intervention by actors in lower levels—even though these higher levels have a crucial bearing upon the strategic selectivity of the context in which they realise their strategic intentions.

At the highest level of structuration—for the purposes of this book 'the global'—there is an analytical problem of an object without a (discrete) subject. In other words, in the absence of any higher levels of structuration there are no decisive actors in the same way as there are at lower levels. There is a deficit of actors capable of refashioning global political economy directly. Instead, there are a multitude of actors at lower levels whose actions and interactions with each other ultimately contribute to a series of global process—for the purposes of the current era: globalisation. This implies that globalisation per se should not be used as an independent variable in the sense that it is a process of tendencies and counter-tendencies that vary over spatial and temporal contexts (Hay 2014). Whilst globalisation plays a role in shaping state capacity and autonomy, accounts need to be made that are sensitive to the fact that globalisation as a process shapes and constrains different actors in different ways, whilst simultaneously being open to shaping by those very actors that are constrained by it, also to differing degrees at different times.

In summary, governance shapes and is shaped by a complex process of structuration across multiple spatial levels. As the previous chapter demonstrated, the state has a key role as a site of institutional integration of power relations and social domination; but, structuration clearly shows that it simultaneously exists in a complex, heterogeneous, and multilevel network. On the one hand, the state is but one spatial level in this model, but on the other, when combined with the analysis of the previous chapter, the state can be seen as more than this. What structuration gives us is not a state that is of equal ontological weight but analytical weight. In other words, the state is clearly not a sovereign authority in a single hierarchical command structure, but rather it can be considered to be an institution that is primus inter pares (Jessop 2016: 185). Furthermore, governance involves not only institutional design but also the transformation of subjects and their orientations to the world. Therefore, the role of power and knowledge in shaping the attributes, capacities, and identities of social agents becomes important to understand.

In order to flesh out the implications of this analysis the rest of this chapter will complete two tasks. In essence, the analytical starting point of structuration presents two problems that must be overcome. The first is to understand the nature of the highest level of structuration: the global. A robust understanding of this object without a subject must be constructed. This will be achieved through an application of Cox's concept of World Order (see, e.g., Cox and Sinclair 1996). The second task is then to understand the implications of this for the state, thus sharpening our understanding of contemporary expressions of state capacity and autonomy in emerging markets in an era characterised by globalisation. A final section concludes about how these forces coalesce in order to generate discreet state projects—which in the context of this book are state projects in capitalist states at early stages of development that drive towards rapid, catch-up development. This is in order to complete the groundwork needed to construct a robust theory for understanding 21st-century developmentalism in the next chapter.

Governance from Above: Globalisation and World Order

The ideological character of governance from the Second World War onwards shows itself in the aspiration to impose a greater degree of uniformity and convergence on the rest of the world than would otherwise exist. Ideologies have always played a major role in shaping contemporary governance of the international (political) economy, which makes possible international orders. Such orders depend upon the role played by leading states: in the current era the USA and *Pax Americana* but historically it has been other hegemons such the UK and its attendant *Pax Britannica*. As such, it is their ideologies which become translated to the international sphere and become accepted as the new common sense (Gamble 2014: 16; see also Cox 1996a).

Change in international society results from state-level movements, which then get internationalised through passive revolution

(Cox 1996b; Gramsci; 1971). 'World hegemony is thus in its beginnings an outward expansion of the internal (national-state) hegemony'. It is the articulation of 'universal norms, institutions, and mechanisms which lay down general rules of behaviour for states and for those forces of civil society that act across national boundaries, rules which support the dominant mode of production' (Cox 1996a: 137). This allows a much more subtle and complete definition of world hegemony to be constructed: 'World hegemony can be described as a social structure, an economic structure, and a political structure; and it cannot be simply one of these things but must be all three' (Cox 1996a: 137).

This theoretical analysis allows the formation of an alternative ontology of World Order (Cox 1981). Understood as the product of the interrelationship of three mutually constitutive spheres—ideas, material capabilities, and institutions—World Order constitutes the top level of structuration in the context of the subject matter of this book. Material capabilities are understood as the productive and destructive potentials of any given state. Ideas are either (a) intersubjective meanings associated with specific constellations of social relations or (b) collective images of social order held by different groups of people that tend to coalesce around concepts such as justice or the public good. Institutions are the physical manifestation of World Order and the process of institutionalisation is a means of stabilising and perpetuating a particular order (Cox 1996b: 98). This has important implications for hegemony, as institutions become 'particular amalgams of ideas and material power which in turn influence the development of ideas and material capabilities', or, they are 'the anchor of hegemony' (Cox 1996b: 99). The hegemony of capital can thus be shown as more than just the power of its economic relations, revealing the underpinning intellectual and moral structures that help create consensus towards that hegemony.

This heuristic device gives analytical purchase on global governance and its concomitant institutions. Combined with structuration this gives us the means by which to understand the interrelationship between the state and other spatial levels of analysis in the contemporary global political economy: ultimately facilitating a robust Developmental Regime approach to understanding states and their desire to develop in the 21st century. The drive towards convergence by global governance was normatively justified as delivering a public good (Kindleberger 1986), although has also been critiqued as serving a particular set of interests (Harvey 2003) . In the context of *Pax Americana*, this can be interpreted as a Western agenda grounded in the philosophical traditions of the Enlightenment and the ideas of universality and cultural superiority. Enlightenment thinkers such as Immanuel Kant show this with concepts such as the doctrine of the categorical imperative. The essence of the Kantian categorical imperative is that actions themselves contain a distinctly moral character, thus reflecting an ethic of conviction as opposed to a more utilitarian ethic of responsibility where suitably moral ends can justify the means (Hampsher-Monk 1992: 318). Thus, this categorical imperative supposes that 'reason can discover an Archimedean moral standpoint that transcends the distortions and limitations of time and place' (Linklater 1998: 48). This thick conception of cosmopolitanism was dominant in Western philosophical thought and strongly believed that the precise content of a single universalisable conception of the good life could be determined. Rousseau's concept of the general will is formulated upon similar arguments (Riley 1978: 432).

There has long been a belief in Western thought of its own cultural superiority. From the writings of the first Western historian Herodotus (Herodotus 1996; see also Hall 1989) this can be discerned. Throughout Herodotus' *Histories*, there runs a constant theme, which displays the Greeks as naturally superior to their Persian counterparts. More contemporary manifestations can be understood through the work of Edward Said and his analysis of the concept of 'Orientalism' (Said 1978): 'a form of knowledge through which Eastern civilisations were seen as subordinate to the West' (Cox 2002: 9). Western thought has therefore sought to portray its own form of civilisation as the dichotomy to foreign forms of barbarism. As a result, colonial history, along with other epochs of Western civilisation, can be seen as a 'civilising process' which was conceived as a universal phenomenon characterising the Enlightenment of eighteenth-century Europe, at one with universal reason and natural laws applicable in physical sciences, economics, law, and morality. The finality of the process was civilisation in the singular.

Whilst in the post-Enlightenment period there was a Romantic reaction to the cosmopolitanism of Enlightenment thought that led to a resurgence of communitarianism in Western philosophy, it became obscured by the role of the Cold War. 'As the Cold War came to dominate thinking about the future of the world, the choice seemed to be between two universalisms, capitalism and communism, both derived from the European Enlightenment. The sense of a coexistence of a plurality of civilisations was obscured' (Cox 2002: 3). Another reaction to this distinctly Western cosmopolitanism emerged at the end of the Cold War. The Enlightenment belief that reason could morally and politically unify the human race was highly criticised due to its tendency towards the potential for domination by areas of thought such as postmodernism and feminism. However, for Cox (2002: 4), 'these new burgeoning identities were contradicted by the triumphant universalism of the Cold War victor: the ideology of economic globalisation'. As a result of this triumphalism, Fukayama's (1992) thesis concerning the 'End of History' being one manifestation of this, 'the universalistic notion of civilisation has...remained a characteristic of Western consciousness and an intellectual obstacle to recognition of the ontological equality of other civilisations' (Cox 2002: 3).

Enthusiasm for the expansion of the liberal, capitalist global order occurs not just because of the belief in cultural superiority, but because of the inherent logic contained within liberal theory that maximum gains can only be achieved if the system is universalised, thus Kant's conclusion that a world of states that have republican, civil constitutions will be one of 'perpetual peace'. This is due to his belief that democracies share a cosmopolitan morality, which is 'assisted through history by the Great Artist Nature herself' (Kant 1991/1795: 108). This is referring to the fact that economics is also a driving factor as the costs of war in an interdependent world increase to the extent that reason dictates that it is no longer profitable. Therefore, moral reason dictates, due to the categorical imperative, that states with shared democratic norms and values will not go to war with each other. Furthermore, liberal economic theory dictates that the real benefits of capitalism will only be fully realised after the global dissemination of its distinctive form of political economy. Efficiency is a strong theme in liberal analysis and the globalisation of liberal principles facilitates its realisation in two senses. Firstly, there is a more efficient global allocation of resources, 'international economics holds that the freeing of trade and capital flows leads to a more efficient allocation of the worlds scarce resources, generating greater output than would be possible under protectionism' (Kapstein 2000: 362). Secondly, there is a more efficient production of goods in the world economy through the 'gains from trade'. Here is not the place to go into detailed analysis of Ricardo's model of comparative advantage (see Ricardo 1973 [1817]), it is enough to say that the model dictates that 'trade permits countries more effectively to exploit their factor endowments and to gain from specialisation' (Hurrell and Woods 1995: 448). Thus, liberal logic proposes that a truly globalised world economy will lead to the most efficient distribution of goods and services on a global scale, reducing inequality to the maximum possible extent.

Global governance can be (re)interpreted as the contemporary institutional manifestation of this philosophical drive towards uniformity, guided by principles of economic (neo)liberalism. Global Governance institutions become key institutions in understanding 'one mechanism through which the universal norms of a world hegemony are expressed' (Cox 1996a: 137). Cox outlines five features of international organisation that express its hegemonic role. Firstly, 'the institutions embody the rules which facilitate the expansion of hegemonic world orders'; second, 'they are themselves the product of the hegemonic world order'; third, 'they ideologically legitimate the norms of the world order'; fourth, 'they co-opt the elites from the periphery countries'; and fifth, 'they absorb counter hegemonic ideas' (Cox 1996a: 138).

The Bretton Woods monetary institutions represent Western efforts to realise this first goal of the expansion of the hegemonic order of global capitalism. Structural adjustment was a governing principle behind the IMF's decisions on who it should lend money to. Countries that refused to initiate reform based around the liberalisation and democratisation of their economic and political institutions were denied access to the IMF's funds (Underhill 1996: 234–235). Furthermore, in the late 1990s the World Bank shifted its focus to a specifically political agenda as it moves away from completely free market policies and begins to embrace New Public Management (NPM). 'In such formulations, the World Bank verges on expressing a directly political agenda, recommending some forms of democracy rather than others' (Hansen et al. 2002: 116). Furthermore, the whole *raison d'etre* of the WTO is the continuing liberalisation and opening of the world economy, thus conforming to a Western-originated universal international norm that free trade will benefit all who take part. The fact that this is in direct contradiction to the path that many Western economies chose in order to develop, i.e. protectionism until international competitiveness is assured, is not lost on the elites of many developing states, or indeed on radical intellectuals in the West.

The economic institutions of global governance are not the only way in which the hegemony of global capitalism is spread, as the more political institutions also play a role. For example, the institution of human rights 'embodies the promise inherent in the logic of *one* conception of global civil society, understood as the space of un-coerced human association' [emphasis added] (Hopgood 2000: 1). Thus, 'human rights... are not morally self-sufficient: a concept of the good life (of the way people ought to live) is always required to underwrite them'. Whilst NGOs and institutions such as the UN and its Universal Declaration of Human Rights 'appear to deal with *people as they are*, [they deal with] them as they *have already been remade*' (Hopgood 2000: 2). These bodies that promote liberal human rights 'are just as much part of a totalising project, and not, as they appear to be, part of the antidote' (Hopgood 2000: 21). Indeed, as a moral institution human rights inherently reflect the priority of the private over the public, and of choice over constraint. It is this prioritisation of the private over the public that is so essential to aiding the spread of global capitalism. They are a crucial ideological pillar of capitalism: property relations and market capitalism were fundamentally private and not public matters. Civil society... [is] the 'space' in which individuals, now the moral building blocks of any collective project, pursues their private interests' (Hopgood 2000: 4).

The second function of international organisation that expresses its hegemonic role, as outlined by Cox, is the fact that these institutions are themselves a product of the hegemonic World Order. This is true of many major contemporary international organisations. As this chapter has shown, the Bretton Woods institutions—IMF, World Bank, GATT/WTO—were all products of a new Western capitalist hegemony after the Second World War; the same is true for the UN. One method that hegemonic states use to secure their dominance over these institutions is through weighing formal participation in their favour. For example, 'IMF member states provide the fund with resources through a system of quotas more or less proportional to the size of respective national economies, and they received votes in the Fund relative to these quota contributions. In this way the power of the richest countries was entrenched' (Underhill 1996: 235). This fact is also demonstrated by the constitution of the Security Council in the UN and its five permanent members who were the dominant world powers during the time of its inception. Another is through 'an informal structure of influence reflecting the different levels of real political and economic power which underlies the formal procedures for decisions' (Cox 1996a: 138). This is also demonstrated by the workings of the Security Council of the UN, and the ways in which America has bought many of the more peripheral countries votes on the rotating membership of the Security

Council through its superior economic power, such as Syria's vote for Resolution 1441 concerning Iraqi disarmament of supposed Weapons of Mass Destruction (WMD) stocks.

Global governance also plays an ideological role of legitimating the norms of the existing world order. Examples of this include the World Bank Development Reports. For example in 1997, the Development Report, entitled *The State in a Changing World*, advocates a non-interventionist role for the state in a modern, capitalist, global economy. 'For many, the lesson of recent years has been that the state could not deliver on its promises: transition economies have had to make a wrenching shift toward the market economy, and much of the developing world has had to face up to the failure of state dominated development strategies. Even the mixed economies of the industrialised world, in response to the failures of government intervention, have opted for a decided shift in the mix in favor of market mechanisms' (World Bank 1997: iii). Cox also points to further examples of this ideological legitimisation such as the OECDs recommendation of monetarism, thus endorsing 'a dominant consensus of policy thinking in the core countries and strengthened those who were determined to combat inflation this way against others who were more concerned about unemployment' (Cox 1996a: 138–139).

The fourth function of international organisation that highlights its hegemonic role is the fact that it 'co-opts the elites from peripheral countries'. The inclusion of this factor reveals Cox's underlying methodology, which owes much of its intellectual heritage to the writings of Antonio Gramsci. Thus, Cox writes 'elite talent from peripheral countries is co-opted into international institutions in the manner of *transformismo*' (Cox 1996a: 139). *Transformismo* is one aspect of 'passive revolution', a distinctly Gramscian concept that suggests that many countries (societies) had 'imported or had thrust upon them aspects of a new order created abroad, without the old order having being displaced' (Cox 1996a: 129). Therefore, *transformismo* refers to 'individuals from peripheral countries, though they may come to international institutions with the idea of working from within to change the system, are condemned to work within the structures of the passive revolution' (Cox 1996a: 139).

This concept of *transformismo* is also the key to understanding Cox's fifth point, which is the absorption of counter-hegemonic ideas. '*Transformismo* can serve as a strategy of assimilating and domesticating potentially dangerous ideas by adjusting them to the policies of the dominant coalition and can thereby obstruct the formation of class based organized opposition to established social and political power' (Cox 1996a: 130). This point of the absorption of counter-hegemonic ideas is derived from Cox's (and Gramsci's) expanded concept of hegemony above and beyond that simply 'power over' (Gill and Law 1993: 93). Gramsci's separation of historical materialism from historical economism allows a broader methodological process to be used which takes into account social, economic, and political spheres. Thus, with regard to the international arena, 'world hegemony can be described as a social structure, an economic structure, and a political structure; and it cannot simply be one of these things but must be all three' (Gill and Law 1993: 137). This idea of consensus as a fundamental part of hegemony is drawn from the Machiavellian concept of power being like a centaur: half man and half beast (Cox 1996a: 127). Coercion is only applied in the marginal cases, as hegemony by this definition is only possible through consent. States have traditionally performed this function, shown by the existence of social democracy in Europe (Gill 1986: 205–221). Thus, what was originally a clear political choice becomes treated as an immutable and uncontroversial aspect of the way things are (Gamble 2014: 16). However, whilst counter-hegemonic ideas can be absorbed to some extent, they must not reach levels where they fundamentally contradict the hegemonic programme.

This Western universal emancipatory project of liberal democracy and (neoliberal) capitalism is far from complete, as globalisation has also led to 'bottom-up' resistance and therefore involves a 'dialectic of homogenisation and diversification' (Gill 1986: 205). Therefore, this book rejects the Fukayama (1992) thesis of the triumph of liberal democracy, as no such universal system exists. The book also rejects scholars, such as Huntingdon (1997: 78) and his conclusion that a universal culture does not exist in any significant sense, as modernisation does not necessarily mean Westernisation. Rather, following a Strategic-Relational Approach as outlined in the previous chapter, globalisation—and its vehicles for the articulation of a global hegemony of capital in the form of global governance—should be viewed not so much as an end state, but as a tendency to which counter-tendencies may be mobilised (Hay 2014: 43). Contemporary global governance and the World Order that it acts on behalf of is not monolithic, and has many internal contradictions that generate sites of resistance; but its power is also undeniable

(Gamble 2014: 29). How the state operates within this changing terrain of shifting hegemony and counter-hegemony will now be explored in the next section.

The State in World Order

Different states clearly have different influence in this World Order. Hegemonic states have the most influence. In the context of the current era, this is the USA and *Pax Americana*. The institutions of World Order are reflections of the ideas and ideologies that underpin the correlation of forces that is also a crystallisation of that state in terms of its social relations. Emerging states, by virtue of the fact that they are emerging economies in a globalising world, operate under the conditions of contemporary World Order, which is shaped and defined largely elsewhere in the global political economy. Their agency is not merely a reflection of the broader structures that characterise World Order. Following neopluralists such as Cerny (2014: 49), the outcome of processes such as globalisation is not determined by the a priori existence of cohesive, vertically unified projects of hegemonic states as such. Instead, they stem from the interaction of a range of individual and collective actors below, outside, and surrounding (hegemonic) states and societies. These actors have very different kinds of social bonds, levels of social, economic, and political power resources, understandings of how to use that power, material interests, normative values, and political projects (Cerny 2014: 49).

From the opposite end of the agent-structure debate, states are not simply able to pursue any national-based agenda free from the multitudinous influences at different levels of structuration either. But what is important to note is that this influence not only changes depending upon the level of material capabilities of states; but also that the power of World Order—expressed partially through institutions of global governance—waxes and wanes over time. For example, it can be seen at its strongest in times of economic downturn and austerity (Gamble 2014: 29; see also Crouch 2008). Any account that seeks to understand the role of the state in a 21st-century development process must be sensitive to the nature of World Order, and its ever-changing influences and shaping of the limits of the possible for Emerging markets.

Governance involves not only institutional design appropriate to different objects of governance, but it has also been argued to involve the transformation of subjects and their orientations to the world. Foucauldians have contributed to this field, drawing attention to the role of power and knowledge in shaping the attributes, capacities, and identities of social agents and how, through a process of governmentality (Foucault 2008/2004), these agents become self-governing and self-reforming. In the context of neoliberalism, for example, this entails a reflection of the self as an entrepreneurial producer and a demanding consumer, 'aware of their choices and rights as well as of actions that can shift the respective scope and powers of the market mechanism and state intervention' (Jessop 2016: 173).

Drawing together both this Gramscian understanding of World Order and more Foucauldian understanding of subject, the theoretical and analytical implications for the state can be more completely understood. The previous chapter suggested that the state plays a key role as a site of institutional integration of power relations and the concomitant sites of social domination. However, this chapter has drawn attention to the contemporary process of structuration, and the inherently political nature of this process due to a stratified social ontology. This set of processes reminds us that the state is not a supreme form of command set in a single hierarchical command structure. However, the classic view that state power is in decline (Ohmae 1990), is not appropriate either. For this argument ignores the transformation of state power in the context of structuration, both above and below the state. Other modalities of state power manifest themselves as alternative social structures and institutions of rule, rather than any kind of 'retreat of the state' per se (Douglas 2000).

Attention must be drawn to the way that governance is always conducted under the primacy of the state's unique role in managing the tension between economic and political advantages and its ultimate responsibility of managing social cohesion (Jessop 2016: 177). This facilitates an understanding of the state as an institution that is primus inter pares in a complex, heterogeneous, and multilevel network (Jessop 2016: 185). The myriad social forces and structures that facilitate globalisation certainly exert pressure on the state, but it is the state that remains the institution with particular capabilities and capacities that must be shaped in order to exert power through social domination. In essence, in shaping state capacities and its (relative) autonomy, the world market also modifies the balance of forces within states; and therefore, it is states that become the primary node of governance for analysis.

Conclusions: Integrating Globalisation in the Political Economy of Development

The process of structuration governs theorisation of spatial levels of analysis. Whilst it draws attention to the fact that not all levels of structuration are equally constraining at all times for all agents, it does not per se provide the tools to establish the how and why of this. If combined with the concepts of the state as a social relation(ship) and power understood as a manifestation of domination by a wide variety of agents and concomitant social relationships (see the previous chapter), these questions can begin to be answered. For if the state is understood as a residue of social relationships that means examination of how those relationships manifest themselves at the different levels of structuration and within their attendant institutions. In addition, the role that expressions of social power at one spatial level of structuration play in influencing those at another must be taken into account. It also points to an understanding of the processes of institutionalisation, and how those relationships change in both spatial and temporal contexts.

At the top level of structuration, the lack of discreet agents facilitates a need to develop a distinct ontology of World Order. The evolution of the international system thus becomes one of the changing natures of World Order (Cox and Sinclair 1996). This World Order and its attendant institutional manifestations in the form of international organisation are not homogenous and totalising projects: they are hegemonic, but this means more a shaping of the limits of the possible (Santiso 2006) through bending and moulding domestic social relations and being shaped by them—with the state as both the spatial level and institution that is primus inter pares. Empirical analysis must therefore be broadened out to include not only global institutions as key actors (IMF, WB, WTO, TNCs, etc.) but also the ideological and material influences on social relations that underpin those institutions. From this is distilled a broadened understanding of the state within global neoliberalism, contained but not bound by the different elements of contemporary World Order.

Governance practices can be seen to range from the expansion of international and supranational regimes through national and regional public-private partnerships to more localised networks of power and decision-making. However, the state acts as the institution that is the core site of expression of social forces of domination, and therefore must become the key site of analysis. Developing robust analytical tools for this task becomes imperative. The next chapter will attempt such a task in the context of emerging markets and catch-up development, through the expansion of a Developmental Regime model.

References

Cerny, P. (2010). *Rethinking world politics: A theory of transnational neopluralism*. Oxford: Oxford University Press.

Cerny, P. (2014). Neoliberalism: Alive and well? *International Studies Review, 16*(4), 645–646.

Chudnovsky, D. (2007). *The elusive quest for growth in Argentina*. London: Routledge.

Cohen, B. J. (2006). The macrofoundations of monetary power. In D. Andrews (Ed.), *International monetary power* (pp. 31–50). Ithaca: Cornell University Press.

Colás, A. (2005). Neoliberalism, globalisation, and international relations. In A. Saad-Filho & D. Johnston (Eds.), *Neoliberalism: A critical reader* (pp. 70–80). London: Pluto.

Cornia, G. A., Jolly, R., & Stewart, F. (1987). An overview of the alternative approach. In G. A. Cornia, R. Jolly, & F. Stewart (Eds.), *Adjustment with a human face, Vol. I: Protecting the vulnerable and promoting growth*. Oxford: Clarendon Press.

Cox, R. W., & Sinclair, T. (Eds.). (1996). *Approaches to world order*. Cambridge: Cambridge University Press.

Cox, R. W. (1996a). Gramsci, hegemony and international relations: An essay in method. In R. W. Cox & T. J. Sinclair (Eds.), *Approaches to world order*. Cambridge: Cambridge University Press.

Cox, R. W. (1996b). Social forces, states, and world orders: Beyond international relations Theory. In R. W. Cox & T. J. Sinclair (Eds.), *Approaches to world order*, Cambridge: Cambridge University Press.

Cox, R. (1981). Social forces, states, and world orders: Beyond international relations theory. *Millennium: Journal of International Studies, 10*(2), 126–155.

Cox, R. W. (2002). Civilisations and the twenty first century: Some theoretical considerations. In M. Mozaffari (Ed.), *Globalisation and civilisations*. London: Routledge.

Crouch, C. (2008). What will follow the demise of privatised Keynesianism? *The Political Quarterly, 79*(4), 476–487.

Dos Santos, T. (1971). The structure of dependence. *American Economic Review, 60*, 231–236.

Douglas, I. R. (2000). Globalisation and the retreat of the State. In B. K. Gills (Ed.), *Globalization and the politics of resistance* (pp. 110–131). Basingstoke: Palgrave Macmillan.

Foucault, M., (2008/2004). *The birth of biopolitics. Lectures at the college de France , 1978–1979.* Hampshire: Palgrave Macmillan.

Frank, A. G. (1960). Human capital and economic growth. *Economic Development and Cultural Change, 8*(2), 170–173.

Fukayama, F. (1992). *The end of history and the last man.* London: Penguin.

Gamble, A. (2009). *The spectre at the feast: Capitalist crisis and the politics of recession.* Hampshire: Palgrave.

Gamble, A. (2014). Ideologies of governance. In A. Payne & N. Phillips (Eds.), *The handbook of the international political economy of governance.* Cheltenham: Edward Elgar.

Gill, S. (1986). Hegemony consensus, and trilateralism. *Review of International Studies, 12,* 205–222.

Gill, S. (2008). *Power and resistance in the new order.* Basingstoke: Palgrave Macmillan.

Gill, S., & Law, D. (1993). Global hegemony and the structural power of capital. In S. Gill (Ed.), *Gramsci, historical materialism and international relations.* Cambridge: Cambridge University Press.

Gramsci, A. (1971). *Selections from the prison notebooks of Antonio Gramsci* (Q. Hoare & G. Nowell-Smith, Ed. & Trans.). London: Lawrence and Wishart.

Grugel, J., Riggirozzi, P., & Thirkell-White, B. (2008). Beyond the Washington consensus? Asia and Latin America in search of more autonomous development. *International Affairs, 84*(3), 499–517.

Gwynne, R. N., & Kay, C. (1999). *Latin America transformed: Globalisation and modernity.* New York: Oxford University Press.

Hall, E. (1989). *Inventing the barbarian: Greek self-definition through tragedy.* Oxford: Oxford University Press.

Hampsher-Monk, I. (1992). *A history of modern political thought.* Oxford: Oxford University Press.

Hansen, H. K., Salskov-Iversen, D., & Bislev, S. (2002). Transnational discourse communities and new public management. In M. Ougaard & R. Higgott (Eds.), *Towards a global polity.* London: Routledge.

Harvey, D. (2003). *The new imperialism.* USA: Oxford University Press.

Harvey, D. (2005). *A brief history of neoliberalism.* Oxford: Oxford University Press.

Harvey, D. (2011). *The enigma of capital and the crises of capitalism.* London: Profile Books.

Hay, C. (2014). Levels of governance and their interaction. In A. Payne & N. Phillips (Eds.), *The handbook of the international political economy of governance.* Cheltenham: Edward Elgar.

Herodotus (1996). *The histories* (Vol. 78). London: Verso.

Hopgood, S. (2000). Reading the small print of global civil society: The inexorable hegemony of the liberal self. *Millennium: Journal of International Studies, 29*(1), 1–25.

Huntingdon, S. P. (1997). *Clash of civilisations and the remaking of the world order*. Oxford: Oxford University Press.
Hurrell, A., & Woods, N. (1995). Globalisation and inequality. *Millennium, 24*(3), 447–470.
Jessop, B. (2016). *The state: Past, present, and future*. London: Polity.
Kapstein, E. B. (2000). Winners and losers in the global economy. *International organisation, 54*(2), 359–384.
Kant, I. (1991/1795). Perpetual peace: A philosophical sketch. In H. S. Reiss (Ed.), *Political Writings*. Cambridge: Cambridge University Press.
Kindleberger, C. P. (1986). International public goods without international government. *The American Economic Review, 76*(1), 1–13.
Krasner, S. D. (1983). *International Regimes*. Ithaca, NY: Cornell University Press.
Lapavitsas, C. (2005). Mainstream economics in the neoliberal Era. In A. Saad-Filho & D. Johnston (Eds.), *Neoliberalism: A critical reader* (pp. 30–40). London: Pluto.
Linklater, A. (1998). *The transformation of political community*. Cambridge: Cambridge University Press.
Munck, R. (2005). Neoliberalism and politics, and the politics of neoliberalism. In A. Saad-Filho & D. Johnstone (Eds.), *Neoliberalism: A critical reader*. London: Pluto.
North, D. (1981). Structure and change in economic history. New York: W.W. Norton.
Ohmae, O. (1990). *The borderless world: Power and strategy in the interlinked economy*. New York: Harper Business.
Palley, T. I. (2005). From keynesian to neoliberalism: Shifting paradigms in economics. In A. Saad-Filho & D. Johnstone (Eds.), *Neoliberalism: A critical reader* (pp. 20–29). London: Pluto.
Polanyi, K. (1944). *The great transformation*. Boston: Beacon Press.
Prebisch, R. (1950). *The economic development of Latin America and its principal problems*. New York: Columbia University Press.
Ricardo, D. (1973/1817). *The principles of political economy and taxation*. New York: Dent & Sons.
Riley, P. (1978). The general will before Rousseau. *Political theory, 6*(4), 485–516.
Ruggie, J. (1983). International regimes, transactions, and change: Embedded liberalism in the post-war economic order. In S. Krasner (Ed.), *International regimes* (pp. 195–233). Ithaca: Cornell University Press.
Saad-Filho, A. (2005). The political economy of neoliberalism in Iatin America. In A. Saad-Filho & D. Johnstone (Eds.), *Neoliberalism: A critical reader* (pp. 222–229). London: Pluto.
Said, E. (1978). *Orientalism*. New York: Pantheon.

Santiso, J. (2006). *Latin America's political economy of the possible.* Massachusetts: MIT Press.

Soloman, M. S., & Rupert, M. (2002). Historical Materialism, ideology, and the politics of globalising capitalism. In M. Rupert & H. Smith (Eds.), *Historical materialism and globalisation.* London: Routledge.

So, A. Y. (1990). *Social change and development: Modernisation, dependency, and world-system theories.* London: Sage.

Strange, G. (2014). *Towards a new political economy of development: States and regions in the post-neoliberal world.* Basingstoke: Palgrave Macmillan.

Stiglitz, J. (2002). *Globalisation and its discontents.* London: Penguin Books.

Sunkel, O. (1973). Transnational capitalism and national disintegration in Latin America. *Social and Economic Studies, 22*(1), 132–176.

Underhill, G. (1996). IMF: International monetary fund. In I. McLean (Ed.), *The Oxford concise dictionary of politics.* Oxford: Oxford University Press.

World Bank. (1997). *World Bank development report 1997: The state in a changing world.* New York: World Bank.

Williamson, J. (1990). *Latin American adjustment: How much has happened?* Washington, DC: Institute for International Economics.

CHAPTER 4

Developmental Regimes in the 21st Century

The previous chapters have explored fully the twin concepts of capacity and (relative) autonomy. This has been for the purpose of working towards a reinvigorated theory of the Developmental State, fit for the 21st century. The Developmental Regime approach attempts to overcome theoretical inadequacies associated with the traditional Developmental State literature, whilst at the same time recognising the fact that it is through this work that such an approach is possible. Analysis of a regime tripod as first outlined by Pempel (1999) and subsequently developed by Wylde (2012, 2014) showed the nature of the tripod's three legs: socio-economic relations, institutions, and a public policy profile. Traditionally understood in terms of Evans' embedded autonomy and the associated Developmental State literature, this can be complemented through consideration of the related concepts of capacity and autonomy (Wylde 2016).

Capacity and autonomy can be best understood on three levels. First, through an understanding of the state as a social relation(ship) (see Chap. 2). Through embracing the lessons of relative autonomy, a Developmental Regime concept is able to 'bring class back in' to the analysis through a nuanced understanding of the state as a social relation; that is a condensation of social relations of previous strategically selective terrains. Second, through an understanding of power that lies between (neo-)Marxism and (neo-)Pluralism (also see Chap. 2). Power as an expression of domination manifests itself both in class understood in relational terms and in other more plural ways such as in the family,

C. Wylde, *Emerging Markets and the State*, International Political Economy Series, DOI 10.1057/978-1-137-55655-4_4

religion, ethnicity, as well as in more Weberian terms such as party or organisation. This combines with the state as a social relation to facilitate a better understanding of the creation and maintenance of state projects. Third, through an understanding of governance that is one of complex, multi-tiered structures and concomitant agents that are embedded through a process of structuration (see Chap. 3). Whilst the state is primus inter pares, it operates on strategically selective terrain that is present at multiple simultaneous spatial levels that interact through structuration. These facilitate and/or constrain certain actions and actors over others, which in turn has an impact on the nature of the state and the strategically selective terrain in which it itself operates within.

One form of strategically selective terrain that a state can take is that of a developmental persuasion. That is, a state that sets to the task of engaging in catch-up development, defined within the contours of its own history but broadly involving rapid (decades rather than centuries) industrialisation and attendant—although not necessarily *post hoc ergo propter hoc*—increases in the key social indicators of development. The key concern of this book is to understand the conditions under which this has facilitated success, and therefore on the other side of the coin understand those where it has not. This task began within the Developmental State tradition (see Chap. 2), distilling down into a core concern for the twin concepts of capacity and autonomy. This chapter will suggest that a modified approach is needed to adequately understand the contours of state capacity and autonomy in the 21st century; that of the Developmental Regime.

The use of the term regime becomes crucial in the sense of not only representing a break with traditional Developmental State theory, but due to the implications of the word itself. 'Regime' involves a sustained fusion among the institutions of the state, social relations, and public policy. In other words, to talk of a regime is to denote the fact that distinct (non-)developmental profiles are distilled from an understanding of state capacity and autonomy. Regimes are based on the complex interactions between the institutions of the state—understood as a social relation—and the relative autonomy that is it able, or not, to carve out. In turn, these fusions of capacity and autonomy are reflected in specific public policy profiles, which result in the character of a regime being determined by the social relations of that state, and the institutionalisation and bias of the public policies that result. The three essential elements of a regime are therefore socio-economic relations, institutions, and a public policy profile (Pempel 1998: 30; see also Wylde 2012, 2014).

The use of the term developmental serves a dual purpose. First, whilst regime denotes a break from the Developmental State tradition the phrase developmental serves the opposite purpose of recognising the intellectual tradition from which this analysis builds upon. Second, the purpose is to restrict the analysis to a specific type of state: an emerging market that is seeking catch-up development in the context of a World Order characterised by neoliberal globalisation. Whilst there can theoretically be many different kinds of regime, those of the developmental persuasion are the ones that fall within the envelope of the analysis of this book.

It is the purpose of this chapter to take each leg of the tripod in turn, with a section on each. These sections will argue that through their analysis an understanding of developmentalism through the twin concepts of capacity and autonomy can facilitate a better understanding of the role of the state. This will contribute to understanding the form and function of state projects in emerging markets associated with national–state development in an era characterised by neoliberal globalisation. This framework can subsequently be operationalised as a theoretical bedrock, anchoring the empirical analysis of Argentina and Malaysia in the second half of this book.

Socio-Economic Relations

The first leg of the tripod thus becomes socio-economic relations. This book views socio-economic relations as important representations of different class (and other) interests and the relational aspects of those interests—both domestically and internationally. Power is a heuristic for understanding social relations (Smith 2009: 87). Due to epistemological, ontological, and empirical differences, a definitive conceptualisation of power is impossible. Rather, a framework for analysing it must be provided. In Chap. 2, this book suggested that power can be best understood through analysing the ways in which power relationships manifest themselves in terms of social domination. This social domination can be perceived in a number of ways, which vary across both time and space.

One way to frame this debate is through the agent-structure dichotomy. Rational Choice Theorists (see, e.g., Riker 1990) see agents as essentially passive, whilst behaviouralists (see, e.g., Clarke and Whiteley 1990) focus on individual behaviour. Both are agent-centred in the sense that power is intentional (Smith 2009: 74). Furthermore, both focus on actions of agents, rather than their perceptions. These are instead the focus of a more Foucauldian analysis. How agents interpret the world and subsequently (socially) construct it are central to understanding power. This is where structure becomes more apparent in theorising power. In the context of postmodernism: 'Individuals have little possibility of breaking out of their particular episteme and therefore the agents have no control over their situation' (Smith 2009: 74). Structural Marxists (see, e.g., Althusser (2001/1970) see agents as mere reflections of the social structures that surround them, which are fundamentally shaped by the capital relation.

Chapter 2 suggested an approach to power, or social domination that recognises the validity of both agency and structure. Bob Jessop's Strategic-Relational Approach reveals that structure consists in differential constraints and opportunities that vary by agent; and that agency in turn depends on strategic capacities that vary by structure as well as according to the actors involved. This further reveals a dialectic between acting routinely or habitually, and 'evaluating the current situation in terms of the changing "art of the possible" over different spatiotemporal horizons of action' (Jessop 2016: 55). Structures are only strategically selective, rather than absolutely constraining. As a result, scope exists for actions to overwhelm structural constraints; subjects are unlikely to absolutely know their own strategic action(s).

Power in this framework becomes a complex amalgam of all forms of social domination, varying across both time and space. For (neo-) Marxists, this is expressed through class domination, with class understood very much in a relational sense and therefore it is social relations that acquire ontological primacy. This is complemented with a more Weberian pluralist analysis which emphasises more social alliances rather than relations, as well as other crosscutting influences ranging from political party, status and religion to—with the help and augmentation of other theoretical contributions—patriarchy and ethnicity. For (neo) pluralists, it is a vast array of resources, identities, and interests across an array of governance levels that form domination.

What all these approaches have in common is a rejection of state power being above society, and class power being anchored wholly in the economy or in civil society. In other words, they reject both hyper-structural and hyper-agential understandings or explanations of power relations. Instead, they understand at a core meta-theoretical level that the relationship between agency and structure is dichotomous. Combining these commonalities with Bob Jessop's Strategic-Relational Approach, power can be understood as a mediated effect of the changing balance of all forces—class, party, status, gender, identities, and interests—in any given scenario. In the context of state power this results in a complex, mutually reconstitutive relationship between agents who strategically navigate the contours of social structures that they themselves helped constitute.

Important for the consideration of socio-economic relations is that the state is not merely a reflection of those forces, rather a complex and ever-changing balance of class (and other) forces—shot through with compromise and contradiction. This also happens at multiple spatial levels of analysis. Those forces are shaped by (and shape) the nature of power as it is directed upon them, and they in turn direct. Whilst World Order clearly exists, its hegemony is one that shapes and constrains rather than necessarily dictates (see Chap. 3). Thus states' involvement in multilevel governance becomes less hierarchical, less centralised, and less directive; instead involving tangled hierarchies and a complex or 'governed' interdependence (Weiss 1998: 189–195; see also Jessop 2016: 185). Through the process of structuration and the attendant procedure of institutionalisation, state capacities are clearly shaped. The form of those institutions will be dealt with in the next section, but their function is understood through this complex process of structuration methodologically and the (re)constitution of power relationships and modes of domination ontologically. In the formation of those power relationships, the state stands as *primus inter pares*. For example, the many social forces and mechanisms that generate globalisation can only exert pressure on—or indeed strengthen—particular forms of state with particular state capacities and liabilities (Jessop 2016: 197). This facilitates study of the particular form a state takes, given the functions it is required to perform on behalf of capital.

Whilst processes at different levels of structuration clearly shape state capacities—regionalism, globalisation—these levels also modify the balance of forces within states; and vice versa. This is the concept of state autonomy, which when understood in terms of relative autonomy (see Chap. 2) is a feature of the state that overcomes its capture by specific interests (both domestic and international) and gives it the ability to serve (as one possibility) the longer term (developmental) interests of society. Autonomy, though, is understood as necessarily limited, or relative to the state's ability to meet the interests of capital given the context of World Order.

One form a state can take, for example, is that of a neoliberal state. There are twin forces at play in its spread across the world: first, international coercive forces, and second, domestic consensual forces. The international forces of transnational capital—represented by TNCs, investors in global capital markets, private organisations in global civil society such as credit ratings agencies, and IFIs—used the hammer of the 'competition state' (Cerny 1997) against the nail of neoliberalism. In this competition state, the welfare of society is understood as secondary to the need to secure capital accumulation, the benefits of which would 'trickle down' to the rest of the population.

The suite of policies associated with forging this neoliberal model of capital accumulation (see below on public policy profile) create a series of domestic winners who facilitate consent to the system through what J.K. Galbraith termed 'the culture of contentment' (Galbraith 1992). Those winners tend to be the transnationally orientated corporate sector; financiers, Western-educated technocratic and policymaking elites, skilled workers such as scientists, managers, academics, and other professionals—often employed in transnational or internationally oriented companies, in other words specific elements of the middle classes. Furthermore, members of the working classes employed in transnational companies and national enterprises that have managed to competitively engage with the global economy and thus shape their relations with fractions of (global) capital also form part of the constellation of socio-economic relations that help embed neoliberalism as a model of capital accumulation in national contexts (Chodor 2015: 61).

In the context of a Developmental Regime, socio-economic relations can be understood to take a different form. This form is qualitatively different in terms of the particular ensemble of relations, and quantitatively different in the sense that the ensemble is much more broader based. The big losers from the shift to neoliberalism—national capital, organised working classes, and minorities—to greater or lesser degrees depending on the national context, find their constellation of social relations and alliances shift through a redrawing of the contours of the state's relative autonomy. This can occur in the form of (re)invigorated corporatist practices, suites of policies towards indigenous peoples (land reform, profit sharing from extractive practices), and/or state-driven industrial policies. Interestingly, not all those winners from a more neoliberal orientated state form of relative autonomy are ejected. This also manifests itself at different spatial levels, with the (re)shaping of regional institutions, for example, or the shaping of the limits of the possible by the hegemony of World Order. Indeed, transnational forces are still engaged with, albeit on a more selective basis. Middle classes are kept on board through maintaining strong macroeconomic fundamentals that facilitate saving and conspicuous consumption. Whilst financial capital and financiers are often marginalised, they are not necessarily totally excluded as capital (both international and domestic) is needed to finance industrial policy and infrastructure investment. Private property is still honoured, the economies remain largely (or even increasingly) open to international trade, and macroeconomic frameworks remain conducive to repayment of international debt obligations.

In summary, the power of social forces as they manifest in social relations and expressed through modes of social domination constitutes the autonomy and capacity of any given regime. These modes of social domination are grounded in, for example, class, ethnicity, religion, party, status, patriarchy, and/or nationalism. This process occurs at multiple levels of structuration. Not all forces are bound equally by this process, facilitating certain behaviours more easily than others. In the context of the global political economy of development, analysis becomes sharpened through an understanding of World Order; a hegemony that manifests itself in terms of consent and coercion in the context of ideological and institutional, as well as material, spheres. Part of this analysis necessarily includes regional institutions: a further level of structuration that develops mutually reconstitutive relationships through its strategically selected terrain that is condensed from the historically specific and contingent constellation of social relations. It is to the analysis of institutions at all levels of structuration that this chapter now turns.

Institutions

The concept of institutionalism is grounded in three core assumptions. The first is that economic orders or systems consist of institutions; structural arrangements that prescribe behaviour in order to pursue social and economic functions (Steinmo and Thelen 1992). The second is that any social and economic order must be created; it does not emerge a priori. It is a product of human agency: 'there is no other credible source' (Palan and Abbot 1999: 27). First Veblen (2003/1899) and then Polanyi (1944) show us a third tenet: that market and state are contextually related to time and place. Polanyi's 'Great Transformation' was a story of industrial change in nineteenth-century Britain and showed that market society and market rules did not evolve naturally or through some process of self-generation (Munck 2005: 61). Indeed, as Polanyi (1944: 258) argues, 'the market has been the outcome of a conscious and often violent intervention on the part of the government which imposed the market organisation on society for non-economic ends'. Polanyi therefore demonstrated that government intervention was crucial to the making of markets in society, rather than the 'natural' processes as suggested by the likes of Hayek (1944).

Institutionalism becomes an essentially evolutionary concept as it stresses the importance of the interaction between economic activities and society. Braudel (1977) shows us that the development of a market-based order does not follow a linear trajectory. This allows for the coexistence of many different modes of political economy and attendant development paths as he charted a 'non-linear movement in the evolution of a global market' (Palan and Abbot 1999: 16). Polanyi (1944) further refined this analysis by showing that conscious political action is required to transform a market economy into a market society. This argument emphasises institutionalism's agent-structure position: social processes are the outcome of the interaction of conflicting social groups, with institutions as the mediators between them. In other words, agency and structure are mutually reconstitutive.

Institutions regularise the organisations of decision-making through which a regime channels and manifests its power. Such institutionalisation of a regime is essential to ensure longevity beyond any single administration. Whilst a regime can, and indeed must, begin with one administration, its longevity beyond a single administration relies heavily on the continuity facilitated by the presence of institutions. This is echoed in the work of Kohli (2004: 16–19), where he suggests that institutions are social patterns that gel only over time; and once gelled, they often endure beyond the forces that brought them into being. In the words of Schumpeter (2003/1942: 12) 'they are coins that do not readily melt'.

Institutions and institutionalisation become of paragon importance in this context. Their study shows how social forces make history in specific institutional contexts through focusing on actors and their interests, identities, and resources in specific institutional contexts, rather than generic, context-free terms. However, whilst they represent a very necessary condition for understanding the regime tripod, they do not constitute a sufficient one. Institutions represent the capacity that a state has to act. Institutionalism sharpens our analysis of the nature of the constitution of those institutions—the nature of the process of institutionalisation—but it does not offer a robust understanding of why some capacities are developed other others. For this, we need to augment—or balance—the tripod with socio-economic relations. As analysed in the previous section, these generate a state's (relative) autonomy and the nature of (non-)developmental state projects in emerging markets in the 21st century.

In essence, what this leg of the tripod seeks to understand in the context of developmentalism is the transformative capacity of the state. In the context of neoliberal globalisation and attendant processes of structuration, this increasingly becomes 'the ability to coordinate industrial change to meet the changing context of international competition' (Weiss 1998: 7). Part of this involves embedding itself into an increasingly complex web of governance institutions across different levels of spatial analysis. Whilst this section will analyse each level of structuration in turn, the state remains the institution that stands *primus inter pares*. It is the state's institutions that offer the most encompassing organisational complex for overcoming a number of obstacles to change: short-term horizons, bounded rationality, antagonistic social relations, as well as—in the modern era—unprecedented time compression in technological transformation (Weiss 1998: 6). Only the state can readily absorb and socialise risk to the extent required by financial sectors and modern production technologies (see Leftwich 2000; Chang 1999).

The core of the debate on capacity concerns the issue of what explains different state capacities; or how can we understand the nature of both diachronic and synchronic influences on the nature of state capacity. One way of approaching this question is through the tradition of corporatism and attendant organisational structures of social interests and relations. This approach suggests that the state facilitates corporatist bargaining via legal recognition of organised interests and provision of policy resources as a *quid pro quo* in labour–industry negotiations over wages. Therefore, corporatist bargaining underpins the state's macroeconomic efforts to control inflation and oversee modest industrial adjustment that could be understood under the aegis of developmentalism. The problem with this approach is it offers an incomplete picture of the state itself. It becomes all too easy for narrowly focused corporatist accounts to see state policy and agency as mere reflections of those corporatist relationships, rather than understanding the relationship between autonomy and capacity to be much more mutually reconstitutive (see Chap. 2). It becomes a necessary, but not sufficient lens through which to understand state capacity.

An alternative conceptualisation of state capacity came in the form of the 'strong state' thesis (see, e.g., Gourevitch 1986; Skocpol and Finegold 1982). This school of thought attributed different responses to industrial adaptation to different balances of power between state and society. It generated a typology that differentiated between 'strong' and 'weak' states, understood in terms of those state–society balances. A strong state is understood to be characterised by a highly centralised, insulated bureaucracy that is staffed by a technocratic elite. Its strength is understood in terms of its power over society, which manifests in three interlocking dimensions: first, the ability to formulate policy goals independent of societal pressure; second, the ability to alter behaviour of important domestic groups; and third, the ability to restructure the domestic institutional environment (Weiss 1998: 26). This account fails to distinguish between the state's ability to formulate its goals from the capacity to devise and implement strategies to achieve them. In other words, it fails to adequately consider the nature of autonomy as well as capacity.

This critique led to the work of Peter Evans and his concept of embedded autonomy (1995). Already explored in detail in Chap. 2, for the purposes of our understanding of state capacity in a Developmental Regime this contribution suggested that capacity depends not only on state internal structures (bureaucracies, etc.) but also on the organisation of groups in society. Linda Weiss developed this work on capacity through her concept of 'governed interdependence' (1998: 189). She suggested that differentiations in state capacities can be understood through thinking of successful state-led developmentalism to have involved *both* strong states and strong societies. Capacity becomes, '…a negotiated relationship in which public and private participants maintain their autonomy, yet which is nevertheless governed by broader goals set and monitored by the state' (Weiss 1998: 188). Furthermore, this was to occur in an international environment characterised by neoliberal globalisation, a factor that constrains relatively rather than absolutely, involving the adaptation of state power rather than the end of the state.

State-Level Institutions

This book has suggested an alternative understanding of state capacity, and therefore a different answer to the question regarding the nature of different state capacities. In addition to relative autonomy, focus on the relational aspect(s) of class interests facilitates an understanding of the state itself as a social relation: a changing balance of class forces. The study must therefore focus on different states 'strategic selectivity' (Jessop 1999: 11) and the factors that shape their strategic capacities. Strategic selectivity can be defined as: '...the ways in which the state as an ensemble of institutions had a specific, differential impact on the ability of various political forces to pursue particular interests and strategies in and through access to and control over given state capacities' (Jessop 2001: 152). The focus becomes the nature of the particular ensemble of institutions that form a real existing state, and mapping the attendant contours of social relations that underpin those institutions as well as being underpinned by them.

Not only must the 'right' (developmental) policies be pursued in any given situation of state autonomy, but they must also be implemented in an appropriate manner; or, the state must possess the necessary capacity. In traditional Developmental State theory, the study of capacity has focused on bureaucracies but, as Chap. 2 analysed, a contemporary (developmental) regime must necessarily embody a set of state–society relationships that move beyond narrow conceptions of bureaucratic autonomy combined with specific ties with business elites. In order to be effectively developmental in the 21st century, the Developmental Regime must take more responsibility, achieve greater autonomy in relation to private elites and the forces of neoliberal globalisation, and construct more complex and demanding forms of embeddedness (Evans 2008: 17). Therefore, successful capacity relies upon a 'very broad range of state-society ties necessary for the effective delivery of capability expanding services' (Evans 2008: 18).

Institutions help capture this concept of capacity within the Developmental Regime framework. At the state level, these can be defined as the formal organisations of the state and society: government institutions, economic institutions, and those that connect government, economy and society (Pempel 1998: 23–26). Government institutions include areas such as the civil service, courts, parliaments, cabinets, the military, and the police. Economic institutions broadly express how the state interacts with the market, both domestically and internationally. Institutions that connect the government, economy, and society include areas such as electoral systems, interest associations, party systems, and economic policy networks. Operationalising the insights from the concept of relative autonomy, the accumulation imperative of the state is facilitated by the repressive institutions such as the government, army, police, tribunals, and administration; whilst the legitimation imperative is served by institutions that legitimate the system materially, such as the welfare state, and ideologically, such as the Church, political parties, schools, mass media, and the family (Poulantzas 1969: 76). Historically such institutions have been prominent mainly in theorising relations described as corporatist—or some variation thereof, but other constellations are possible such as more fluid structures based on grassroots movements in civil society.

A highly individualistic market-driven agenda (i.e. neoliberal) will produce different economic institutions to those that express extensive concentration and coordination of market power by the state (i.e. Developmental Regime). Such constellations will be reflected in areas such as Central Banks, corporate structures, legal economic frameworks, and patent regulations. Examples of neoliberal institutions include independent central banks with sole responsibility for inflation targeting (e.g. the Bank of England), or corporate structures with weak trade unions and strong business associations. Neoliberal states will be dominated by a strong emphasis on judicial rule and strict constitutionality, as solutions and remedies to problems are to be sought by individuals through the legal system (Harvey 2005: 67). This is all connected to the central principle of private property and well-defined property rights, set out in contract and enforced through a strong and clear rule of law.

A more national-based, developmental agenda will possess qualitatively different institutions. The nature of a Developmental Regime's relative autonomy is different, as it is shaped by, and in turn shapes, the contours of its institutional capacities. Central Banks will often have multiple targets written into their constitution—Argentina's, for example, is responsible for inflation, economic growth, and 'stability'—as well as some limitations on strict independence, the Argentine Treasury can pay public debt using Central Bank reserves, for example. Trade unions can be stronger in the sense of greater ties with government in (neo)corporatist relationships. These can exist on macro levels like in Argentina, or more meso-level like in Brazil. Business clearly retains links with government, as they too shape the relative autonomy of the state. However, this relationship is not as one-sided as a neoliberal state, with more complex contours of public policy emerging that represent a compromise between the sometimes competing goals of labour and capital. Relationships other than corporatist could also emerge: the Malaysian state, for example, has pursued a distinctly ethnic agenda since independence (see Chaps. 7, 8). This has led to a series of institutions designed to redistribute economic growth to specific ethnic segments of the population, rather than those grounded in labour–capital relationships per se.

The role of democracy also becomes important here. Over the course of the 1990s, Western thinking became dominated by the thought that democracy was not only a desirable but a necessary feature of development. This culminated into the liberal triumphalism of Francis Fukayama (1992) and the end of history. It became commonplace for Western governments and international institutions 'to attach political conditions to aid so as to "persuade" governments in developing countries to move in a democratic direction' (Leftwich 2000: 9).

The relationship between democracy and development has been very well researched. The classic Modernisation argument (see, e.g., Lipset 1959) suggested that indicators of development such as average wealth, degree of industrialisation, levels of education, and urbanisation are higher in democratic countries; their development comes in a mutually reinforcing manner with democracy due to factors such as the fostering of tolerant values, a growing middle class, a more egalitarian social structure to help mitigate class conflict, and more intermediary institutions as analysed above. Contributing to the sequencing debate, Przeworski and Limongi (1993) investigate democracy and development through analysis of four mutually reinforcing factors: democracy and property rights, democracy and investment, democracy and societal pressures, and democracy and predatory rulers (1993: 52–58). They conclude that regime characteristics (i.e. democratic versus authoritarian regimes) are less useful for unpicking the relationship between democracy and development than the concepts of autonomy and capacity (Przeworski and Limongi 1993: 65). Clearly, both types of regime can possess the necessary autonomy and capacity to generate rapid, catch-up development, but this conclusion facilitated a contemporary research agenda into the relative quality of democracies, and therefore democratic consolidation. Further research by these two authors led them to highlight the importance of distinguishing between exogenous and endogenous democracies (Przeworski and Limongi 1997). They suggest that endogenous democracies are more likely to emerge as countries develop economically, whilst democracies that emerge for reasons other than economic development are more likely to survive in countries that are already economically developed (see also Gasiorowski and Power 1998: 98). Boix and Stokes (2003) further complicate the relationship through a contribution that concludes democracy is not linked to development per se, but to the income equality that accompanies the process of economic development.

The debate progressed into realising a need to distinguish between the impact of development on democratic transition, and democratic consolidation. This led to a focus on the quality of democracy, with a continuum that focused on ordinal variables rather than dichotomous ones. A seminal example of this is William Case's (2002) empirically rich contribution on different democratic regimes in South-East Asia. Part of this distinction became about developing an understanding of the differences between procedural and substantive aspects of democracy; other parts about disaggregating the concept of democracy and recognising the variety of institutional and political forms it can and does take and then see their implications for developmental capacity and autonomy in emerging markets.

Democracy cannot be seen as a mono-system. It manifests itself in a variety of institutional formats, both procedurally and in more nebulous substantive ways. Processes of democratisation can be understood as government's being displaced by aspects of society that have colonised key parts of the state (Ferrero 2014). In other words, social factors such as class, ethnicity, religion, and their combinations shape a myriad of political forces that can have decisive influences on the institutional and political form that democracy may take and hence the particular developmental capacity of the state (Leftwich 2000: 11). Understanding the strategic terrain upon which actors exercise their agency through exploring the nature as well as interrelationship between institutions and socio-economic relations becomes paramount. This generates strong frameworks induced from these empirically rich accounts that further our understanding of 21st-century developmentalism.

Global Level Institutions

In the context of globalisation, institutions 'above' the state clearly exist that have an important role in the process of forging a state's relative autonomy. We must be careful however to distinguish analytically as well as ontologically between global institutions and those of the state (or indeed region, see next section). As Chap. 3 discussed at length, the role of the global level in the process of structuration is analytically distinct due to its privileged position in the structuration hierarchy in terms of being an object without a discrete subject. This dilemma was solved through the application of the principles of World Order (Cox and Sinclair 1996).

World Order is the product of the interrelationship of three mutually constitutive spheres—ideas, material capabilities, and institutions (see the previous chapter). Institutions thus become specific conglomerates of ideas and material power that in turn influence mutually reconstituted ideas and material capabilities. The ultimate source of their power comes from (global) hegemony, which is the result of an expansion of state-based hegemony. This global hegemony, or World Order, is thus when one state is able to control the articulation of universal and global norms, institutions, and practices across different states that support the maintenance of their hegemony through supporting the dominant mode of production.

The evolution of the global institutions of World Order in the post-1945 period was examined in the previous chapter. For the purposes of understanding the ability of 21st-century developmentalism, it is important to distil the fact that the current era is one of US hegemony supporting a neoliberal mode of production. However, given the constraints of global hegemony, the process of globalisation involves a dialectic of homogenisation and diversification (Gill 1986: 205). World Order therefore becomes a series of institutions, ideas, and material power that is able to shape the limits of the possible, certainly for less powerful states like emerging markets.

Whilst an important network of global think tanks, NGOs, financial markets and regimes, TNCs, Off-Shore Financial Centres, etc. operate at this level, the role of the IFIs has been central to the nature of development trajectories pursued by many emerging markets. The IMF,

GATT/WTO, and World Bank have clearly had significant influence in the post-Second World War world, particularly for developing economies and emerging markets. As shown in the previous chapter, as the contours of globalisation shifted so did the form and function of its attendant global institutions. In the wake of the global financial crisis of 2007, these institutions retain, and indeed have seen some functions enhanced, in the nurturing of a global hegemony of neoliberalism. Mapping the contours of their influence in state-level projects therefore becomes essential in order to sharpen our understanding of the concomitant relative autonomy and capacity of any Developmental Regime.

Regional-Level Institutions

The Developmental Regime approach has been critiqued for not developing an appropriately rigorous analysis of regional institutions (Strange 2014: 135). In order to address this lacuna in the Developmental Regime approach, some extended analysis is necessary. Regional institutions differ to global ones, both analytically and ontologically. Due to the existence of the state below it in the spatial analysis hierarchy, and the global level above it, there exists the need to understand the nature of the stratified social ontology from both analytical directions of structuration. This section will therefore address two interrelated tasks. First, it will identify the ontological nature of the discrete subjects present at this spatial level of analysis, i.e. regional institutions. Second, it will develop an appropriate understanding of the analytical relationship between those institutions, World Order, and the state.

This second task represents one of the fundamental fault lines in the literature on regions. The role of the state versus the role of global forces in shaping regional projects has traditionally been explored and expressed in academic research as a dichotomy. The state was seen as inimical to regional integration (Milner and Mansfield 1999); regional agreements were understood as 'locking in' (Haggard 1997) structural reforms in order to overcome the potential pitfalls of domestic politicisation. This highly structural view saw regionalism and globalisation as inherently intertwined; although with a strong one-way causality—or downward causation—where regionalism was often seen as subordinate to the dictates and constraints of globalisation, or at best as a supplementary layer of governance. Subsequently, the structure of global order was fundamental to understanding the construction of regions (Katzenstein 2005).

This 'new regionalism' or 'New Regionalist Approach' (NRA) focused on the pressures of International Political Economy on regions, and the ways in which regions responded to these pressures. As a governance project, new regionalism became a state strategy to develop much closer ties to the market reforms of the Washington Consensus on a regional scale (Gamble and Payne 1996: 251).

'Old regionalism' contrasted sharply with this view. This perspective analysed regionalised forms of high tariffs and regulated markets as a function of post-war economic protectionism (Viner 1950; Meade 1955). Such a view saw the relationship between different layers of governance from the opposite angle; the institutional character of regions was a function of states. Still imbued with a one-way causality, this neo-functionalist perspective analysed the dichotomy between states and regions. Both old and new regionalism were essentially approaching their understanding of the constitution of regions through a state/non-state lens.

Both these perspectives also share an understanding of a region as a construction of authority and order in reflection of regional hierarchy. Whilst they are right to draw attention to the fact that regions are the product of power politics and interests, for Riggirozzi and Tussie (2012: 4) they overlook the question of 'followers'. Other than hegemonic politics grounded in some kind of global order, region can alternatively (or simultaneously) 'be constructed on the basis of consensual views and interests that, although advanced and guaranteed by the leader, reflect the position of the followers' (Riggirozzi and Tussie 2012).

This complements alternative strands of research into regions which understand that the process of regionalism is not only the institutionalisation of trans-border practices, but also reflections of transformations of the regional space. Scholars such as Hettne and Söderbaum (2000) expressed this perspective through their concept of 'regionness'. Looking to move beyond the state/non-state dichotomy they suggested that regionness was a sense of identity and belonging to a particular region based on shared values, norms, and institutions that govern their interaction and the ways they perceive themselves within a given polity. This denotes cohesive action towards the outside; grounded in the material foundations of trans-border relations, the symbolic foundations of common goals and values, and a network of institutions and regulations that enhance the region's ability to interact autonomously in the global arena (Riggirozzi 2011; Riggirozzi and Tussie 2012: 5). Under this perspective, regions can be seen more as a function of both formal *and* informal exchanges and practices more akin to Castells (1996) and his concept of 'network societies'. A focus on states and regionalism remains of importance, but analytical focus must also come to bear on the process of regionalisation itself.

The relationship between regionalism and regionalisation has led to a new synthesis in the literature. Post-hegemonic regionalism (see, e.g., Riggirozzi 2011; Riggirozzi and Tussie 2012) has facilitated a re-mapping of the debates between state versus non-state and formality versus informality: first, a synthesis between regionalism as a reflection of global order versus a form of regulated markets and high tariffs. The intellectual hegemony of new regionalism has led to an overfocus on advanced industrial states as the systemic rule makers *par excellence* (Riggirozzi and Tussie 2012: 12). Regionalism becomes an intensely political process, a legitimising tool for linked strategies and objectives whereby governments seek to coordinate the terms of competition on which rival economic and political agents confront each other (Riggirozzi and Tussie 2012: 11–12). Second, a synthesis between regionalism as formal institutions and regionalisation as the evolution of informal trans-border exchanges between non-state social and business actors. Key regional institutions and their attendant capacities are of clear importance, as are the very processes of regionalisation itself that underpins the crafting of the institutions.

Post-hegemonic regionalism therefore (re)draws attention to regional structures characterised by hybrid practices as a result of partial displacement of dominant forms of US-led neoliberal governance. Regional governance can thus be seen as the result of a mosaic of different regional policies, regional identities, and regional forms of cooperation and competition that are 'transforming the cartography itself' (Riggirozzi and Tussie 2012: 10). This cartography can be mapped as the simultaneous pursuit of three distinct projects within regionalism. First, there are regional projects whose *raison d'être* is the promotion of multilateralism through the reduction of tariffs and non-tariff barriers and attendant promotion of free trade and greater commercial integration. These projects often have low, or no, sociopolitical content (Riggirozzi and Tussie 2012: 11). The second type of project pursued by regional institutions could be promoting trade at its core, but also 'seeking alternative and autonomous trade and post-trade political projects' (Riggirozzi and Tussie 2012: 11).

The third and final distinct project could be an institution that is much more focused on sociopolitical content rather than trade promotion. These could come in the form of new welfare commitments, or economic aspects of social integration. They could also come in the form of 'reclaiming the principles of socialism in direct opposition to neoliberal globalisation' (Riggirozzi and Tussie 2012: 11).

In summary, the relationship between regions and the state must be understood on two complementary levels: analytically and ontologically. Through an analytical distinction between regionalism and regionalisation, the relationship between the state and regions can be seen as mutually reconstitutive. States clearly aid in the (re)constitution of regional projects through regionalisation; simultaneously being influenced by regionalism as these institutions aid in the reflection and refraction of hegemonic projects at the global level (i.e. World Order). This aids in sharpening our understanding of the ontological nature of regional institutions themselves which, following the post-hegemonic taxonomy of Riggirozzi and Tussie (2012: 11), can engage in three distinct projects: free-trade projects, hybrid projects, and sociopolitical projects.

In more concrete terms, at the regional level there has emerged a complex structure of regional norms, rules, and institutions. There are a number of contradictions between different regional projects, and often different constellations in different regions of the globe. 'Regional projects are faced with substantially divergent visions of what regional governance should mean, and how integration projects should respond to current challenges of development in the new construction of the region' (Riggirozzi 2012: 18). Furthermore, shifts in development hegemony mean that some regions are displaying a loss of certainty in the wisdom of orthodox, market-driven strategies for development; responding through the pursuit of projects grounded outside the traditional free-trade area through the state's influence via the process of regionalisation. This facilitates a rich variety of different regional institutions that should be examined and analysed in order to generate robust understandings of the autonomy and capacity of emerging markets in the 21st century. The examples most pertinent to the cases to be analysed in the second half of this book include ASEAN (Association of South-East Asian Nations) for Malaysia, and MERCOSUR (Common Market of the South) and UNASUR (Union of South American Nations)—among others—for Argentina.

Public Policy Profile

Socio-economic relations and their attendant institutionalisation are underpinned and reinforced by policies of the state, or the final leg of any regime tripod. A regime's public policies (both in the political and economic spheres) are 'tangible manifestations of the regime's power configuration' (Pempel 1998: 27). Policies are not simply the product of those socio-economic relationships, as it must always be remembered that the state acts as a mediator between the desires of specific (class) fractions and the policies that these interests crystallise into. In the words of Colin Hay, the state becomes a 'factor of cohesion' (Hay 2006: 62). Public policy profiles are therefore the product of the complex interrelationships between autonomy and capacity as developed and elucidated in the previous chapters. It must never be forgotten that these characteristics are both shaped and mediated by contemporary global political economy and their attendant regional and global institutions.

In a neoliberal state, for example, these policies come in the form of favouring strong individual property rights, the rule of law, and facilitating/creating the institutions of freely functioning markets and free trade (Harvey 2005: 64). Neoliberals are particularly assiduous in seeking the privatisation of assets: an extension of the principle of strong and clear individual property rights. The free mobility of capital between sectors, regions, and countries is regarded as crucial as this improves efficiency, productivity, and lowers prices—therefore combating inflationary pressures. With personal and individual freedom in the marketplace guaranteed, individuals are considered accountable for their own actions; a principle that extends into welfare, education, healthcare, and pensions. This leads to minimal 'safety-net' responses to welfare, rather than comprehensive welfare states associated with social democracy, for example.

In practice, these policies do not always (in fact never) manifest themselves in an ideal form. For example, the EU pushes a free-trade agenda, but not in agriculture through the Common Agricultural Policy (CAP). Similarly, the USA maintains high barriers to trade in areas such as steel or maize—usually because Presidential candidates want to win key battleground states like Pennsylvania or Iowa (Harvey 2005: 71). WTO rounds are riddled with national exceptions and mechanisms for maintenance of myriad forms of non-tariff barriers. The evolution of the IMF's thinking on capital account restrictions (Ostry et al. 2016; Chwieroth 2009) represents a classic case of changing policy. Such oscillations and imperfections are reflections of the inherently complex and contingent nature of power as it is exercised by different agents across different strategically selective terrains that also have highly complex relationships with different levels of spatial analysis.

In Developmental Regimes, public policy profiles reflect the nature of capacity and autonomy of a different set of social relations. Private property is still central and free trade is still broadly followed. There are, of course, exceptions such as the drive for greater communal land rights for indigenous groups and the use of the state to ensure these. Macroeconomic frameworks are conducive to debt reduction, fiscal conservatism, and (broad) price stability. Welfare policies are usually kept within the safety-net model and come in the form of Conditional Cash Transfer (CCT) programmes—designed to catch individuals from falling into indigence rather than lifting individuals up to a basic standard of living. There is greater scope for state intervention in the economy beyond facilitating market-friendly conditions. This comes in the form of industrial policies such as sector subsidies, infrastructure investment, currency manipulation, or selective protectionism. Collectively these can be considered as developmental in the sense of the state guiding and coaxing markets to work for the national interest, rather than that of international capital.

Under globalisation, the level of state autonomy from the forces of globalisation and the interests that they represent are limited, or 'passive' (Cohen 2006: 46); they exist de jure in different configurations of formal sovereignty, but increasingly less de facto in terms of the capacity to act with operational independence. Key institutional capacities at all levels of structuration—global, regional, and state—exercise power over the state to act in the interests of the hegemonic force of neoliberal capital. Nevertheless, these forces often shape what Santiso (2006) called the 'political economy of the possible', rather than being absolutely constraining forces. States are still able to reflect constellations of autonomy and capacity that can actively resist the forces of neoliberalism. In the context of emerging markets, this manifests itself in terms of Developmental Regimes.

Conclusions

Emerging markets are confronted by a number of different challenges when faced with the need to engage in catch-up development when compared to their twentieth-century counterparts. There is therefore a clear need to refresh our understandings of the Developmental State in the 21st century. The Developmental Regime approach represents such a device: a reinvigorated analytical framework for understanding Emerging Markets and their possibilities for successful catch-up development in a world characterised by changing regional and global trends. The three legs of the tripod—socio-economic relations, institutions, and public policy profiles—generates an analysis that helps map the contours of a state's capacity and (relative) autonomy. This map facilitates clearer understandings of the nature of a given state's development trajectory, offering analytical rigour into possible mosaics of (un)successful political economies of development.

Socio-economic relations are representations of different class and non-class interests that can be understood through an analysis of power. Power is understood as a mutually reconstitutive dichotomy between structure and agency that manifests itself in different forms of domination that is mediated through the state as per the Strategic-Relational Approach (see Chap. 2). This mediation is influenced by multiple spatial levels of analysis, ultimately crafting a state's relative autonomy and the development trajectory it pursues. This is by definition contingent, subject to change, and always constrained (although not absolutely) by World Order.

Institutions and attendant processes of institutionalisation shape state capacity. They also have a mutually reconstitutive relationship with socio-economic relations. Actors exercise their power through agency, which is partially constrained by the strategic terrain upon which that agency is exercised—as well as helping change the nature and shape of that terrain. These processes are once again to be understood as operating at different spatial levels if a complete analysis is to be drawn. State-based institutions have specific relationships with its constellation of socio-economic relations through the nature of its capacity and autonomy. Regional institutions are placed in the middle of the structuration schema, and are therefore influenced by states through regionalisation whilst simultaneously influencing them as a result of regionalism itself. Global institutions are (re)constituted and possess attendant influence over states as per the concept of World Order.

Finally, public policy profiles are tangible manifestations of the contemporary constellations of power and how they have shaped (and been shaped by) the state's capacity and autonomy. They represent the policies that a Developmental Regime implements that facilitate a (non-)developmental agenda. In the context of successful catch-up development, proactive industrial policy and sound macroeconomic management are common profiles. Once again, the influence of different levels of spatial analysis must be understood, with World Order offering a 'political economy of the possible', rather than being absolutely constraining, that states are able to operate within.

Having generated a robust framework for understanding contemporary Developmental Regimes this book will now turn to the empirical cases that first led to these insights. The cases of Argentina and Malaysia represent two emblematic examples of contemporary emerging markets, yet situated in very different geostrategic and regional political economies with distinct historical processes. The second half of this book will seek to first offer a stylised account of the development trajectories of these two emerging markets, in order to apply the Developmental Regime approach to their examples of forging distinct political economies of development in the context of contemporary neoliberal globalisation.

References

Althusser, L. (2001/1970). *Lenin and philosophy and other essays.* New York: Monthly Review Press.

Boix, C., & Stokes, S. C. (2003). Endogenous democratization. *World Politics, 55*(4), 517–549.

Braudel, F. (1977). *Afterthoughts on material civilization and capitalism.* Baltimore: John Hopkins University Press.

Case, W. (2002). *Politics in South East Asia: Democracy or less.* Oxford: RoutledgeCurzon.

Castells, M. (1996). *The network society.* Oxford: Blackwell.

Cerny, P. G. (1997). Paradoxes of the competition state: The dynamics of political globalization. *Government and Opposition, 32*(2), 251–274.

Chang, H.-J. (1999). The economic theory of the developmental state. In M. Woo-Cummings (Ed.), *The developmental state* (pp. 182–199). New York: Cornell University Press.

Chodor, T. (2015). *Neoliberal hegemony and the pink tide in Latin America: Breaking up with Tina?* Basingstoke: Palgrave Macmillan.
Chwieroth, J. M. (2009). *Capital ideas: The IMF and the rise of financial liberalization*. Princeton: Princeton University Press.
Clarke, H., & Whiteley, P. (1990). Perceptions of macroeconomic performance, government support and Conservative Party strategy in Britain 1983–1987. *European Journal of Political Research, 18*, 97–120.
Cohen, B. J. (2006). The macrofoundations of monetary power. In D. Andrews (Ed.), *International monetary power* (pp. 31–50). Ithaca: Cornell University Press.
Cox, R. W., & Sinclair, T. (Eds.). (1996). *Approaches to world order*. Cambridge: Cambridge University Press.
Evans, P. (1995). *Embedded autonomy: States and industrial transformation*. Princeton: Princeton University Press.
Evans, P. B. (2008, December). *In search of the twenty first century developmental state*. (CGPE Working Paper Series, No. 4).
Ferrero, J. P. (2014). *Democracy against neoliberalism in Argentina and Brazil: A move to the left*. Basingstoke: Palgrave Macmillan.
Fukayama, F. (1992). *The end of history and the last man*. London: Penguin.
Galbraith, J. K. (1992). *The culture of contentment*. Boston, MA: Houghton Mifflin.
Gamble, A., & Payne, A. (Eds.). (1996). *Regionalism and global order*. Basingstoke: Macmillan.
Gasiorowski, M. J., & Power, T. J. (1998). The structural determinants of democratic consolidation evidence from the third world. *Comparative Political Studies, 31*(6), 740–771.
Gill, S. (1986). Hegemony consensus, and trilateralism. *Review of International Studies, 12*, 205–222.
Gourevitch, P. (1986). *Politics in hard times: Comparative responses to international economic crises*. Ithaca: Cornell University Press.
Haggard, S. (1997). Regionalism in Asia and the Americas. In E. Mansfield & H. Milner (Eds.), *The political economy of regionalism* (pp. 20–49). New York: Columbia University Press.
Harvey, D. (2005). *A brief history of neoliberalism*. Oxford: Oxford University Press.
Hay, C. (2006). (What's Marxist about) Marxist state theory. In C. Hay, M. Lister, & D. Marsh (Eds.), *The state: Theories and issues*. Basingstoke: Palgrave.
Hayek, F. A. (1944). *The road to serfdom*. London: George Routledge and Sons Ltd.
Hettne, B., & Söderbaum, F. (2000). Theorising the rise of regionness. *New Political Economy, 5*(3), 457–474.

Jessop, B. (1999). The strategic selectivity of the state: Reflections on a theme of Poulantzas. *Journal of Hellenic Diaspora, 25*(1–2), 1–37.

Jessop, B. (2001). Bringing the state back in (yet again): Reviews, revisions, rejections, and re-directions. *International Review of Sociology, 11*(2), 149–173.

Jessop, B. (2016). *The state: Past, present, and future.* London: Polity.

Katzenstein, P. (2005). *A world of regions: Asia and Europe in the American Imperium.* Ithaca: Cornell University Press.

Kohli, A. (2004). *State directed development.* Cambridge: Cambridge University Press.

Leftwich, A. (2000). *States of development: On the primacy of politics in development.* London: Polity.

Lipset, S. M. (1959). Some social requisites of democracy: Economic development and political development. *American Political Science Review, 53,* 69–105.

Meade, J. E. (1955). *The theory of customs union.* Amsterdam: North Holland.

Milner, H., & Mansfield, E. (1999). The political economy of regionalism. *International Organization, 53*(3), 589–627.

Munck, R. (2005). Neoliberalism and politics, and the politics of neoliberalism. In A. Saad-Filho & D. Johnstone (Eds.), *Neoliberalism: A critical reader.* London: Pluto.

Ostry, J. D., Loungani, P., & Furceri, D. (2016). Neoliberalism: Oversold? *Finance and Development, 53*(2), 38–41.

Palan, R., & Abbott, J. (1999). The state in the global political economy. In R. Palan & J. Abbott (Eds.), *State strategies in the global political economy* (pp. 32–54). London: Pinter.

Pempel, T. J. (1998). *Regime shift: Comparative dynamics of the Japanese political economy.* London: Cornell University Press.

Pempel, T. J. (1999). The developmental regime in a changing world economy. In M. Woo-Cumings (Ed.), *The developmental state* (pp. 137–181). New York: Cornell University Press.

Polanyi, K. (1944). *The great transformation.* Boston, MA: Beacon Press.

Poulantzas, N. (1969). The problem of the capitalist state. *New Left Review, 58,* 67–78.

Przeworski, A., & Limongi, F. (1993). Political regimes and economic growth. *Journal of Economic Perspectives, 7*(3), 51–69.

Przeworski, A., & Limongi, F. (1997). Modernization: Theories and facts. *World Politics, 49*(2), 155–183.

Riggirozzi, P. (2011). Region, regionness, and regionalism in Latin America: Towards a new synthesis. *New Political Economy, 17*(4), 421–443.

Riggirozzi, P. (2012). Reconstructing regionalism: What does development have to do with it? In P. Riggirozzi & D. Tussie (Eds.), *The rise of post-hegemonic regionalism: The case of Latin America* (pp. 17–41). New York: Springer.

Riggirozzi, P., & Tussie, D. (2012). *The rise of post-hegemonic regionalism: The case of Latin America*. New York: Springer.
Riker, W. H. (1990). Political science and rational choice. In J. E. Alt & K. A. Shepsle (Eds.), *Perspectives on positive political economy* (pp. 163–181). Massachusetts: Harvard University Press.
Santiso, J. (2006). *Latin America's political economy of the possible*. Massachusetts: MIT Press.
Schumpeter, J. (2003/1942). *Capitalism, socialism, and democracy*. London: Routledge.
Skocpol, T., & Finegold, K. (1982). State capacity and economic intervention in the early new deal. *Political Science Quarterly, 97*(2), 255–278.
Smith, M. (2009). *Power and the state*. Basingstoke: Palgrave Macmillan.
Steinmo, S., & Thelen, K. (1992). *Structuring politics: Historical institutionalism in comparative analysis*. Cambridge: Cambridge University Press.
Strange, G. (2014). *Towards a new political economy of development: States and regions in the post-neoliberal world*. Basingstoke: Palgrave Macmillan.
Veblen, T. (2003/1899). *The theory of the leisure class: An economic study of institutions*. Pennsylvania: Pennsylvania State University.
Viner, J. (1950). *The customs union issue*. New York: Carnegie Endowment for International Peace.
Weiss, L. (1998). *The myth of the powerless state*. Cambridge: Polity.
Wylde, C. (2012). *Latin America after neoliberalism: Developmental regimes in post-crisis states*. Basingstoke: Palgrave Macmillan.
Wylde, C. (2014). The developmental state is dead, long live the developmental regime! Interpreting Nestór Kirchner's Argentina 2003–2007. *Journal of International Relations and Development, 17*(2), 191–219.
Wylde, C. (2016). Post-neoliberal developmental regimes in Latin America: Argentina under Cristina Fernandez de Kirchner. *New Political Economy, 21*(3), 322–341.

CHAPTER 5

Argentina Under the Kirchner Administrations

Mapping the theoretical terrain of the role of the state in development in an era characterised by the hegemony of neoliberal globalisation has resulted in a robust framework for understanding 21st century developmentalism. As the previous chapter demonstrated, this is best distilled into the Developmental Regime concept. It is now the purpose of the second half of this book to survey the empirical landscape, so that it can be mapped onto this theoretical bedrock. This will be achieved through the examination of two emblematic cases of developmentalism in the global south: Argentina and Malaysia.

This chapter will give a detailed account of the trajectory of Argentine economic development policies, and will be structured through a periodisation of post-crisis Argentina grounded in Maristella Svampa's concept of the 'Four Moments' (Svampa 2014). The First Moment is the crisis of neoliberalism and its immediate aftermath, the Second Moment the administration of Nestor Kirchner, the Third Moment starts with the *crisis del campo* under the tenure of Cristina Fernandez de Kirchner (hereafter CFK), and the Fourth Moment the second administration of CFK. This will create the necessary empirical basis to generate detailed analysis of the changing nature of the strategic selective limits of the Argentine state and how they changed in the 21st century, an analysis that is best conducted using a Developmental Regime framework and to be completed in the next chapter.

C. Wylde, *Emerging Markets and the State*, International Political Economy Series, DOI 10.1057/978-1-137-55655-4_5

The First Moment: The Crisis of Neoliberalism (2001–2003)

The crisis of 2001 resulted in extreme economic and social dislocation in Argentina, culminating in a default on the national debt and the collapse of the hard peg (or *Convertibilidad*), with a subsequent devaluation of the peso. Economic impacts of this crisis were catastrophic with severe contraction of the economy and output, as were the social consequences in terms of poverty and immiseration. As Table 5.1 demonstrates, the immediate macroeconomic consequence of the crisis was an acute recession throughout 2002 and early 2003, with the figures improving in the second half of 2003. Official unemployment peaked at 21.5%, with underemployment and informal employment levels (18.6% by May 2002) also increasing, thus contributing to the immiseration of the people. Many that were left in work saw wages plummet, and Cavallo's zero-deficit budget meant public sector employees were forced to take a 30% pay cut. As Table 5.1 demonstrates, output plummeted and Gross Domestic Product (GDP) took year-on-year falls, peaking in 2002 with a catastrophic 10.9% contraction of the domestic economy. This was reflected in the investment figures, with real levels of investment only getting back into positive figures by 2003. Inflation also reignited after 2002 as a result of exit from the US dollar peg, with stagflation (negative growth and inflation) being experienced in 2002.

The immediate impact of the crisis on goods and services was catastrophic, with output in almost all industries collapsing. *El Argentinazo* was not a widely foreseen crisis (IMF 2000a: 6; IMF 2000b: 5; Chudnovsky 2007: 145), and many commentators actually anticipated

Table 5.1 Macroeconomic indicators during the crisis period

Year	*Unemployment (%)*	*Real GDP growth (%)*	*Gross fixed capital formation (% change)*	*Inflation (CPI) (1995 = 100)*	*Interest rates (deposits)*
1999	14.3	−3.4	−15.4	99.2	10.0
2000	15.1	−0.8	−7.5	99.5	12.3
2001	17.4	−4.4	−18.0	98.4	15.0
2002	21.5	−10.9	−0.4	123.9	39.3
2003	14.5	8.8	49.0	140.5	10.2

Source Ministry of Economy and Production (2015)

positive growth as the economy was seen to be emerging from the recession resulting from Brazilian devaluation in 1998. As demand plummeted many businesses either went out of business or massively scaled down production. This is reflected in the high levels of unemployment at the time (see Table 5.1), as well as the significant falls in output experienced across the industrial manufacturing sector. The financial sector fared no better, due to the twin policies of the *corralito* and asymmetric pesification. The *corralito* was a weekly withdrawal limit on Argentine's bank accounts of first 250 Argentine pesos, then 300. Asymmetric pesification was where bank credits (or its assets), were exchanged at one Peso to one US dollar, and its deposits (or its liabilities) at one Peso to 1.40 US dollar. For the financial sector, this resulted in wide losses.

The depositors, the ordinary Argentine people, felt the effects of this asymmetric pesification much more severely. This was due to the fact that the majority of domestic contracts were denominated in dollars (Chudnovsky 2007: 140), and therefore it was not only banking deposits but also rents, tariffs on public services and utilities that were affected (Bezchinsky 2007). Not able to get to their money due to the *corralito*, Argentines saw their deposits that they thought were guaranteed as interchangeable with the US dollar, initially converted at 1.4 Pesos to one US dollar, and, after devaluation, the market rate had settled at closer to 3 Pesos to one US dollar. As Table 5.2 shows, this had a profound impact on poverty and indigence levels in Argentina.

The combined impact of the *corralito* and asymmetric pesification was not the only reason for the profound impact that the crisis had on poverty. A further reason was the nature of the system of *Convertibilidad* itself.

Table 5.2 Individual poverty and indigence (%) in Argentina in selected regions, 2001–2003

Region	*October 2001*		*October 2002*		*October 2003*	
	Indigence	*Poverty*	*Indigence*	*Poverty*	*Indigence*	*Poverty*
Urban total	13.6	38.3	27.5	57.5	26.3	54.7
Mendoza	11.5	36.7	28.4	58.4	27.1	56.1
La Rioja	10.3	44.5	28.6	66.2	28.7	60.4
Salta	18.3	48.3	42.5	70.3	34.8	68.4
Corrientes	25.1	58.7	43.1	74.4	37.7	73.0

Source Ministry of Economy and Production (2015)

Due to its longevity, it had become more than simply a fixed exchange rate, and had become the contractual basis for the whole economy (Levy 2004). Many contracts were denominated in dollars, as were company liabilities and individual debt. Therefore, when forced devaluation came, many saw their assets shrink and their liabilities grow to unsustainable levels. This led to a downward spiral of unemployment, shrinking incomes, and poverty. High levels of poverty and indigence are not necessarily directly correlated to increased social rebellion. However, in Argentina, where citizenship has been associated with a range of social and economic rights since Peronist days, the political impact of this rapid and abrupt pauperisation is hard to exaggerate (Grugel and Riggirozzi 2007: 94).

There was also an impact on income distribution in Argentina, as the extremely wealthy were able to avoid the effects of the crisis having traditionally held their assets abroad in tax havens, or European countries such as Spain. Throughout the convertibility years (1991–2001) the gap between the 10% richest and the 10% poorest Argentine's was increasing, but after 1998 and the beginnings of economic trouble, and especially in 2001 and the crisis itself, the gap increases dramatically. Even the gap between the 20% richest and 20% poorest has increased, reflecting greater polarisation in society (BCRA 2015). This evidence is complemented by the evolution of the Gini index. The Gini index for household income inequality rose to a high of 54.2 in 2002 at the height of the impacts of the crisis (CEPAL 2015). This increase was not as severe as the impact on poverty and indigence levels due to the fact that the deterioration of real wages as a result of the crisis was generalised across workers of difference sectors and qualifications (Beccaria et al. 2007: 23).

The Political Economy of the Crisis Period

The magnitude of the economic crisis and its social consequences forced many Argentines to re-evaluate domestic politics in the search for the causes of such a crisis. The crisis facilitated an inordinate degree of apathy and a concomitant low degree of commitment to the political process in Argentina. This was mostly due to the fact that the socio-economic crisis had had a 'very corrosive effect on politics' (Sanchez 2005: 461), generating profound scepticism about the political process. The fleeing of the *Casa Rosada* by De la Rua in the Presidential helicopter at the height of the protests, the regime's general impression of incompetence and paralysis in the run-up to the crisis, and the power vacuum that ensued with several Presidents in several days until Duhalde emerged all served to give the perception of political meltdown during the crisis in 2001. However, the fact that democracy survived at all, especially given the recent Argentine history of military coups and dictatorship, is a testament to the strength of democracy in Argentina in comparison with the 1970s. Nevertheless, these unique events did arguably have a significant impact on the trajectory of Argentine political economy. The crisis of neoliberal hegemony and associated disintegration of the dominant model that struck Argentina at the end of 2001 presented a great historical opportunity for society to construct another way of organising. An autonomist narrative emerged which inspired a new political activism that was characterised by an opening-up to new experiences and direct democracy. Horizontal decision-making structures and the rejection of hierarchy characterised the neighbourhood assemblies (*barrias asembleas*), unemployed workers movements (*piqueteros*), wave of worker-recovered factories (*fabricas recouperados*), and mass experiences with using barter clubs (*trueque*) all embodied these ideas.

'*Que se vayan todos*' can be interpreted as a measure of the enormous distance that had opened up between government and society (Oxhorn 2002: 499; Grugel and Riggirozzi 2007: 94; Dinerstein 2014). According to Laura Tedesco (2002: 481), the forms of 'resistance politics' that emerged in response to the crisis were the result of a lack of horizontally accountable institutions in Argentine society due to its traditional vertical accountability through strong presidential and personal politics (O'Donnell 1998). Therefore, the crisis represented a fundamental rejection of the Menemist model based on elements of neoliberal thinking and the separation of state from society. The large political impact of the crisis can be attributed to the legacy of poverty and social exclusion in a country where citizenship had been associated with a range of social and economic rights since Peronist days (Grugel and Riggirozzi 2007: 94). A whole new stratum of society had been impoverished both by the neoliberal restructuring of the 1990s and by the events of the crisis itself. This 'new poor' (Chudnovsky 2001; Grugel and Riggirozzi 2007: 94) were politicised, vocal, and numerically significant.

The crisis had clear implications for the Argentine state. The hegemonic constellation of social relations from the Menem period that had coalesced around broad neoliberal principles had been shattered.

Middle-class prosperity ended with the destabilisation of the macro-economic environment through asymmetric pessification; finance capital was devastated by huge losses; working classes were hit with mass unemployment and government cuts to social programmes. The attendant expressions of power through the state dissipated as the various autonomist movements outlined in the previous section increasingly dominated everyday Argentine life. The old state project had clearly ended in a spectacular fashion, with an ongoing reconfiguration of social power that had yet to manifest itself in terms of the strategic limits of state terrain. However, this reconfiguration was to occur in the second moment.

The Second Moment: The Rise of *Kirchnerismo* (2003–2008)

The vision of a new resistance politics of horizontally accountable institutions in Argentine society that emerged in The First Moment was not to be. By the end of the first year of Nestor Kirchner's presidency, many of these movements barely existed and were in full retreat. The factory takeover movement was all but over, the *Piqueteros* movement was split with fractions supporting Kirchner and the FPV (*Frente para la Victoria*), *trueque* was undermined by a proliferation of social currency that helped facilitate forgery and scandal, and the *assambleas barrias* degenerated into talking shops and participation plummeted after the middle classes were once again able to access their savings after the ending of the freezing of their bank accounts. It was Kirchner's deliberate forging of a new social contract that co-opted many of these movements, either through integration of their concerns into policy, removal of original grievances through reform, incorporation of new social fractions into the social basis of Kirchner's power through adoption of new policy, and also through more direct forms of clientelism. The strategic terrain of the Argentine state was busily being re-mapped through the new expressions of social power that emerged in the immediate aftermath of the 2001 crisis.

In the post-crisis administrations of Néstor Kirchner (2003–2007) and Cristina Fernandez de Kirchner (2008–2015), this re-mapping of the state's strategic terrain manifested in the search for a new model of capital accumulation. This search represented a critical juncture for the trajectory of Argentine development, although the evolution of the national-popular ideology of *Kirchnerismo* was gradual. At the start of 2003 the decline of the new popular protest movements that had emerged in The First Moment, combined with the break-up of the *piquetero* organisations gradually diluted the expectations of a political reconstruction 'from the bottom up' and replaced by demands for order and normality. This crystallised into Kirchner's campaign slogan '*un pais en serio*'. In adopting this social message Kirchner advocated the construction of a progressive discourse 'from the top': the removal of Menemist judges from the Supreme Court, the prioritisation of human rights in relation to the violations committed by the dictatorship during the 1970s and 1980s, and the pursuit of a strong role for the state alongside fiercely anti-neoliberal and pro-Latin Americanist rhetoric.

The Policies of Nestor Kirchner

When GDP figures are examined for the Nestor Kirchner administration it is clear that Argentina experienced a dramatic recovery in terms of economic growth (see Fig. 5.1). The reasons for this dramatic recovery change according to which period one examines, but Damill et al. (2007: 18) identify three stages to the recovery. The first stage is the immediate recovery period of the second and third quarters of 2002. The actual GDP recovery during this period was relatively weak, and GDP levels remained significantly below pre-crisis levels until 2004,

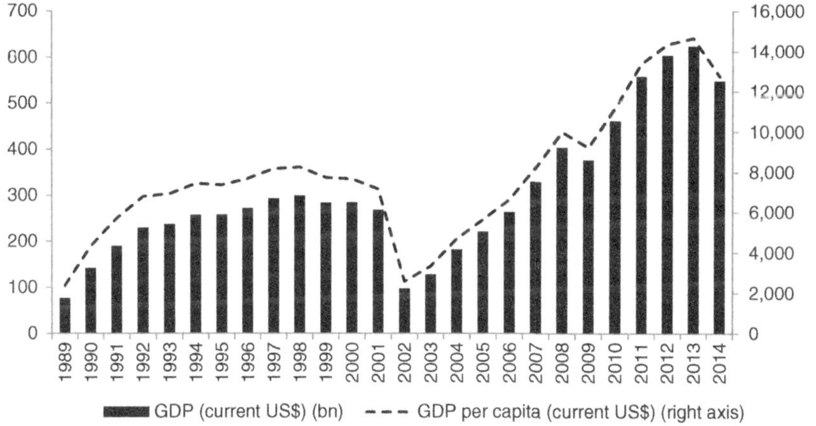

Fig. 5.1 Argentine GDP and GDP per Capita in current US$, 1989–2014. *Source* World Bank (2016)

due to suppressed aggregate demand as a result of falling employment, falling wages, liquidity constraints as a result of the *corralito*, and economic uncertainty (Riggirozzi 2009: 103; Bezchinsky et al. 2007: 19). The second period of recovery from the last quarter of 2002 to the second quarter of 2004 was very much to do with increases in aggregate demand (Heymann 2006: 58). Employment ceased falling, wages began to increase again, liquidity returned to the economy as the *corralito* was finally totally lifted, and some sense of normality and certainty began to return (Damill et al. 2007: 19; Bezchinsky et al. 2007: 21).

The third and final period of recovery, from the third quarter of 2004 onwards, was due to the fact that exports started a period of faster expansion. This can be attributed in no small part to the government's interventions in the foreign exchange market and the stated policy of maintaining a competitive exchange rate (Damill et al. 2007: 20; CEPAL 2006: 69), although other factors were certainly involved; these include the rise in global primary commodity prices and the reversal in the terms of trade both for Argentina and Latin American countries as a whole (Petras and Veltmeyer 2009: 11–13; Panizza 2009: 225–249), as well as stronger external demand (CEPAL 2006: 70).

The three main sectors that fuelled this growth were construction, agriculture, and industrial manufacture. The dynamism of the construction and industrial manufacture was reflected in both significant Gross Fixed Capital Formation (GFCF) and in the imports of capital goods (Bezchinsky et al. 2007: 21). As a weighted index where 1997 = 100 construction activity increased from a crisis low of 57.8 in 2002 to 134.3 by 2007, thus far exceeding pre-crisis highs in the 1990s (Wylde 2013). Therefore, whilst the economic recovery had a consumption component, investment across sectors played a significant role in the return of growth (Gerchunoff and Aguirre 2004: 4). Agribusiness grew by 11.9% and industrial manufacturing grew by 7.7% (CEPAL 2007a) in the 2004–2005 period, with a weighted index of the physical volume of industrial manufactures growing from a crisis low of 70.2 in 2002 to 121.9 by 2007 (INDEC 2007).

There was also a shift in emphasis in the management of the Argentine economy since 2003. This was to encourage production, more specifically the industrial sectors of the economy, at the expense of the financial sector, especially the banking and capital markets (Ferrer 2005: 370–371). There were dozens of mechanisms and promotion programmes that offered tax breaks, subsidies, sponsored credit, and technical assistance which formed the core of Kirchner's industrial policy, and thus facilitated this change in the structure of the Argentine economy (Baruj and Porta 2005; see also Ortiz and Schorr 2009: 5). In addition, there were a number of public works programmes such as road building and bridge construction in order to promote private levels of economic activity (EIU 2007; Heidrich and Tussie 2009: 45). This represented a key source of change in the structure of the post-crisis Argentine economy in comparison with the Menem period. Banking and capital markets that took centre stage during the 1990s, whilst not actively discouraged, were relegated in importance in comparison with industry and the 'real' economy broadly defined.

Ortiz and Schorr (2009: 3) suggest that industrial policy was based largely on the movements of the exchange rate post-*Convertibilidad*, rather than any active industrial policy on the part of the Kirchner administration. Policies only involved very specific measures 'bounded in its effects and poorly coordinated' (Ortiz and Schoor 2009: 3). Nevertheless, programmes did exist and represented aggregate demand stimulation policies based on Keynesian principles of 'fiscal pump priming'; where the government could create jobs in a variety of ways, which stimulated demand for goods and services and therefore led to the private sector expanding output, creating both economic growth and employment (Clarke 2005: 58).

The efficacy of such an approach in the Argentine context has been brought into question. Fernando Porta (2005) has suggested that much of the industry in Argentina suffers from the twin problems of low value-added production and low levels of complementarities. Ortiz and Schorr (2009: 5) complement this analysis as their suggestion of a lack of coordinated industrial policy led to an absence of active policies aimed at strategic reconstitution of production chains. Therefore, whilst on a quantitative level the structure of the Argentine economy shifted post-*Convertibilidad*, in a qualitative sense it has stayed the same. The change in the exchange rate and the associated decreased cost of labour, whilst having encouraged the development of activities historically neglected did not substantially changed the relationship between different production linkages within the industrial network (Santarcángelo et al. 2011: 103). The trend of declining industrial output relative to total output that occurred in the 1990s was partly reversed but the configuration of the industrial sector did not change in a meaningful way (Bugna and Porta 2008: 41). Taking advantage of the shift in currency and some limited industrial policies aided the macro level in terms of industry's share of GDP but there was limited progress in support of a reindustrialisation that would redefine Argentine specialisation in terms of its production profile; nor has was there a drastically different insertion of Argentina into the international division of labour (Azpiazu and Schorr 2010: 136).

The third phase of recovery also involved a substantial expansion of Argentine exports. This expansion represented a centrally important feature of the nature of the economic recovery in post-2001 crisis Argentina and had a major impact on the structure of the Argentine economy. This is due to the fact that throughout the post-War period there has been a structural imbalance in the economy of Argentina: the asymmetry between the export contribution of the smaller agricultural sector (in terms of contribution to GDP) and that of industry (Di Tella and Dornbusch 1989: 6–7; Chudnovsky 2007). Under Kirchner the value of exports rose steadily from the start of 2003 onwards, and, unlike the period preceding the crisis in 2001, the total value of exports exceeded the total value of imports, which is reflected in the Argentine current account surplus post-2001 crisis (Heymann 2007; Wylde 2013).

Not only did the value of exports rise but Argentine exports increased from a maximum of 10% of GDP throughout most of the 1990s to between 22 and 25% of GDP from 2003 onwards (Heymann 2007). Whilst part of this is certainly down to the massive contraction of GDP experienced by the crisis, as well as the statistical effect of the devaluation of the peso, the coefficient has remained above 20% through into 2006 after GDP recovered to pre-crisis levels. Therefore, manufacturing exports formed a large and growing part of the Argentine economy for the first time (Heymann 2006: 55).

Nestor Kirchner facilitated this structural shift after abandoning the currency peg through a proactive policy in the form of intervention in the foreign exchange markets. From mid-2002, and up until mid-2003, there was a period of appreciation that only came to a halt as the result of a deliberate policy decision by the Kirchner administration: the maintenance of a 'Stable and Competitive Real Exchange Rate' (SCRER) (Frenkel and Rapetti 2008; Damill et al. 2007: 3; CEPAL 2007b: 104–105). In practice, this resulted in an exchange rate with the US dollar of between 2.8 and 3.1 pesos, and a steady depreciation of the Real Exchange Rate.

This maintenance of an SCRER can therefore be argued to represent the administration's single most important contribution to Argentine GDP growth in the 2003–2007 period (Frenkel and Rapetti 2008: 215). This policy was intended not only to aid the import substitution process that had begun after devaluation, but also to promote exports (especially those of a manufacturing origin) and therefore accelerate the growth of the economy and thus the recovery (Riggirozzi 2009: 103). This strategy can also be read as a desire to restructure the economy in order to reduce dependence on international commodity prices through the promotion of exports of a non-traditional origin for Argentina, namely those of manufacturing origin. Furthermore, this policy also reduced Argentine dependence on the global economy by facilitating the accumulation of foreign exchange for debt servicing, giving Argentina a financial cushion from potential future external shocks.

Exports of primary products represented 71.3% of total exports, and manufacturing represented 28.7% in 2004 (CEPAL 2005: 105–106). Figure 5.2 demonstrates the increased level of exports, as well as the increased share of manufacturing as a percentage of total exports. Data from the United Nations Development Programme (UNDP) also mirror these trends, with a significant increase of exports as a percentage

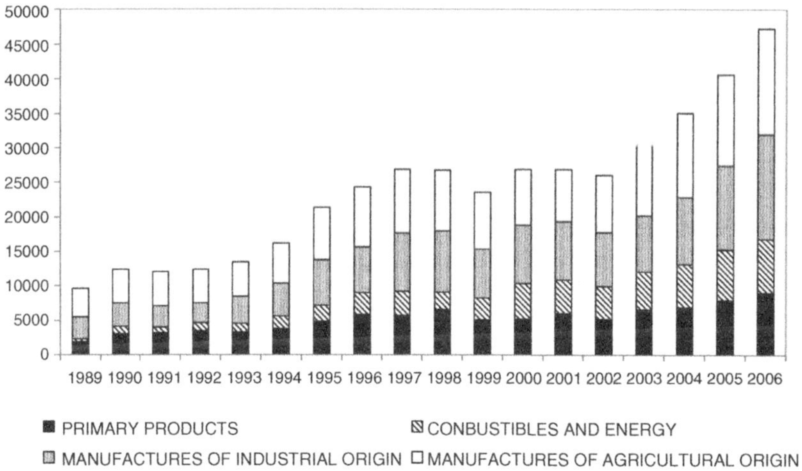

Fig. 5.2 Exports by type of good in Argentina, 1989–2006 (US$bn). *Source* Bezchinsky et al. (2007)

of GDP from 10% in 1990 to 25% from 2003 onwards (UNDP 2005, 2006, 2007–2008). Furthermore, a growing proportion could be attributed to exports from a manufactured origin, growing from 27% in 1990 and 2003 to 31% by 2005.

The contribution of increasing global commodity prices should not be underplayed, and certainly represents one of the reasons for such significant increases in agricultural exports in particular. Indeed, it was not only Argentina that experienced a strong growth record grounded in exports but also much of Latin America as a whole during this period, with the continent growing at an average of 5.6% in 2006 (CEPAL 2007a: 1). This growth was fuelled by a highly favourable external environment (Petras and Veltmeyer 2009: 84; CEPAL 2007a: 18), which included the steady expansion of the world economy (prior to the onset of the global financial crisis in 2007–2008), China and India's increasing importance in world demand, and the role of increasing commodity prices that created increasingly favourable terms of trade for Argentina and Latin America as a whole. CEPAL calculations suggest that these factors were the equivalent to 3.4% of GDP growth for the Southern Cone region in 2006 (CEPAL 2007a: 11).

One of the main themes in the literature is that the dramatic recovery and growth experienced by Argentina in the 2003–2007 period was more due to the convergence of these international conditions, rather than the result of proactive and successful government policy. However, whilst the international conditions were clearly favourable, their role should not be overstated. Whilst exports in Argentina grew impressively from 2003 onwards, gross domestic investment grew at much higher levels (Tussie 2009: 72). This was mostly due to the construction boom, as well as strong growth in manufacturing. This strong growth in manufacturing also demonstrates that not all export growth in Argentina during the period 2003–2007 was in the primary sector, with exports of manufacturing origin representing a significant proportion of the growing export base (Bezchinsky 2007). Therefore, manufacturing growth served to help a limited 'decoupling' of the Argentine economic recovery from international commodity prices. However, agriculture remained Argentina's chief source of export revenue and therefore the limited nature of this decoupling should be stressed.

In fiscal terms the administration of Nestor Kirchner saw a significant and sustained improvement, leading to both a primary surplus and a surplus in the public accounts throughout from 2003–2007. Not only were there significant improvements in the federal budget surplus and primary surplus but also as a percentage of GDP in a growing economy (EIU 2007). On the other side of the balance sheet is expenditure. Both primary and non-primary spending increased at approximately the same rates, with primary spending increasing from 19.6% of GDP in 2003 to 20.1 in 2006 (Ministry of Economy and Production 2009). Whilst spending increased fairly dramatically in absolute terms, as a percentage of GDP government spending has changed very little. Sound public finances were the chief characteristic of the Argentine fiscal situation in the period 2003–2007.

There were several reasons for the turnaround in the public accounts during the 2003–2007 period, which had been plagued by deficits in the years running up to the crisis and in the recession period after the crisis in 2001–2002. By far the largest impact on the surplus was the improvement due to debt restructuring. Interest payments on debt as a percentage of GDP fell from a high of 3.8% in 2001 to 2% in 2007, a level comparable with the median average of developing countries (World Bank 2004). This was due to Kirchner's policies with regard to debt restructuring. The improvements in the primary surplus were derived from increasing tax receipts. There was a steady increase in tax receipts since 2003, partly the result of a growing economy and partly the result of increased efficiency of tax collection and consequent reductions in tax evasion. In 2006 alone, tax receipts rose by 25.85% (CEPAL 2007a: 104), and as a percentage of GDP, tariffs on exported goods rose from an insignificant 0.02% in 1998, to 2.5% in 2007 (Ministry of Economy and Production, 2009). These increases in tax receipts were the result of Argentina's export boom and were especially beneficial to the fiscal surplus created by the agricultural sector due to the boom in international primary commodity prices during that period (Petras and Veltmeyer 2009: 61; CEPAL 2007a: 11).

Favourable international circumstances for major Argentine primary commodity exports certainly contributed to these increases. However, favourable international circumstances are not the only reason for this expansion of revenue from export tariffs. Kirchner's SCRER can be interpreted as deliberate government policy to stimulate exports of a manufacturing origin (Interview with Heymann 2007; Gerchunoff and Aguirre 2004: 6), combined with increasing the competitiveness of agricultural exports, partially due to the same policy. Therefore, this increase in the competitiveness of Argentina's exports can be traced not only to international factors but also directly to deliberate government policy.

During Nestor Kirchner's administration, there was a reduction of the external debt from $164.6 billion in 2004 to $107.8 billion in 2006 (CEPAL 2007a, b). Furthermore, the relationship between total debt and GDP improved, falling from a high of 153.6% in 2003 to 62% in 2006 (CEPAL 2007b: 104). The relation between exports and debt also improved, both as a result of falling debt obligations and rising exports. Interest rate payments as a percentage of exports fell from 29% in 2003, or a high of 39.4% in 2001, to 9.8% in 2006 (CEPAL 2007a, b), reflecting both rising exports and the increased sustainability achieved by Kirchner's negotiations in the debt swap of 2005.

The fundamental reason for the sound public finances was the result of Kirchner's renegotiation of Argentina's debt burden. Debt was used as a way of funding the current account deficit throughout the 1990s and combined with the recent experience of the 2002 default it was clear that Argentina not only required a major reappraisal and restructuring of its international debt portfolio but also a change in attitude towards debt in order to facilitate the conditions for a sustainable future in the form of a long-term sustained reduction of the debt. Both of these issues were addressed by Kirchner, managing to negotiate both a significant haircut (i.e. a partial cancellation) of its outstanding debt and a favourable restructuring of interest and maturity (Tussie 2009: 73; Damill et al. 2007; Kosacoff 2008: 39) as well as removing the stress on sustainability (Riggirozzi 2009: 102–104).

This policy of hard negotiation and the eventual removal of Argentina from IMF-inspired economic policy represented a departure from the history of Argentine policy since the *Desarrollismo* governments of Frondizi (1958–1962) and Illia (1963–1966). For example, IMF advice was taken by Frondizi and Illia when attempting to tackle inflation in the economy, and *Convertibilidad* in the 1990s was maintained under continued IMF advice. Reaching a peak during the Menem years, many Argentine commentators, including Kirchner himself, blamed the IMF and its policies in Argentina for the crisis of 2001 and its aftermath (Tresca 2005, 2009: 73). Therefore, in both related policy areas of debt reduction and IMF influence, the Kirchner administration represented a substantial departure from the 1990s under the administration of Menem, as well as from earlier administrations as this accumulation of debt in the economy and associated IMF influence in its economic affairs has been a trend from much earlier in history.

Immediately after the crisis, there was a large spike in inflation, as prices adjusted to post-*Convertibilidad* conditions. At the time there were widespread fears that the economy would enter a hyper-inflationary period similar to that experienced in the late 1980s; this did not occur mainly due to suppressed demand through reduced wages and high unemployment. Since this period inflation has been rising steadily, with increased prices for both goods and services in a context of high and sustained economic growth. From a base of 100 in 1999, the CPI (Consumer Price Index) reached 194.89 by 2007 (Ministry of Economy and Production 2008). In percentage terms, from 2003 onwards Argentina experienced official annual year-on-year rates of approximately 10%.

The issue of inflation represents the single greatest challenge for contemporary Argentine macroeconomic policy given the task of maintaining high growth rates through a depreciated real exchange rate in the context of an open capital account. This problem represents the classic 'trilemma' (Fleming 1962; Mundell 1963) or 'impossible trinity', where in the absence of capital controls and a policy of a fixed exchange rate regime, governments give up sovereignty of monetary policy. The solution in the Argentine context was for the Central Bank to concentrate more on price stability by raising interest rates and letting the peso appreciate (Frenkel and Rapetti 2006: 21). In the short run, Argentina was able to deal with this dilemma from the currency side of the equation (i.e. preventing real appreciation of the peso) through using its fiscal surplus to buy foreign exchange generated by the trade surplus and using it to pay foreign debt or accumulate foreign exchange reserves (Mercado 2007: 11). The inflation issue, however, was more difficult in the context of high GDP and decreasing spare capacity. From the supply side the relatively low investment levels, especially in the energy sector, reduced the elasticity of supply over time (Mercado 2007: 12) This was exacerbated by the demand side, as the increases in consumption and investment associated with accelerated growth, as well as the continuing trade surplus, all put short-run pressures on the rate of inflation (D'Amato et al. 2007: 7; Mercado 2007: 12).

The traditional levers of inflation dampening, increasing interest rates or an appreciation of the exchange rate, were unavailable to Argentina given its stated policies of a low RER—the result of the unholy trinity issue. Instead, monetary policy involved sterilisation efforts to limit the growth of monetary aggregates (Frenkel and Rapetti 2006: 22) and limited capital controls introduced in June 2005, inspired by Chile's policies in the mid-1990s to discourage short-term capital inflows. Fiscal policy also played a role in the inflation conundrum of contemporary Argentina. As analysed elsewhere in this chapter, fiscal discipline and conservatism, as well as a reluctance to see large wage increases and the management of inflation expectations through price controls, all served to help dampen inflation. Indeed, according to Martin Redrado (2008), former governor of the Argentine central bank, the evolution of fiscal and wage policy was critical, along with monetary aspects, when making judgements about the Argentine macro economy.

Many have commented that the levels of inflation under Nestor Kirchner were not problematical, given the expansion of GDP (Mercado 2007; Frankel and Rapetti 2006). Notwithstanding alleged attempts to manipulate the official rate through presidential bribes to the government statistical body INDEC (due to large amounts of newly denominated debt being linked to domestic inflation) (Petras and Veltmeyer 2009: 85), and the subsequent perception on the street that prices were rising much higher than the official rate and creating wage demands in the workplace, this is true. However, the historical mechanisms for previous hyper-inflationary situations were government deficits and upward pressures on the exchange rate, two factors that were not present in the contemporary macroeconomic framework of Argentina with a government fiscal surplus, and an exchange rate that was not appreciating. Combined with a trade surplus and a high level of foreign reserves the situation in Argentina did not show the typical triggers for an explosion of inflation. Nevertheless, many of the measures adopted by the government were short-term solutions at best and problems began to manifest themselves under the subsequent administration of Cristina Fernandez de Kirchner.

Under Nestor Kirchner, Argentina saw large falls in the unemployment level, which was largely the result of sustained economic growth after 2003. This also resulted in a significant decline in unemployment and underemployment in Argentina from over 20 to 12%, respectively, to around 7 and 6% by Q4 2007 (Ministry of Economy and Production 2009), leading Beccaria et al. (2007) to conclude that the intensity of the net generation of jobs associated with the recovery constituted the most remarkable characteristic of the period. Furthermore, much of the new employment generated was in the private sector, with public employment expanding less than 5% in the 2003–2007 period (Heidrich and Tussie 2009: 47).

Real wages were hit particularly hard after devaluation in January 2002 and the subsequent change in relative prices. Due to the inflationary pressures on the economy present at the time, the government was very conscious of not wanting to add to them through wage increases), as well as the fact that Kirchner wanted to contain public expenditure (Heymann 2006: 52). Public sector salaries were almost static throughout 2003 and 2004, and real salaries were still 40% below their 2001 levels in 2006 (Heidrich and Tussie 2009: 47; see also Riggirozzi 2009: 89–113). Therefore, one of the main effects of exit from *Convertibilidad* was the change that resulted in relative prices and the subsequent enormous cost that this entailed for the working class due to the fall of real wages to a historic low in the last 30 years. However, in the 2003–2007 period there were more significant wage increases in the private sector: from a weighted index of 121.89 in 2003 (where 2001 = 100) to 264.46 by 2007 (Ministry of Economy and Production 2009). The end result was that the average remuneration for work by the second quarter of 2005 was 17% below 2001 (i.e. pre-crisis) levels and 9% below in the more dynamic manufacturing and construction sectors (Beccaria et al. 2007).

Kirchner's strategy of job creation through economic growth resulted in a relative lack of specific anti-poverty measures. Whilst poverty reduced significantly from its crisis highs (see Table 5.3), this was largely due to the employment trends, with the effectiveness of Kirchner's anti-poverty strategies fairly limited. During his administration, he maintained and partially extended minimal social safety nets. The universal policy of *Plan Jefes,* originated in the Duhalde administration in response to the extreme poverty impact of the 2001–2002 crisis, was actually run down throughout his administration. This programme was replaced with other, much smaller schemes such as *Planes Trabajar* and *Plan Familias.* Therefore, despite his traditional Peronist power base, and his extensive use of associated rhetoric, this was not backed up with systematic attempts to deal with poverty. Instead, Kirchner preferred to use expansions in employment and private wages in order to help reduce the very high levels of poverty in Argentina.

Table 5.3 Social indicators under the Kirchner administration

Year	*Urban poverty rate (households) (%)*	*Urban poverty rate (persons) (%)*	*Urban unemployment rate (%)*	*Urban underemployment rate (%)*	*Registered private sector wages (2001 = 100)*	*Unregistered private sector wages (2001 = 100)*	*Public sector wages (2001 = 100)*
2003	36.5	47.8	14.5	11.4	135.32	104.23	106.23
2004	29.8	40.2	12.1	9.7	150.21	116.25	110.78
2005	24.7	33.8	10.1	8.4	189.20	130.88	125.06
2006	23.1	31.4	10.4	8.1	215.68	146.97	132.55

Source Ministry of Economy and Production (2009)
Note Wages are in money terms (i.e. non-inflation adjusted)

Table 5.4 Minimum wage compared to the basic basket of goods for a typical family (constant pesos)

Year	*Basic basket of goods (1)*	*Minimum wage*	*Minimum wage as a % of the basic basket*
2003 March	668.87	200	29.9
2003 September	656.61	270	41.1
2004 March	672.02	350	52.1
2004 September	684.82	450	65.7
2005 March	720.36	450	62.5
2005 September	754.37	630	83.5
2006 March	799.25	630	78.8
2006 September	810.57	780	96.2
2007 March	854.18	800	93.7
2007 September	896.57	900	100.4

Source Ministry of Economy and Production (2009)
Note (1) Estimation for the total country based on INDEC data and the 2001 Census

Despite demonstrating this relative lack of systemic intervention, the Kirchner administration was proactive in its minimum wage policy. The minimum wage in Argentina had been at the same level since 1993, until Duhalde increased it in 2002. This policy was continued by Kirchner with incremental increases throughout his presidency (see Table 5.4). These steady rises in the minimum wage had an important impact on extreme poverty, especially, as in March 2003 the minimum wage of 200 pesos represented 29.9% of the money needed to purchase what was considered a basic basket of goods; whereas, by September 2007 the minimum wage of 900 pesos was 100.4% of that same basket in real terms.

All of these measures together can be read as government designed 'catch-up' policies in order to facilitate increasing purchasing power of key socio-economic groups in Argentine society. *Kirchnerismo* involved a significant dose of state-led development, grounded in industrial policy that favoured domestic capital and established foreign corporations and a macroeconomic policy of fiscal conservatism and sound money. Impressive GDP growth (see Fig. 5.1) resulted in the context of favourable international circumstances—particularly in terms of global commodity prices. However, this positive picture began to deteriorate, the dynamics of which will be explored in the rest of this chapter.

The Third Moment: The '*Conflicto Del Campo*' (2008–2011)

In 2007, Nestor Kirchner surprised many by announcing that he would not be standing for re-election. Instead, his wife and Senator Cristina Fernandez de Kirchner (CFK) would stand as the Presidential candidate for their Peronist political party the *Frente para la Victoria*. CFK was elected to power with nearly 45% of the vote on the campaign promise of a desire to 'deepen the model' that was initiated under her husband and analysed in detail in terms of policy in the above section. This message of continuity was underpinned by the fact that seven of the twelve appointed ministers were from her husband's administration, and also that Nestor himself would stay active in Argentine politics, working closely with CFK as advisor and confidant.

The start of The Third Moment is identified in the conflict between the national government and the rural sectors in 2008 over a planned increase in the export duties placed on agricultural products (*retenciones*), which occurred shortly after CFK's inauguration. The road blocks, strikes, and lockouts during the economic conflict had clear political dimensions: both in terms of the inflexible response of the government and the speedy reaction of some sectors of the middle classes in Buenos Aires, who took to the streets in support of agrarian sectors whilst questioning the authoritarian political style of the government. This led to a renewal of old polarised oppositions, which are a key part of Argentine historical tradition and are deeply anchored in the national-popular discourse: civilisation or barbarism, Peronism or anti-Peronism, people or anti-people (Levey et al. 2014). This established a rhetoric on the part of the administration that in turn facilitated an associated development of increasingly antagonistic relationships between the state and fractions of Argentine capital.

The broader IPE context at the time of these domestic tensions was the global financial crisis and subsequent 'Great Recession'. The collapse of international demand that followed the global financial crisis hit Argentine exports hard. A key cornerstone of Argentine political economy post-2001 was the rise in exports. As well as the direct impact on exports of a manufacturing origin, this dynamic also served to restrict the revenues gained from agricultural exports due to an associated declining term of trade. This was exacerbated in 2012 by severe drought which affected yields. In turn, this impacted on Argentina's public finances.

Since export taxes (*retenciones*) were reintroduced in 2002 they became an important source of state income, representing an average of 12% of budget revenues (INDEC 2010). The increase in *retenciones* by CFK in 2008 can be seen as a direct response to these changing international dynamics, coupled with a desire to maintain fiscal surpluses in the face of declining revenues. This served to create a backlash among rural oligarchs and TNCs that dominate Argentine agro-industry (especially in soya and soya derivatives production) (Rivera-Quiñones 2014).

The drop in international demand for Argentina's exports also facilitated downward pressure on her nominal exchange rate. This trend was further exacerbated by the need to import increasing amounts of energy to fuel Argentina's rapid economic expansion in the absence of domestic investment in energy production. In turn, this eroded Argentina's current account surplus. A drop in the nominal exchange rate combined with increasing inflation to increase Argentina's Real Exchange Rate (Table 5.5), further eroding export competitiveness and thus further eroding the current account surplus.

This erosion of the current account surplus (to near zero by 2012) threatened to undermine one of the key cornerstones of *Kirchnerismo*. Persistent current account deficits in the 1990s during neoliberal restructuring led to excessive foreign debt accumulation. Ultimately this helped precipitate economic meltdown in 2001–2002 and the associated dislocation of Argentine politics and society (Svampa 2014; Wylde 2014). Frenkel and Rapetti (2008) point to the accumulation of substantial foreign exchange reserves from 2003 onwards, which gave monetary

Table 5.5 Key economic indicators in Argentina 2008–2014

	2008	*2009*	*2010*	*2011*	*2012*	*2013*	*2014*
GDP growth (%)	3.1	0.05	9.1	8.5	0.9	2.9	2.8
Inflation (%)	7.2	7.7	10.9	9.5	10.2	10.6	
Inflation (%)[a]	–	–	–	22.64	25.25	28.27	38.53
Primary balance (% GDP)	2.8	1.4	1.5	−0.1	−0.1	−1.4	−2.0
REER (2005 = 100)	97.2	99.3	98.5	99.5	94.8		
Unemployment (%) (ILO)	7.8	8.6	7.7	7.2	7.2	7.5	
Current account balance (% GDP)	1.6	2.2	0.3	−0.4	−0.2	−0.7	

Source Rows 1 and 6: World Bank (2016); row 2: INDEC (2016); column 3 Congreso Nacional (2016)[a]; rows 4 and 5: CEPAL (2016)

[a]Since 2011, opposition members of the National Congress published inflation data that were an aggregate of eight different independent consultants

authorities greater flexibility to absorb negative external shocks and to avoid sharp exchange rate corrections in contexts of low liquidity of foreign exchange. In addition, outstanding debt burdens were significantly lower than in the 1990s, and at historically low levels. This served to give Argentina much more room for manoeuvre, room that they used in terms of the different policies of the CFK administration.

Of greater concern was the associated steady appreciation of the Real Exchange Rate. Historically, sustained RER appreciation has had a negative effect on industrial employment and output. Typically, this led to the destruction of firms and employment, human and organisational capital, vertical and horizontal linkages and access to foreign markets (Frenkel and Rapetti 2011: 9). This represented a clear challenge to the post-crisis *Kirchnerismo* model, with a number of CFKs policies designed to prevent this from happening again. However, the problem was not necessarily as bad as it was in the 1990s. Whilst the bilateral RER between the Argentine peso and the US dollar appreciated significantly in this period, Argentina's REER (a more accurate representation of the competitiveness of the Argentine peso) was more muted. A country's REER index is calculated by weighing its real bilateral exchange rate indices with each of its trading partners by each partner's share in the country's total trade flows in terms of exports and imports. A currency depreciates in real effective terms when this index rises, and appreciates when it falls (CEPAL 2010: 82). An appreciation of the Real Exchange Rate indicates that the foreign price (in dollars) of a bundle of goods has risen relative to the domestic price. If the real exchange rate appreciates it means that the real value of the dollar has depreciated; that is, the purchasing power of the dollar has fallen in relative terms. The REER data as shown in Table 5.5 were largely due to Argentina's currency appreciation being offset by currency appreciation in Argentina's main trading partners, especially Brazil (Frenkel and Rapetti 2011: 11; see also CEPAL 2010: 98). Furthermore, diversification of Argentine exports—both geographically away from the USA and sectorally with a sharp increase in exports of a manufactured origin from 2003 onwards—gave the economy the strength and capacity to deal with large negative external shocks (Wylde 2012: 200–203).

A number of CFK's policies can therefore be interpreted as attempts to correct these pressures on the current account balance. A series of foreign exchange restrictions to prevent domestic US dollar hoarding facilitated tensions with middle-class elements of Argentine society as foreign travel and holidays become more expensive, and saving domestically became more difficult. In addition, a number of import restrictions, as well as measures to require businesses that import to also export goods, widened these tensions to domestic bourgeois elements of the middle classes. The renationalisation of YPF in an attempt to reignite energy investment and thus reduce the levels of imported energy (which in turn will help relieve pressure on the current account balance) also created tensions with elements of international capital.

The Fourth Moment: CFKs Second Mandate (2011–2015)

These adverse external economic headwinds, and the Argentine administration's policies to deal with them, dominated the rest of CFK's tenure all the way into her second term. This final section will first outline key trends and trajectories in the Argentine economy, followed by an analysis of the political economy of the period in order to understand the development of *Kirchnerismo* up to the election of Mauricio Macri in October/November 2015.

The Fourth Moment is characterised by the beginning of Cristina's second mandate and reveals new incarnations of the national-popular project. Having achieved an overwhelming 54% of the vote in 2011, the government steadily weakened over the period. This was reflected in the breakdown of its meticulously constructed social alliances and slowdown in growth alongside persistently high inflation. Relations with significant sectors of the middle classes soured, as demonstrated by the mass anti-government mobilisations undertaken between September 2012 and April 2013. These expressed discontent vis-a-vis a range of institutional issues: the rejection of the possibility of changing the constitution to allow a third term for Cristina, a series of corruption scandals, and support for a politically impartial judiciary, government currency control policies, and the perception of rising crime.

The following analysis of this period of Argentine political economy will interpret many of the administration's policies in the context of her husband and predecessor's post-crisis model of twin surpluses in the current account and the fiscal account. Under the Presidency of CFK, these twin surpluses came under attack. The onset of global recession and subsequent drop in demand for Argentine exports, combined with severe drought in the 2011–2012 period, the current account surplus shrunk to effectively zero before falling into deficit thereafter in CFK's second term (see Table 5.5).

On the monetary policy front inflation continued to rise which, coupled with nominal depreciation of the peso (the result of effects from the trade channel), meant a steadily appreciating Real Exchange Rate. This gradual but steady real appreciation of Argentine peso further eroded the competitive edge of the country's exports. Table 5.5 demonstrates this by showing the trend of appreciation in Argentina's Real Effective Exchange Rate (REER). Such an appreciation appears inevitable in the face increased demand due to both increased export levels and low rates of return on capital in the West due to headline interest rates at or near zero.

This in turn impacted on the fiscal surplus. Reduced export tax intake combined with increasing spending reduced the primary surplus to the point where in 2009 expenditure exceeded income for the first time since 2002. This trend has continued to the present day, with a primary deficit registered from 2011 onwards (see Table 5.5). There were a number of sources of increasing expenditure during the presidency of CFK. Firstly, in the context of the impact of the global financial crisis in 2009, a fiscal stimulus package was initiated. This involved, inter alia, expansion of a number of welfare programmes, generous state subsidies in public transport and utilities that grew exponentially as inflation reignited, and increasing public sector wage demands as a result of that inflation. This meant that employment stood up well in the face of strong headwinds (see Table 5.5). In addition, according to official data, real wages increased significantly. Since 2011 opposition members of the National Congress have published inflation data that is an aggregate of eight independent consultants, data that is significantly above the official INDEC rate (see Table 5.5). As a result, whilst significant real income gains were achieved since the crisis of 2001–2002, 2012 witnessed a 3.5% decline from 2011 levels (The Economist 2013).

The presidency of CFK can therefore be seen as a desire to continue the same policies as her husband. The economic policies that Néstor Kirchner pursued in office had spectacular success in terms of sustaining economic growth over several years whilst managing, at the same time, to reduce the country's debt burden and keep inflation under control. This recovery occurred in the context of both a severe multifaceted domestic crisis in 2001–2002 and a favourable international context: i.e. benign and stable geopolitics as well as record highs for international commodity prices.

This benign international context was not sustained beyond 2007. As the previous section analysed, the global financial crisis of 2007–2008 led to the Great Recession as it impacted the real economy in the form of overproduction and demand contraction. This in turn depressed the prices of global commodities as global demand contracted. The following years were marked by sluggish recovery in much of the developed world, systemic and ongoing debt crisis in the eurozone, a ballooning deficit and debt burden in the US, and fiscal austerity in the UK into 2020 according to the latest budget statement (and likely to increase further as a result of Brexit). These forces hit Argentina in 2009 through a slowdown in capital flows, large declines in stock price indices, significant currency adjustments, and an increase in debt spreads (Bustillo and Velloso 2009: 35). As Table 5.5 shows, the Kirchner model of capital accumulation weathered this storm well with the economy returning to growth in 2010.

Argentina's economy thus passed an important stress test. However, the underlying trends outlined above were exacerbated by relatively high inflation. Inflation was high in this period for a number of reasons: first, expansionary fiscal policy. Under Nestor Kirchner, Argentina witnessed increased state spending, although as a percentage of GDP it remained fairly constant and the regime was able to maintain a significant fiscal surplus throughout his tenure (Wylde 2013: 118). Under CFK the general fiscal stance was more expansionary. This started in 2009 with a large fiscal stimulus in the wake of the global financial crisis, but continued beyond 2010/2011 despite a shrinking fiscal surplus. Second, the regime maintenance of its SCRER policy led to some inflation being imported, especially from Brazil. This problem represents the classic 'trilemma' or 'impossible trinity' where in the absence of capital controls and a policy of a fixed exchange rate regime, governments give up sovereignty of monetary policy. The solution for a number of analysts was for the central bank to concentrate more on price stability by raising interest rates and letting the peso appreciate (Frenkel and Rapetti 2006: 21). In the short run, Argentina was been able to deal with this dilemma from the currency side of the equation (i.e. preventing real appreciation of the peso) through using its fiscal surplus to buy foreign exchange generated by the trade surplus and using it to pay foreign debt or accumulate foreign exchange reserves (Mercado 2007: 11). From the supply side the relatively low investment levels, especially in the energy sector, reduced the elasticity of supply over time (Mercado 2007: 12). Cristina's policy of nationalising YPF could be read in this light: i.e. an attempt to overcome key energy investment bottlenecks to help relieve inflationary pressures, as well as current account pressures as a result of significant increases in energy imports. A third source of inflation in Argentina was from the demand side. Increases in consumption and investment associated with accelerated growth, as well as the continuing trade surplus, all put short-run pressures on the rate of inflation (D'Amato et al. 2007: 7; Mercado 2007: 12).

In summary, CFK continued some of the policies started in 2003 by her husband, but diverted in other important areas. Expansionary fiscal policy in the form of welfare provision and public subsidies in public transport and electricity tariffs were complemented with a macroeconomic framework to stimulate exports. However, this occurred in a changing international context, characterised by global financial crisis and declining commodity prices. This exacerbated underlying trends in inflation present due to expansionary fiscal and monetary policy set at the domestic level. This inflation impacted on the twin surpluses in the current and fiscal accounts that underpinned the post-crisis model of capital accumulation. The myriad of heterodox policies of CFK analysed in this section can all be interpreted as measures designed to protect those surpluses, and have been designed in a manner that continues to underpin an understanding of capital accumulation that places the state as an important driver of economic growth.

Conclusions

The crisis of 2001 clearly had a significant and lasting impact on the Argentine state and its political economy of development more broadly. The collapse of the neoliberal model of political economy during the Menem and de la Rua administrations in the 1990s was replaced with one grounded in the principles of *neodesarrollismo* (Katz 2006; Wylde 2011). State-led industrial policy that favoured domestic capital and established foreign investors helped nurture GDP growth and a significant expansion of employment. This was aided through sound macroeconomic management: a Stable and Competitive Real Exchange Rate policy was adopted, along with sound money and fiscal conservatism. Poverty reductions came largely from the expansion of employment rather than any comprehensive welfare programmes.

This model then underwent a series of challenges as a result of both internal and external shifts in conditions during Argentina's Third and Fourth Moments. CFK's desire to 'deepen the model', combined with significant international headwinds in the form of the global financial crisis and Argentina's continued expulsion from international capital markets, led to a series of macroeconomic imbalances that led the state to attempt increasingly heterodox methods to rectify. These policies were unable to hold back recession in 2014, and CFK's hand-picked successor—Daniel Scioli—lost to the centre-right led by Mauricio Macri.

This neo-developmentalist model present from 2003 to 2015 in Argentina was underpinned by a different constellation of power relationships, which in turn reshaped the contours of the Argentine state. Interpretation of these changes and the attendant impact upon Argentina's development trajectory are best understood through the application of the Developmental Regime model, a task to which this book will now turn.

References

Azpiazu, D., & Schorr, M. (2010). La industria Argentina en la post convertibilidad: Reactivacióm y legados del neoliberalismo. *Problemas del Desarrollo, 41*(161), 111–139.

Baruj, G., & Porta, F. (2005). *Politicas de Competitividad en la Argentina y su Impacto Sobre la Profundizacion del Mercosur*. Santiago de Chile: CEPAL.

BCRA. (2015). *Boletin Estadistico*. BCRA: Buenos Aires.

Beccaria, L., Esquivel, V., & Maurizio, R. (2007). *Crisis y recuperación: Efectos sobre el mercado de trabajo y la distribución del ingreso*. Argentina: Universidad Nacional de General Sarmiento.

Bezchinsky, G., Dinenzon, M., Guissani, L., & Caino, O. (2007). *Inversion extranjera directa en la Argentina. Crisis, reestructuracion y nuevas tendencias despues de la convertibilidad. Documento de Proyecto*. Santiago: CEPAL.

Bugna, F. C., & Porta, F. (2008). 'El crecimiento reciente de la industria Argentina. *Nuevo regimen sin cambio estructural', Realidad Económica, 233*, 63–105.

Bustillo, I., & Velloso, H. (2009). *The global financial crisis: What happened and what's next* (Vol. 4). Estudios y Perspectivas. Washington: ECLAC.

CEPAL. (2006). *Economic survey of Latin America and the Caribbean*. United Nations: Santiago, Chile.

CEPAL. (2005). *Economic survey of Latin America and the Caribbean*. United Nations: Santiago, Chile.

CEPAL. (2007a). *Statistical Yearbook for Latin America and the Caribbean—2007* (Santiago, Chile: United Nations).

CEPAL. (2007b). *Economic survey of Latin America and the Caribbean.* United Nations: Santiago, Chile.
CEPAL. (2010). *Economic survey of Latin America and the Caribbean: 2010–2011.* Santiago de Chile: CEPAL.
CEPAL. (2015). *Economic Survey of Latin America and the Caribbean.* United Nations: Santiago, Chile.
CEPAL. (2016). *Economic survey of Latin America and the Caribbean.* United Nations: Santiago, Chile.
Chudnovsky, D. (2001) Interview with Daniel Chudnovsky of CENIT, conducted in 2001 by Prof. Ruth Pearson.
Chudnovsky, D. (2007). *The elusive quest for growth in Argentina.* London: Routledge.
Clarke, S. (2005). The neoliberal theory of society. In A. Saad-Filho & D. Johnson (Eds.), *Neoliberalism: A critical reader* (pp. 50–59). London: Pluto.
D'Amato, L., Garegnani, L., & Paladino, J. M. S. (2007, August). Inflation persistence and changes in the monetary regime: The Argentine case. Paper given at the Euro area seminar in Buenos Aires at the Central Bank (BCRA), 23–24.
Damill, M., Frenkel, R., & Maurizio, M. (2007). *Macroeconomic policy changes in Argentina at the turn of the century.* Buenos Aires: CEDES.
Dinerstein, A. (2014). *The politics of autonomy in Latin America: The art of organising hope.* Springer: New York.
Di Tella, G., & Dornbusch, R. (1989). Introduction: The political economy of Argentina 1946–1983. In G. Di Tella & R. Dornbusch (Eds.), *The political economy of Argentina: 1946–1983* (pp. 6–7). Hampshire: Macmillan.
EIU. (2007). Country report—November 2007. http://www.eiu.com. Accessed 5 January 2016.
Ferrer, A. (2005). *La economía Argentina.* Buenos Aires: Fondo.
Fleming, M. J. (1962). Domestic financial policies under fixed and floating exchange rates. *IMF Staff Papers, 9,* 369–379.
Frenkel, R., & Rapetti, M. (2006). *Monetary and exchange rate policies in Argentina after the convertibility regime collapse* (p. 20). Nuevos Documentos: CEDES.
Frenkel, R., & Rapetti, M. (2008). Five years of competitive and state real exchange rate in Argentina 2002–2007. *International Review of Applied Economics, 22*(2), 215–226.
Frenkel, R., & Rapetti, M. (2011). Fragilidad externa o desindustrialización: ¿Cuál es la principal amenaza para América Latina en la próxima década? *Serie Macroeconomía del desarrollo,* N° 116 (LC/L.3423), Santiago de Chile, Comisión Económica para América Latina y el Caribe (CEPAL), noviembre.
Gerchunoff, P., & Aguirre, H. (2004). La política economía de Kirchner en la Argentina: varios estilos, una sola agenda. DT No. 35/200, Madrid: Real Instituto Elcano.
Grugel, J., & Riggirozzi, P. (2007). The return of the state in Argentina. *International Affairs, 83*(1), 87–107.

Heidrich, P., & Tussie, D. (2009). Post-neoliberalism and the new left in the Americas: The pathways of economic and trade policies. In L. MacDonald & A. Ruckert (Eds.), *Post-neoliberalism in the Americas* (pp. 37–53) Basingstoke: Palgrave Macmillan.

Heymann, D. (2006). Buscando la tendencia: Crisis macroeconómica y recuperación en la Argentina. Estudios y perspectivas, No. 31, Buenos Aires: CEPAL.

Heymann, D. (2007). Notas sobre la evolucion macroeconomica de la Argentina'. Unpublished document presented during interview by this author.

IMF (2000a). Selected issues and statistical index. IMF Staff Country Report 00/160. http://www.imf.org/external/pubs/ft/scr/2000/cr00160.pdf. Accessed 18 August 2016

IMF (2000b). *Argentina: 2000 article IV consultation and first review under stand-by arrangement, and request for modification of performance criteria—staff report and public information notice following consultation.* http://www.imf.org. Accessed 18 August 2016.

INDEC. (2007). *Anuario Estadístico de la República Argentina.* Buenos Aires: INDEC.

INDEC. (2010). *Anuario Estadístico de la República Argentina.* Buenos Aires: INDEC.

INDEC. (2016). *Anuario Estadístico de la República Argentina.* Buenos Aires: INDEC.

Katz, C. (2006, April 19). Las Tendencias de la Economia Argentina. *Argenpress.* http://rebelion.org/docs/25473.pdf. Accessed 16 August 2016.

Kosacoff, B. (2008). *Development of technological capabilities in an extremely volatile economy. The Industrial Sector in Argentina*, Vol. 40. Estudios y perspectivas. New York: United Nations Publications.

Levy, M. L. (2004). *We are millions: Neo-liberalism and new forms of political action in Argentina.* London: Latin American Bureau.

Levey, C., Ozarow, D., & Wylde, C. (2014). *Argentina since the 2001 crisis: Recovering the past, reclaiming the future.* Basingstoke: Palgrave Macmillan.

Mercado, P. R. (2007). *The Argentine recovery: Some features and challenges.* VRP Working Paper, LLILAS.

Ministry of Economy and Production. (2008). *Argentine economic indicators.* http://www.mecon.gov.ar. Accessed 3 Nov 2008.

Ministry of Economy and Production. (2009). *Argentine economic indicators.* http://www.mecon.gov.ar. Accessed 16 Aug 2016.

Ministry of Economy and Production. (2015). *Argentine economic indicators.* http://www.mecon.gov.ar. Accessed 16 Aug 2016.

Mundell, R. A. (1963). Capital mobility and stabilization policy under fixed and flexible exchange rates. *Canadian Journal of Economic and Political Science, 29*(4), 475–485.

O'Donnell, G. (1998). Horizontal accountability in new democracies. *Journal of Democracy, 9*(3), 112–136.
Ortiz, R., & Schorr, M. (2009). *Crisis internacional y alternativas de reindustrialización en la Argentina*. Número 7, Documentos de Investigación Social, IDAES.
Oxhorn, P. (2002). History Catching up with the Present? State–society relations and the Argentine crisis. *Cambridge Review of International Affairs, 15*(3), 499–514.
Panizza, F. (2005). Unarmed Utopia revisited: The resurgence of left-of-centre politics in Latin America. *Political studies, 53*(4), 716–734.
Panizza, F. (2009). *Contemporary Latin America: Development and democracy beyond the Washington Consensus*. London: Zed.
Petras, J., & Veltmeyer, H. (2009). *What's left in Latin America? Regime change in new times*. Surrey: Ashgate.
Redrado, M. (2008, March). *On Argentina's monetary policy*. Letter to the Economist, 19.
Riggirozzi, P. (2009). After neoliberalism in Argentina: Reasserting nationalism in an open economy. In J. Grugeland & P. Riggirozzi (Eds.), *Governance after neoliberalism in Latin America* (pp. 89–113). New York: Palgrave Macmillan.
Rivera-Quiñones, M. (2014). Macroeconomic governance in post-neoliberal Argentina and the relentless power of TNCs: The case of the soy complex. In C. Levey, D. Ozarow, & C. Wylde (Eds.), *Argentina since the 2001 crisis: Recovering the past, reclaiming the future* (pp. 67–88). London: Palgrave Macmillan.
Sanchez, O. (2005). Argentina's landmark 2003 presidential election: Renewal and continuity. *Bulletin of Latin American Research, 24*(4), 454–475.
Santarcángelo, J. E., Fal, J., & Pinazo, G. (2011). Los motores del crecimiento economic en la Argentina: rupturas y continuidades. *Investigación Económica, LXX*(275), 93–114.
Svampa, M. (2014). Revisiting Argentina 2001–2013: From "*¡Que se vayan todos!*" to the peronist decade. In C. Levey, D. Ozarow, & Wylde, C. (Eds.), *Argentina since the 2001 crisis: Recovering the past, reclaiming the future* (pp. 155–175). New York: Palgrave Macmillan.
Tedesco, L. (2002). Argentina's turmoil: The politics of informality and the roots of economic meltdown. *Cambridge Review of International Affairs, 15*(3), 469–481.
Tresca, G. (2005). *El collapso de la convertibilidad y el Nuevo modelo de desarrollo argentino*. Buenos Aires: Ateneo.
The Economist. (2013, January 19). *Sparks in the Dark.*
Tussie, D. (2009). Economic governance after neoliberalism. In J. Grugel & P. Riggirozzi (eds.), *Governance after neoliberalism in Latin America* (pp. 67–89). New York: Palgrave Macmillan.

UNDP. (2005). HDR—International cooperation at a crossroads: Aid, trade and security in an unequal world. http://hdr.undp.org. Accessed 4 May 2016.
UNDP. (2006). HDR—Beyond scarcity: Power, poverty, and the global water crisis. http://hdr.undp.org. Accessed 4 May 2016.
UNDP. (2007–2008). HDR—Fighting climate change: Human solidarity in a divided world. http://hdr.undp.org. Accessed 4 May 2016.
World Bank. (2004). *Global development finance: Harnessing cyclical gains for development*. New York: World Bank.
World Bank. (2016). *World development indicators*. http://data.worldbank.org/data-catalog/world-development-indicators. Accessed 9 Aug 2016.
Wylde, C. (2011). State, society, and markets in Argentina: The political economy of *neodesarrollismo* under Nestor Kirchner, 2003–2007. *Bulletin of Latin American Research, 30*(4), 436–452.
Wylde, C. (2012). *Latin America after neoliberalism: Developmental regimes in post-crisis states*. Basingstoke: Palgrave Macmillan.
Wylde, C. (2013). *Continuidad o cambio?: Política económica argentina posterior a la crisis y el gobierno de Néstor Kirchner, 2003–2007* (Vol. 43, pp. 109–133) Íconos: Revista de Ciencias Sociales.
Wylde, C. (2014). 'The developmental state is dead, long live the developmental regime! Interpreting Nestór Kirchner's Argentina 2003–2007. *Journal of International Relations and Development, 17*(2), 191–219.

CHAPTER 6

Argentina's Developmental Regime

Post-2001 crisis Argentina underwent significant change with regard to its development trajectory. This may be once again changing in the context of the election of Mauricio Macri in 2015, but at the time of writing this book it is certainly too early to tell. It must not be forgotten that this shift in focus was embedded in a continent-wide shift in models of capital accumulation, dubbed the 'pink tide' (see, e.g., Lievesley and Ludlam 2009). The rise of left and left-of-centre governments across Latin America, particularly in the first decade of the 21st century, has resisted attempts to classify its different aspects. Setting aside the more obvious polemical attempts, such as that of Castañeda (2006), more balanced approaches have been able to shed further light on the nature of these models.

The concept of 'post-neoliberalism' has provided the most convincing framework (see Grugel and Riggirozzi 2007; MacDonald and Ruckert 2009), defined as: 'more than simply the return of the state in terms of the economy... it is also a call for a new kind of politics, rooted in, and responsive to, local traditions and communities and an attempt to forge a new pact between society and the state (Grugel and Riggirozzi 2012: 3). Post-neoliberalism captures the broad thrust of this phenomenon, offering a useful framework for understanding a very real shift in Argentine (and Latin American) political economy that is neither a return to the old Import Substituting Industrialisation (ISI) models of the twentieth century nor a simple continuation of neoliberal policies. Much like Williamson's phrase 'Washington Consensus' captured the

C. Wylde, *Emerging Markets and the State*, International Political Economy Series, DOI 10.1057/978-1-137-55655-4_6

global shift in political economy in the 1990s, post-neoliberalism captures the continental shift in Latin American political economy in the 21st century. Also like the term Washington Consensus, the term post-neoliberalism can be critiqued for not being sufficiently sensitive to national-level idiosyncrasies. One solution to this is to reject these frameworks and embrace the sui generis nature of different national contexts.

What this book has suggested is that what is needed to make greater sense of the shift towards developmentalism, both in Argentina since 2001 (and Latin America more widely) as well as Malaysia more historically and contemporaneously, is a more robust framework. This framework must move beyond polemical accounts (see, e.g., Castañeda 2006) whilst simultaneously offering extra detail and analysis beyond broad characterisations of important trends such that post-neoliberalism captures (see, e.g., Grugel and Riggirozzi 2012). Such an analysis has become essential for any further advance of the post-neoliberal project in Latin America. Theories should be nurtured that allow an understanding of the real historical situation that the region confronts, 'with its strengths and weaknesses, the real, concrete and global balance of force, the challenges and possible solutions' (Sader 2011: 75).

In order to accurately and precisely map the contours of its new political economy, the insights of the first half of this book will be applied to generate an understanding of 21st-century developmentalism in Argentina. This will be achieved through the Developmental Regime framework as set out in Chap. 4, distilled from the mutually reinforcing and illuminating concepts of the state as a social relation, a robust theory of power grounded in theoretical pluralism through a Strategic-Relational Approach, and an understanding of different spatial levels of analysis through the complex processes associated with structuration. In so doing, it will not only demonstrate the efficacy of the Developmental Regime concept in analysing contemporary Argentina but also shed further light on the dynamics of that country through analysis of its regime tripod.

Public Policy Profile

One leg of a regime tripod is its public policy profile, or its tangible manifestations of regime power. In post-crisis Argentina this manifested itself in a redefinition, and associated strengthening, of the state in two core aspects: first, the role of the state as an agent of redistribution for social justice; and second, the state as regulator of markets. The redefinition of the role of government was in the context of the neoliberalism of Carlos Menem in the 1990s, where the government was an 'absent state' (Kirchner, cited in Cohen 2012: 106). This facilitated redistribution policies through improving revenue collection that would be used for increases in public expenditures—with an increase in the net total of tax collection as a percentage of GDP increasing from 23.43% in 2003 to 33.66% by 2010 (Ministry of Economy and Production 2010). These public expenditures were focused on poverty reduction and social deprivation through a variety of *Planes*. Whilst the first—*Plan Jefes y Jefas de Hogar*—was initiated under Duhalde, under Nestor Kirchner this programme was actually run down by preventing new entrants and instead placing them on his own *Planes* (Beccaria et al. 2007): *Planes Trabajar* and *Plan Familias*. These were expanded under CFK in terms of the number as well as the scope. One particularly important flagship policy was the AUH (*Asignacion Universal por Hijo*). Initiated in 2010, this programme provides approximately 200 Argentine pesos a month for nearly 4 million children and families (Grugel and Riggirozzi 2012: 9). Collectively, these policies facilitated a reduction in the poverty rate ($2/day at PPP) from 16.4% in 2003 to 2.9% by 2011 (see Table 6.1), although this must be treated with caution given the government manipulation of INDEC—the official statistical agency of the state (see later section on institutions)—after 2007. However, even if alternative data is used—such as the Catholic University data set—whilst the figures are higher, they still display the same general downward trend (see Table 6.1). Increases in per capita public spending (in USD at current prices) from $1301 in 2003 to $2002 by 2007 (CEPAL 2010) reflected this emphasis on social welfare programmes in the form of the various *Planes* as detailed above.

In addition to redistributive policies, Argentine political economy shifted its public policy profile in terms of the state as an agent of redistribution for social justice came through its policies towards the labour market. Precipitous drops in unemployment from 16.1% in 2003 at the start of Nestor Kirchner's administration to 7.5% in 2013 (see the previous chapter), steadily increasing real wages (in spite of significant inflation post-2007), several increases in the minimum wage throughout the period, a reduction in the informal labour sector, and a new form of 'segmented neocorporatism' (Etchemendy and Collier 2007: 363) to manage relations between the state, labour, and business

Table 6.1 Key economic indicators in Argentina 2003–2014

	2003	*2004*	*2005*	*2006*	*2007*	*2008*	*2009*	*2010*	*2011*	*2012*	*2013*	*2014*
GDP growth (%) (World Bank)	8.8	9.0	9.1	8.3	8.0	3.1	0.05	9.1	8.5	0.9	2.9	2.8
Inflation (%) (INDEC)	4.9	6.1	12.3	9.8	8.5	7.2	7.7	10.9	9.5	10.2	10.6	
Inflation (%) (Congreso Nacional)[a]	–	–	–	–	–	–	–	–	22.64	25.25	28.27	38.53
Primary Balance (% GDP) (CEPAL)	2.1	3.2	2.3	2.7	2.7	2.8	1.4	1.5	−0.1	−0.1	−1.4	−2.0
REER (2005 = 100) (CEPAL)	96.9	100.2	100	101.9	101.4	97.2	99.3	98.5	99.5	94.8		
Poverty at $2/day (PPP) (%) (World Bank)	16.4	12.3	9.8	7.4	6.4	5.7	5.4	3.9	2.9	–	–	–
Poverty (%)[b]	–	–	–	–	–	–	–	17.6	14.3	15.5	16.5	
Indigence at $1.25/day (PPP) (World Bank)	9	6.3	4.6	3.8	3.0	2.7	2.7	1.7	1.4	–	–	–
Indigence[b]	–	–	–	–	–	–	–	7.3	6.2	5.8	5.5	
Unemployment (%) ILO	16.1	12.6	10.6	10.1	8.5	7.8	8.6	7.7	7.2	7.2	7.5	
Current Account Balance (% GDP) (World Bank)	6.2	2.1	2.3	2.9	2.2	1.6	2.2	0.3	−0.4	-0.2	-0.7	
Central Government Gross Public Debt (% GDP) (CEPAL)			60.2	51.7	44.2	39.0	39.6	36.1	33.3	35.4	37.9	39.6
GINI index (World Bank)	53.54	50.18	49.27	48.26	47.37	46.27	45.27	44.5	43.57			
Commodity Prices (ex. oil and precious metals) (2000 = 100) (EIU)	99.7	103.6	106.9	110.7	116.1	123.1	117.4	123.1	133.0	133.5	133.0	132.3

[a] Since 2011 opposition members of the National Congress have published inflation data that is an aggregate of eight different independent consultants

[b] Data produced by Universidad Católica Argentina *Observatorio de la Deuda Social Argentina*. Figures are individual urban poverty and indigence based on ability to buy a basic basket of goods

(see later sections) all facilitated a state that was active and interventionist in the labour market in order to help facilitate redistribution of wealth for social justice reasons.

The second core aspect of the post-crisis Argentine public policy profile under Néstor Kirchner came in the form of market regulation. Under Néstor Kirchner, Argentina experienced substantial economic growth, with GDP exceeding pre-crisis levels within a year of the start of his administration. The policies that achieved this growth can be grouped under the two main themes of macroeconomic policy and industrial policy. In terms of macroeconomics, the administration adopted an exchange rate policy that Frenkel and Rapetti (2008: 217) have termed a 'Stable and Competitive Real Exchange Rate' (SCRER). This was one of a suite of policies that led to a significant boost in exports, manifesting in a sustained surplus in the current account (see the previous chapter). Furthermore, given the presence of export taxes, this policy also helped to provide sustained fiscal surpluses, as well as expansions of state spending in areas such as welfare (see above), reduction of national debt, and also industrial policy. Whilst the role of record international commodity prices cannot be ignored, Kirchner was still able to harness these forces to maximum benefit, as well as the fact that a significant proportion of the economic growth seen during the period 2003–2007 was in the manufacturing sector (Bezchinsky et al. 2007; Wylde 2011: 439) and therefore independent of the reversal in terms of trade during this time.

Industrial policy centred on encouraging production, or more specifically the industrial sectors of the economy, at the expense of the financial sector, or more specifically banking and capital markets. Large public works programmes, selective protective tariffs, selective subsidies for industries, the promotion of SMEs through favourable access to credit, combined with the central plank of the SCRER, all represented a coordinated attempt to promote Argentine national capitalism under Néstor Kirchner. This all occurred under a broad acceptance of core neoliberal principles—the importance of conservative fiscal policy and budget surpluses, steady inflation (at least under Nestor Kirchner), an awareness of inefficiencies associated with many forms of state intervention and state ownership, the acceptance of the primacy of the market in setting prices, the abandonment of economic protectionism in favour of at least relative economic opening and regional integration, and—albeit cautious and selective—welcoming of foreign direct investment (Wylde 2011: 439–440). In other words, state power was exercised upon a strategic terrain shaped by previous models of political economy—not least neoliberalism.

During the presidency of CFK from 2008 onwards, a number of underlying issues manifested themselves into a number of strain points that facilitated shifts in this broad public policy profile. The first area of tension was concerning relations with domestic rural oligarchs, agricultural TNCs, and the state, signifying the start of Argentina's 'third moment' (see the previous chapter). In 2008 there was widespread social unrest as farmers all over the country blocked major routes and roads to ports and cities, preventing the passing of trucks transporting agricultural commodities. This was in response to the government's announcement of an extension of *retenciones* on soya bean products from 35% to 45%, greatly affecting soya, maize, wheat, and sunflower seed producer's interests. Due to the flat nature of the tax, it produced an unlikely coalition of interests between rural oligarch's, TNC's, and medium- and small-scale producers (Cohen 2012: 133).

Second, there were those creditors who did not agree to the debt swap and haircut in 2005 (and in 2010 after a second deal was struck by CFK with 93% of the holdouts from 2005), or at least the vulture funds (such as Elliott Management) who bought the outstanding debt on secondary markets. These firms have been using legal systems in friendly countries to try to force Argentina to repay on defaulted debt in full, including accrued interest. This has led to a 'technical default' in August 2014, and the protracted locking out of Argentina from international capital markets—facilitating a shortage of foreign currency domestically.

Third, there was widespread unrest from September 2012 across the country, including rioting and looting in December 2012 (The Economist 2012: 47; 2013a: 32). The rioters were a mix, involving middle classes protesting against foreign exchange restrictions, curbs on imported goods, and high inflation making it impossible to save. Also present were organised labour movements protesting against lower real wages as a result of high inflation, demanding further extensions in welfare provision, and wanting greater involvement in the creation of state policy like they did in under previous regimes such as those of Péron (The Economist 2012: 48).

The collapse of international demand that followed the global financial crisis hit Argentine exports hard. A key cornerstone of Argentine political economy post-2001 has been the rise in exports. As well as the direct impact on exports of a manufacturing origin, this dynamic also served to restrict the revenues gained from agricultural exports due to an associated declining term of trade. This was exacerbated in 2012 by severe drought which affected yields. In turn, this impacted on Argentina's public finances. Since export taxes (*retenciones*) were reintroduced in 2002 they became an important source of state income, representing an average of 12% of budget revenues by 2010 (INDEC 2010). The attempt to increase *retenciones* by CFK in 2008 can be seen as a direct response to these changing international dynamics, coupled with a desire to maintain fiscal surpluses in the face of declining revenues.

The drop in international demand for Argentina's exports facilitated downward pressure on its nominal exchange rate. This trend was further exacerbated by the need to import increasing amounts of energy to fuel Argentina's rapid (although by now the rate of GDP growth was declining) economic expansion in the absence of domestic investment in energy production. In turn, this eroded Argentina's current account surplus. A drop in the nominal exchange rate combined with increasing inflation to increase Argentina's Real Exchange Rate (see Table 6.1), further eroding export competitiveness and thus a further drop the current account surplus. This fall in the current account surplus (to a small deficit by 2011) threatened to undermine one of the key cornerstones of *Kirchnerismo*. Persistent current account deficits in the 1990s during neoliberal restructuring led to excessive foreign debt accumulation, mounting on top of an already significant debt accrued during the bureaucratic-authoritarian period. Ultimately this helped precipitate economic meltdown in 2001–2002 and the associated dislocation of Argentine politics and society (Svampa 2014).

A number of CFK's policies can therefore be interpreted as attempts to correct these pressures on the current account balance. A series of foreign exchange restrictions to prevent domestic US dollar hoarding facilitated tensions with middle-class elements of Argentine society as foreign travel and holidays become more expensive. In addition, a number of import restrictions, as well as measures to require businesses that import to also export goods, widened these tensions to domestic bourgeois elements of the middle classes. The renationalisation of YPF in an attempt to reignite energy investment and thus reduce the levels of imported energy (which in turn will help relieve pressure on the current account balance) also created tensions with elements of international capital.

High inflation after 2007 was a persistent trend (see Table 6.1), causing further tensions among different socio-economic relations in Argentine society. The middle classes, once again, were hit through difficulties in saving given the level of inflation in the economy; especially when combined with the foreign exchange restrictions that made it difficult to use the US dollar as a more inflation proof store of value. The working classes and trade unions were hit as a result of the erosion of real wages that this began to facilitate. Whilst there was some redistribution to these elements of Argentine society as a result of the state taking responsibility for economic growth, these began to be undermined by 2012 as growth stalled but the inflationary trend persisted. Many of the poorest in Argentina were protected from this trend through a persistently expansionary fiscal stance that saw the extension of welfare benefits beyond the more traditional clientelist links with trade union organisations (Grugel and Riggirozzi 2012: 9). Therefore, whilst important in the political context of increasing tensions between the Argentine state and organised labour, the impact of inflation on real income levels of the poor should not be over exaggerated.

In summary, the policies of CFK represented departures from her husband's more cautious and pragmatic approach. They were the result of twin forces at play in contemporary Argentina. First, the deteriorating international economic conditions, in contrast to the relatively benign international economic environment that prevailed in the 2003–2009 period; the collapse of international demand in the wake of the global financial crisis severely impacted on Argentina's export-driven growth model. This was also exacerbated by a fall in international commodity prices in 2009 (see Table 6.1) as agricultural commodities still represented by far the largest share of Argentine exports. However, this should not be overemphasised as Table 6.1 also shows that international commodity prices soon bounced back after 2009, and also a number of other countries in the region were not as affected by the same changes in prices (Bolivia, for example). The second factor that has played a significant role in the deterioration of GDP growth (see Table 6.1) was Cristina's policies intended to 'deepen the model'. This came in the form of extending welfare—through, for example, the AUH—and extension of the minimum wage to non-unionised workers, counter-cyclical fiscal spending in the wake of the global financial crisis, and maintaining (even increasing) subsidies and price controls in a number of areas—especially transport, energy, and fuel. Cristina's heterodox policies prevented outright recession, maintained reductions in poverty, and reductions in the GINI (see Table 6.1), but at the expense of rampant inflation, and the key loss of the twin surpluses in the current and fiscal accounts.

Socio-economic Relations

The public policy profile of the Kirchners served a new set of socio-economic relations present in post-crisis Argentina. Begun by Duhalde, and continued and consolidated under Néstor Kirchner this led to the forging of a new social contract between the state and the Argentine people. This new social contract can be understood within the Strategic-Relational Approach. First, it is the product of previous contours of political economy, with institutional residue's shaping the trajectory of Argentine social relations. However, it is also the product of actors (with the state as primus inter pares) navigating that terrain by exercising agential power. As power is a heuristic for understanding social relations (Smith 2009), analysing its impacts through the lens of social domination—understood in a broad range of ways from the capital relation through to ethnicity and gender—becomes paramount. This section will therefore analyse the developments, trends, changes, and trajectories of Argentine socio-economic relations in order to facilitate a deeper understanding of the post-crisis Argentine political economy of development.

The first important development was with regard to the poor and working classes, who benefited from both expanding welfare combined with expanding employment opportunities. In addition, substantial increases in the minimum wage complemented these trends. Second, trade union groups have formed part of the alliance, although not as central a role as under former models of capital accumulation such as *Peronismo*. This is due to the fact that welfare provision moved beyond formal unionised sectors of society and into family life, thus reducing the influence of clientelistic links present between the state and the trade union movement present under *Peronismo* (Grugel and Riggirozzi 2012). This issue will be further discussed in the section on institutions. Third, middle-class elements were brought into the regime. The stabilisation of the macroeconomic environment from 2003 onwards combined an exchange rate policy that favoured domestic bourgeoisie elements (and especially exporters) brought these elements into the *Kirchnerismo* model. Furthermore, the consumer boom that such policies facilitated fed into underlying middle-class support, ensuring that the state brought widespread benefits across different class fractions rather than simply representing any one discreet class or class fraction. Finally, stimulation of exports also favoured agro-industrialists. Given that the agro-industry in Argentina is dominated by TNCs (especially soya) this policy also brought these interests of international capital into the model.

The post-neoliberal model of political economy in Argentina can be summarised as a desire to re-install the productivist pact between labour and capital as seen under *Peronismo*, with the state acting as the key arbiter of those interests (Grugel and Riggirozzi 2012: 5), although with some key differences in terms of more antagonistic relations with labour and a less fractious relationship with business (Etchemendy and Collier 2007). In other words, *Kirchnerismo* and the constellation of socio-economic relations that underpinned its attendant (neo)developmentalist state project were a condensation of a bending and moulding of previous contours of Argentine political economy.

The Strategic-Relational Approach as outlined in the first section of this book draws attention to just such a sedimentation (and occasional metamorphosis) of social relations, and how agents are able to shape those structural contours through institutionalisation whilst simultaneously being shaped by those institutions. This happens across multiple levels of spatial analysis. In order to trace out specifically the shaping of historical contours in *Kirchnerismo* the analysis will seek to draw specific linkages between different modes of capital accumulation present in Argentina's historical record. The first, *Peronismo*, represents the emblematic original *desarrollismo* political economy of Juan Domingo Peron; the second, *Menemismo*, the emblematic neoliberal mode of capital accumulation that was at its height in the mid-1990s. Analysing the broad redrawing of Argentina's social relations in the post-crisis period in the context of these historical forces and residues will help illuminate the broad trends identified in this introduction with regard to *Kirchnerismo*: a redrawing of social relations between the elements of the poor and (organised) labour, between domestic bourgeoisie industrialists and international capital, and between different fractions of the middle classes.

Points of Departure Between Peronismo and Kirchnerismo

Peronismo was an ideology that contained many manifestations, but during the first two administrations (1946–1955) of Perón at least some important key principles can be located. *Peronismo* included both authoritarian and populist components, which were a blend of the ideologies of the 1930s and a traditional Argentinean style of leadership (a charismatic strongman leading from the front). Perón and *Peronismo* (Peronism) therefore represented a form of leftist–populist nationalism, rooted in an urban working-class movement that was allied to elements of the domestic bourgeoisie as well as the military. Therefore, for Portantiero (1989: 18) '[t]he first Peronist administration based its legitimacy on a pact between the trade unions and the armed forces, but its most important axis was the arbitrating figure of Perón as a symbol of the new state'. Perón's economic model of the late 1940s and 1950s was based on a *desarrollismo* model, and therefore favoured national over foreign capital, and urban wage labour over agro-exporting elites (Vellacott 2006; see also Gambini 2007). Indeed, Torre and Riz (1991: 78) outline Perón's economic policy as having three core objectives: 'the expansion of public spending, giving the state a stronger role in production and distribution; the alteration of relative prices to encourage a more egalitarian distribution of national income; and the progressive accumulation of a system of incentives and rewarded activities orientated towards the internal market and discouraged production destined for international markets'.

These economic policies of ISI initially produced an impressive growth record, and combined with his generous legislation in favour of worker rights and redistribution of the proceeds of growth to the workers, generated huge popularity. Peronism's fundamental political appeal therefore lay in its ability to redefine the notion of citizenship within a broader, and ultimately social, context (Blanksten 1969: 249; Di Tella 1983: 15; Portantiero 1989: 17; Gambini 2007). Citizenship was not defined in terms of individual rights and relations within political society, but was redefined in terms of the economic and social realms of civil society (Di Tella 1983: 17). Citizenship, therefore, was more about social equity, rather than the individual pursuit of wealth (Segura-Ubiergo 2007: 60–61; Gambini 2007). This social equity, however, was limited to the urban working classes due to the institutional links of the PJ (*Partido Justicialista*) with the trade unions. As Grugel (2009: 50) puts it, '...since social policies and labour law during the ISI period had reinforced the links between governments and trade unions and social protection had been mainly directed to the workforce (rather than the poor), the social policy regime had tended to neglect the rural population and the poorest groups in society'.

The first major difference between *Kirchnerismo* and Perón's policies was in the nature of the link between citizenship and social welfare, and the attendant social relations that underpinned this. As summarised by Grugel and Riggirozzi (2007: 88), 'Peronism changed the terms of citizenship in Argentina by establishing the pueblo, made up of unionised workers the urban poor, and the lower-middle classes, as a political actor with rights to economic and social inclusion'. Despite using rhetoric that echoed this link between citizenship and social welfare, Kirchner has not engaged in widespread social programmes, instead preferring to target specific social groups (Petras 2006: 283; Grugel and Riggirozzi 2007: 98; Beccaria et al. 2007). Therefore the welfare programmes present in Argentina in the 2003-2007 period such as *Plan Familias* and *Planes Trabajar*, combined with the running down of *Plan Jefes y Jefas* were not designed as proactive policies to systematically tackle poverty in traditional Peronist constituencies, as the state-society relationship under *Kirchnerismo* is not based on such principles; rather, they have much more in common with neoliberal style safety-net models of social welfare, designed to 'catch' individuals and prevent them from falling into complete poverty and destitution (Beccaria et al. 2007). Whilst CFK sought to extend this net under the AUH programme, is remained qualitatively different to Perón's policies of providing social protection and political patronage through clientelism for the urban working classes as a whole.

A prioritisation of inflation control over wage increases for the working classes also reveals a second difference between *Kirchnerismo* and *Peronismo*. Traditional Peronism 'was unable to construct a social consensus around the principles of nationalist/statist development' (Panizza 2005; Grugel and Riggirozzi 2007: 89; Roberts 2007; Riggirozzi 2009: 102). As Riggirozzi (2009: 90) puts it: 'the nationalistic rhetoric and the political economy of Peronism redefined citizenship in terms not of individual rights but as economic rights and social inclusion'. State intervention was about control over the key sectors of the economy and to engage in social programmes in line with the state-society relationship present. *Kirchnerismo*, on the other hand, was a strategy for growth based on selective protectionism and targeted state intervention in order to facilitate macroeconomic stability and economic growth through stimulation of an export industry and limited diversification away from traditional reliance on agro-exports. The state took on the responsibility for economic growth, and specifically facilitated this through the SCRER policy and stimulation of exports (Frenkel and Rapetti 2008), as well as an accumulation of reserves to create confidence in the domestic economy (Grugel and Riggirozzi 2007: 97–98). This important principle was to be largely abandoned under CFK, something that will be addressed in the net section.

A third difference concerns the issue of poverty. The rise in poverty in Argentina first under Menem (see next section), and then as a result of *El Argentinazo*, was spectacular. Whilst these levels receded from crisis highs under Kirchner's administration, this was largely due to decreasing unemployment in the context of high and sustained economic growth (Grugel and Riggirozzi 2007: 104). Therefore, the middle-class elements that were driven into poverty as a result of the events of 2001–2002, and who joined the ranks of the 'new poor', were relatively quick to recover. However, high degrees of poverty that were created in the 1990s as a result of structural reforms—as well as the result of the process of neoliberal globalisation and greater international competition—remained, with individual poverty and indigence at 20.6 and 5.9%, respectively, in 2007 (Ministry of Economy and Production 2008). This poverty was not systematically addressed by Nestor Kirchner's administration (Beccaria et al. 2007), with modest increases in coverage under CFK. Such policies would perhaps have required a more fundamental shift in political economy, and *Kirchnerismo* was characterised by a strategy of 'bending and moulding' the existing political institutions and economic model rather than changing it altogether (Panizza 2005: 15).

A fourth and final difference concerns the orientation of the domestic economy towards the global market. The cornerstone of *Kirchnerismo* rested on the development of Argentina's export economy, largely facilitated through the maintenance of an SCRER. This represented a fundamental break with the Peronist model. Peronismo was based on ISI, and therefore largely closed to external economic forces through tariff and non-tariff barriers (NTBs). *Kirchnerismo* stood in stark contrast to this model, with active promotion of an open economy through effective state management (Gerchunoff and Aguirre 2004).

Points of Departure Between Kirchnerismo and Menemismo

Menemismo in the 1990s was very different to traditional *Peronismo*. Despite being elected on a Peronist platform, as soon as he was in power he initiated a programme of 'neoliberalism by surprise' (Stokes 2001). Consistent with this project, Menem himself expressed the intention to 'pulverize the crisis'. He warned his fellow citizens to brace themselves for 'a tough, costly, and severe adjustment', requiring 'major surgery without anaesthesia' (Smith 1991: 46). Indeed, 'from a deceptively simple assumption that the state—understood as a complex social and political process as well as an economic one—was to produce development in the 1950s and 1960s, it came itself to be seen as the principal obstacle to development, responsible for both crisis and stagnation' (Grugel and Riggirozzi, 2009: 5).

The neoliberal regime installed in Argentina, and Latin America more widely, had a distinct four-point agenda (Munck 2003: 53). First, trade liberalisation was pursued, which culminated in the creation of MERCOSUR in 1991 (Argentina, Brazil, Paraguay, and Uruguay). During this time (1991–1997) Argentina dismantled or removed many of its remaining tariff and non-tariff barriers, thus opening its economy to international markets and competition. Trade liberalisation had actually begun under Alfonsín in 1988, and served to reduce the weighted average tariff rate to 48% (from a high of 141% in 1959) (Chudnovsky 2007: 34). Menem therefore carried out a 'second phase' of trade liberalisation, which served to reduce the weighted average tariff rate to 19% by 1991.

The second was the promotion of privatisation and a consequent reduction in the role of government. Due to the legacy of ISI and *Peronismo* Argentina at the start of the 1990s was dominated by SOEs (e.g. YPF, *Gas del Estado*, *Ferrocarriles Argentinos*, *Empresa Nacional de Telecomunicaciones*) and nationalised industrial sectors. Therefore, privatisation saw the transfer of ownership of huge swathes of the Argentine economy; including the telecommunications sector, water and sewerage, natural gas distribution, electricity generation and distribution, state firms in the manufacturing sector including steel and petrochemicals, ports, airports, railways, the postal service (*Correo Argentino*), the national airline (*Aerolíneas Argentinas*), and a number of provincial banks. These mass privatisations generated substantial cash reserves and were used to help fund consistent balance of payments deficits due to the suppression of exports as a result of the currency peg (*Convertibilidad*). However, there were also more political reasons for such actions. 'Privatisation was considered a powerful instrument that could be used to gain a good reputation, quickly, among the local and international establishment' (Chudnovsky 2007: 66). This need to gain a good reputation was crucial in the context of a traditionally populist party in government and the fact that it had come to power in the middle of hyper-inflationary conditions.

Third, labour reforms to introduce 'flexibility' so as to lower the cost of labour were implemented. New controls over the labour movement were therefore introduced (Grugel and Riggirozzi 2007: 91).

In 1991, fixed-term and special training contracts were introduced for the young (Law No. 24,013), as well as creating an unemployment benefit system. Employer wage taxes were reduced in 1994, and in 1995 Law No. 24,013 was expanded and introduced 6-month trial period into new employment contracts (Chudnovsky 2007: 90). These reforms helped to deregulate the labour market, and increase the flexibility of the labour force. At the same time, it also served to increase the precariousness of employment (Cortés 2009: 57).

Fourth, and finally, policies of financial liberalisation involving liberalisation of cross-border capital movements, and domestic bank deregulation to promote greater integration into the international capital market were introduced. Therefore, the Argentine economy was further linked to the global economy and was prone, as scholars such as Ffrench-Davies and Reisen (1998), Rock (2002), Dinerstein (2002: 21), and Stiglitz (2002) argue, to speculative flows of financial capital. For O'Donnell (1973: 122) and Ferrer (2005: 107) this has been a long-term structural characteristic of Argentine economic history. Initially the result of Argentine prosperity resting on the export of agricultural products, under Menem it was the result of increasing incorporation into the global economy through tariff reduction, both in industrial sectors and, importantly for understanding the impacts of the 2001 crisis, in the financial sector.

To achieve these goals Menem constructed and maintained a coalition between the economic right and the working class, forged through an emphasis on a discourse around the idea of economic emergency. The context of hyperinflation and chronic instability that ensued allowed Menem to persuade these groups that desperate times called for desperate measures (Tedesco 2002: 474–475; Chudnovsky 2007: 65; Grugel 2009: 39). Indeed, Menem sought to put 'politics directly at the service of economic priorities' by presenting economic stabilisation as the most important means to steady democratic society (Tedesco 2002: 478). He therefore manipulated politics in order to achieve economic ends. Combined with the generally worsening situation in terms of unemployment, poverty, and widening income inequality, contributed to the erosion of the traditional bonds between the poor/working class and Peronism. However, these bonds were, whilst reduced, still very much present, and help explain the populist redistribution policies and use of patronage to mitigate some of the costs of labour restructuring and unemployment (Grugel and Riggirozzi 2007: 91).

Whilst *Menemismo* contained important populist elements, it also contained distinctive elements that could be characterised as neoliberal. Indeed, state-society relations in the 1990s under Menem were often considered to be distant and this was manifested in removal of social safety nets and the deregulation of the labour market. Kirchner did not engage in policies involving redistributive taxation, inequalities increased or simply stayed the same depending upon the sector, and the structures of socio-economic power stayed in place. Therefore, 'Kirchner has not distributed property income or power—except among different segments of the capitalist class' (Petras 2006: 284). *Kirchnerismo's* approach to poverty also reflects a continuation of the Menem era (Petras 2006: 283), as 'welfare essentially remains in the safety-net model of neoliberalism which can at best only ameliorate some of the worst manifestations of poverty' (World Bank 2001: 10–11; Grugel and Riggirozzi 2007: 105).

Despite these similarities, there were a number of points of departure that allows for a characterisation of the Kirchner administrations that is different to *Menemismo*. The first concerns the emphasis under Menem on stability, through controlling inflation via the *Convertibilidad* regime, and increasing efficiency through policies of liberalisation of the economy and privatisation. This was achieved through moving towards a separation of the state from society in the political economy of *Menemismo*, and thus the erosion of the bonds between the poor/working classes and the Peronist party as represented by *Menemismo*. *Kirchnerismo* 'forged a relationship based more on nationalist/statist development' (Godio 2006: 35, 58; Grugel and Riggirozzi 2007: 89) combined with a nationalistic political project (Rigirozzi 2009: 89). This 'new' relationship came under strain during the tenure of CFK. Middle classes were alienated by import restrictions and high inflation. The benefits of macroeconomic stability that CFK has sought to maintain through various heterodox policies were outweighed by the fallout of those very policies for middle-class interests. In addition, a solution to Argentina's high and persistent inflation continued to elude CFK; she refused to sacrifice short-term economic growth prospects—and therefore unemployment and poverty reductions—on the altar of stable prices, even if stable prices may have facilitated better medium- and long-term growth prospects. This served to further alienate the middle classes.

These different understandings of the state-society relationship were also reflected in *Kirchnerismo's* relationship with the trade unions. The links and conduits between the Kirchner administration and organised labour movements are different to the Menem years and facilitated more cooperation and agreements than under *Menemismo* (Etchemendy and Collier 2007: 381). This in turn fed into differences in the tripartite relationship. Genuine cooperation and negotiation between the business community and organised labour under *Kirchnerismo* was not present in the Menem years, due to the nature of his relationship with the trade unions (for further details see next section). However, this relationship also began to break down under CFK. Formal working classes and trade unions were agitated by real wage declines, the result of the high inflation present in the economy. This outweighed benefits accrued from the expansion of formal employment as a result of a growing economy. In addition, domestic bourgeoisie were alienated by the series of heterodox macroeconomic policies of CFK designed to protect the twin surpluses in the current and fiscal accounts. Rural oligarchs and agro-industrialists saw their profits decline in the face of elevated taxes; international capital remained alienated over the protracted dispute over settlement of outstanding defaulted debt from January 2002. Collectively, these measures served to severely undermine the segmented neo-corporatist (Etchemendy and Collier 2007) productivist pact between labour and business, mediated by the state. With both business (domestic, transnational, industrial, and rural) and labour (formal and informal) further alienated from both the state and each other a key social compromise that constituted a cornerstone of the post-neoliberal social contract in Argentina was fractured.

Argentina's relations with international capital fundamentally changed under *Kirchnerismo*. The sovereign debt default after the 2001 crisis altered the relationship between the Argentine state and international capital, and both Nestor and CFK's administrations served to cement those changes, albeit in different ways. First, Nestor's tough negotiations with the IMF and other creditors (most of which were represented by the Paris Club of creditors) over the restructuring of the defaulted debt served to isolate Argentina from international capital markets. This judicious drawing down of Argentine debt to much more manageable levels represented an attempt to break the structural nature of debt in Argentine economic history, and was arguably unique to *Kirchnerismo* as both Peronism and Menemism oversaw large increases in the Argentine debt burden. Furthermore, the early repayment of the entire outstanding US$9.8 billion debt facility that Argentina had with the IMF meant that the Fund's influence, a factor shaping Argentine international relations since the end of Peron's first administration, all but disappeared. Indeed, the IMF even closed its regional office in Buenos Aires as there was no further need for it after the repayment of the outstanding debt. Whilst this decision 'owes much to the government's need to create an image inside Argentina of a sovereign state' (Grugel and Riggirozzi 2007: 99), the desire to shrug off IMF influence over economic policy, forge a more appropriate relative autonomy, and engage in rhetorically nationalist economic policy was also a strong motivation.

The final consideration in understanding the nature of socio-economic relations that underpinned *Kirchnerismo* is that of foreign investment. More specifically, concerning relations with foreign business—namely Trans-National Corporations (TNCs). Whilst Kirchner was happy to accommodate foreign companies that had existing interests in the domestic economy, he was more hostile towards TNCs looking to initiate interest in Argentina. This approach is different from more traditional policies associated with *Peronismo*, which viewed almost all TNC activity in the domestic economy as potentially damaging. Such an approach by Kirchner was also mirrored in the financial sector. Whilst Kirchner maintained links with the sector in order to help his plans to expand personal credit to facilitate the consumer boom, and there was no hostility towards the banks in particular. There was not, however, the active promotion of their interests as experienced during the Menem years through institutional links with the state, such as personnel in the administration or the central bank. For example, one commentator (interview with Anonymous 2007) suggests that 'there are not the kind of people in the financial sector who move in government circles and can therefore be in a position to influence policy anymore...'. Indeed, this shift in emphasis is in line with the 'competitive change' identified by Heidrich (2005: 5). As a result of Kirchner's desire to promote industrial development through export-led growth, emphasis on the financial sectors of the economy waned relative to the productive sectors. This stood in contrast to the Menem years of the 1990s, which Kirchner viewed as overly focusing on finance capital, precipitating a legacy of social exclusion and poverty present in contemporary Argentina (Ferrer 2005: 370–371; Heidrich 2005: 5).

In summary, in terms of state-society relations, or the social contract, *Kirchnerismo* was a *form* of Peronism, one that reflected the influence of *Menemismo* and contemporary processes of neoliberal globalisation. This has led Grugel and Riggirozzi (2007) to suggest a characterisation of a form of *neodesarrollismo*, constituted fundamentally in principles of statist development; or Riggirozzi (2009) to term it as 'open economy nationalism', a blend of market-friendly economics and a nationalistic political project to help structure state-society relations. Such characterisations are indeed appropriate to the extent that they accurately reflect the Kirchner's forging of a new social consensus.

These shifts must also be understood in terms of Argentine institutions and attendant institutionalisation. The next section will further expand on the analysis of shifting tendencies in the CFK flavour of *Kirchnerismo* as compared to that of her husband's. It will show how socio-economic relations underpin and are underpinned by the shape of the strategic terrain that is created through the agency of the state, both in its contemporary and more historical forms. This will complete the tripod and, like the apparatus itself, forms a stable base that represents our understanding of a Developmental Regime in any given spatial-temporal context.

Institutions

The process of the institutionalisation of *Kirchnerismo* represents the third leg of the post-neoliberal regime tripod. One argument of this chapter has been that Argentina's post-crisis political economy of development under CFK witnessed shifting social relations that manifested in the exercise of public policy. This was the result of the twin forces of a changing international environment (represented by the global financial crisis as well as shifting international commodity prices) as well as the desire on the part of the CFK administration to 'deepen the model'. In other words, the degree and nature of the Argentine state's relative autonomy that was enjoyed under Néstor Kirchner became significantly reduced under CFK. Following analysis presented in Chap. 2, this changing relative autonomy needs to be explained through application of the Strategic-Relational Approach and its attendant meta-theoretical understandings of the agent-structure relationship. In other words, understanding the changing relationships between actors must be complemented with an understanding of the terrain upon which they operate. The understanding of that terrain can be completed through an analysis of the final leg of the regime tripod: institutions. The reducing levels of state autonomy under CFK were the product of a realignment of international forces and, simultaneously, domestic class fractions that internalised the imperatives of global capital.

Revealed by analysis of the first two legs of the regime tripod, this insight can be further complemented with an understanding of institutions, which reveals a lack of state capacity in the Argentine Developmental Regime. Unlike the changing nature of state autonomy between the two Kirchner's, state capacity in the form of institutionalisation was consistently weak across both Presidents. Whilst under Néstor Kirchner this mattered less due to favourable international circumstances and a post-crisis domestic climate conducive to his brand of post-neoliberal developmentalism, under CFK it added to the general malaise of Argentina's post-neoliberal Developmental Regime. In the context of political and social institutions this general weakness does not mean that there were not efforts to consolidate certain aspects: rebuilding the regulatory framework around work and labour (Repetto 2015), expanding rights to civil society groups (such as the improving coverage of social policy, or equalisation of civil rights for sexual minorities), or the introduction of PASO—the open and simultaneous primary elections in national elections.

One particular area of significant institutional change concerns the role of corporatist practices. Svampa's analysis (2008: 83) that *Kirchnerismo* represents a return to old Peronist style corporatism does not tell the whole story, as *Kirchnerismo's* relationships with business and the trade unions possessed qualitatively different characteristics from old Peronist relationships, such as the top-down associations and institutional links between Perón himself, the PJ, and trade union movements. This led Etchemendy and Collier (2007) to term Kirchner's distinct approach as 'neocorporatism', or, more specifically, 'segmented neocorporatism'. This is defined (ibid: 366) as 'a pattern of peak level negotiation in which monopolistic unions, business associations, and the government coordinate on inflation-targeted, sector-wide wage agreements and minimum wage floors, which apply to a substantial minority of the labour force'. It is corporatist due to the tripartite nature of the relationship (government, organised labour, and business), it is 'neo' due to the redefinition of this relationship (see below), and it is segmented due to the fact that the agreements reached only applied to a minority of the workforce (formally employed, organised labour).

A new pattern of tripartite negotiations was therefore present under the administrations of the Kirchner's that was different from both the *Peronismo* of Perón and *Menemismo*. Whereas the relationship between the CGT (*Confederación General de Trabajo*) and the government under

Peronismo was very much top down, *Kirchnerismo* was characterised by more autonomy from both the state and the increasingly fragmented party system (Etchemendy and Collier 2007: 365, 381). The formal links between the Peronist party and the CGT and the political appointments of CGT members to government posts under Juan Perón that facilitated this top-down relationship were not present in *Kirchnerismo*. Whilst there were links and conduits between the Kirchner administration and organised labour movements, they were much more diffused, informal, and decentralised (Etchemendy and Collier 2007: 381). This was demonstrated by the fact that individual unions engaged in industrial action (strikes) in order to manipulate the outcome of negotiations, often against the wishes of government officials (Ibid.). Strikes in Argentina consistently exceeded the levels of the presidency of Menem, and certainly represent more than during Perón's first two administrations (1946–1955). Nestor Kirchner was able to re-institutionalise protest politics in the aftermath of the 2001/2002 crisis, with non-union-led protest dropping dramatically during his administration and in the aftermath of the 2001 crisis. In sum, 'Peronist unionism has displayed in the last three years a degree of autonomy from an allied government and from the Peronist party arguably unknown in Argentine history' (Etchemendy and Collier 2007: 381).

There was also a difference in another aspect of the tripartite relationship, that between the government and the business community. The 'genuine participation of business' (Etchemendy and Collier 2007: 382) in these tripartite negotiations stood in contrast to the governments of Perón, where the genuine involvement of business participation in tripartite negotiations was rare. Even during periods of Argentina's history where directly populist governments were not in power, the involvement of business associations was fragmented. For example, the most important business associations did not support the outcome of the negotiations in the wage bargaining rounds of 1973–1976 and 1987–1989 (Etchemendy and Collier 2007: 382). Under the administration of Kirchner, such negotiations were more systematic, with both the sector-wide wage agreements and the minimum wage agreements of 2005, 2006, and 2007 enjoying the support of the most important sectoral and national business associations (ibid.).

Systematic negotiation and agreements with both organised labour and domestic business were part of Kirchner's greater goal of economic development, due to the need to contain inflation, or more specifically one of the main traditional drivers of Argentine inflation: excessive wage increases. The traditional Peronist and *desarrollismo* policies in Argentina led to sustained wage increases for skilled workers that were ultimately eroded due to periods of systemic inflation. This led to the classic struggle between the monetarists and the structuralists, one that was won by the monetarists and the IMF, who gained control over the direction of Argentine economic policy. There is an important difference here between the dynamics of *Kirchnerismo* compared to those of traditional *Peronismo* in particular. The prioritisation of controlling inflation over wage increases for the (organised) working class is not only demonstrated by this relationship and subsequent institutionalisation of it with the unions. Indeed, it is also present in Kirchner's relationship with the business world. His extensive use of ad hoc price controls can be interpreted as helping in negotiations with the unions over wages as such price controls reduce inflationary expectations (Etchemendy and Collier 2007: 379, 381).

The nature of Argentine democracy during this period also represents an interesting area of institutional development. The constitution of democratic forces in Argentina in the aftermath of the 2001 crisis and during the subsequent Kirchner period have been systematically analysed by J.P Ferrero in his book *Democracy Against Neoliberalism* (Ferrero 2014). He suggests that the move to the left experienced in Argentina, or what he terms as 'a process from disagreement to participation' (Ferrero 2014: 6), was the result of democracy against neoliberalism. The development of democratic forces, or the constitution of the demos, is responsible in the post-transition context of Argentina for the emergence of a counter-hegemonic discourse captured in the literature as the pink tide. The process of this realisation is best captured by the notion of 'democratic subjectivities'. This facilitates a discussion of how the internal articulation of disagreement with neoliberalism led to the construction of a new consensus; what issues and questions formed part of the development of democratic subjectivities; and who were the main protagonists influencing the formation of a new counter-hegemonic discourse.

Ferrero explicitly critiques the transitology literature and instead embraces a radical democracy framework: seeking to integrate the concept of 'the ceaseless enacting of equality' (Ferrero 2014: 7) into the literature. He therefore departs from issues of representation and instead investigates the more foundational arena of self-government. As Ferrero argues (2014: 8): '...both the transition school and the participatory democracy perspectives posit different theoretical limits to the analysis of democratisation as transformative socio-political action... the narrative of democracy needs to engage with the production of democratic subjectivities in order to give account for the potential and the limitations of the ceaseless enacting of equality, that is, the production of politics in post-transition contexts'. Thus, radical democracy as a framework is required in order to successfully integrate complexity, without displacing the question of emancipation.

The ontological starting point of such a position is that societies are differentiated according to their complexity, which in turn makes them bound to the development of certain types of demand over others. Different degrees of institutionalisation, and different types of colonial legacy—among other factors—have had an influence on the configuration of societies. This facilitates a need to re-engage with democratisation in light of emancipation, to challenge the notion of democracy as institutional regime and institute the notion of democracy as the making of transformative politics. In the words of Ferrero (2014: 24): '... to move the study of democracy from that of passive institutional regime [transition school] to democracy as active transformative politics [radical democracy perspective]'. This facilitates a suitable framework for an interrogation of the conditions that generated a democratic movement that challenged the institutionalisation of neoliberalism and associated Washington Consensus policies.

Democracy Against Neoliberalism places radical democracy in relation to existing debates on democracy in general and in the process critiques the conceptualisation of democracy as a 'passive state of arrival' (Ferrero 2014: 208). Democracy is not an end point, but a process. Subsequent empirical exploration of social protest across different organisations and networks concerned with industrial relations facilitates a transcending of the notion of fronts and coalitions and instead positing the emergence of a permanent contentious dynamic. Ferrero talks about relations of 'space' and 'time': the presence of 'networks' with deliberation outside of traditional institutions such as parliament, and the challenge to corporatism through the rejection of typical hierarchies and the empowerment of the grassroots. Power was displaced from the political to the social. Out of this dynamic emerges both the contingent character and the radical possibility of the politicisation of demands. This in turn proves not only the importance of governments in affecting the sociopolitical processes but also the limits within which their policies are generated and implemented. Thus, the configuration of two differentiable moments (disagreement and participation) within the post-transition period provides an accurate account of democratisation in Argentina; a process understood as governments being displaced by aspects of society that have colonised key parts of the state.

These processes of institutionalisation and democratisation were not sufficient to reverse a general situation of institutional weakness, resulting in deficits of state capacities, lack of coordination between different levels of government, lack of mechanisms for the coordination of public policies, and increasing rule through Presidential decree. In their totality, these different factors conspired against the development of an efficient, effective, and transparent democratic state (Gervasoni and Peruzotti 2015). This pattern is repeated when examining economic institutions, which are arguably of greater importance in the context of state capacity under a Developmental Regime. There were certain organisational islands that exhibited a successful process of building state capacities, among which stand out the ANSES, the AFIP, CONICET, the Ministry of Science and Technology and Innovation, and specific programmes such as *Remediation*, *Nacer*, and *Sumar*. In addition, under CFK the central bank constitution was reformed to establish a new mandate 'to promote, to the extent of its ability and in the framework of policies established by the national government, monetary stability, financial stability, jobs and economic growth with social fairness'. This can be seen as a clear example of an economic institution that reflects post-neoliberal developmental concerns, rather than a more neoliberal Central Bank that is only concerned with inflation targeting. However, these institutional reforms were the result of contingencies and opportunities rather than the result of a systematic effort (Gervasoni and Peruzotti 2015). Of particular note in the area of institutional weaknesses was the general areas of economic regulation and state promotion of development. For example, despite continued reference to monopolies the National Tribunal for the Defence of Competition was never created. Also, regulatory agencies such as the National Communications Commission, the National Gas Regulatory Body, or the National Transportation Regulatory Commission experienced systemic political interventions and were bureaucratically subordinated to the Executive. The absence of a national development bank was also striking, facilitating poor institutionalisation of the system of public credit for productive investment.

Perhaps the most high-profile example of institutional weakness that facilitated a lack of development of Argentine state capacity was the saga of the INDEC. Ever since 2008 it has produced dubious data, not least its inflation measurement. The disparity between the official rate and the unofficial rate is shown in Table 6.1. This has further impacts on poverty data, as their calculation depends on inflation numbers; these disparities are once again shown in Table 6.1. This manipulation became so unsustainable that INDEC even stopped publishing poverty statistics. The continued manipulation of inflation data, among other key economic indicators, led to an official reprimand by the IMF on 1 February 2013 (The Economist 2013b). Whilst a new, supposedly accurate, inflation measurement was introduced in January 2014 (called the CPINu), there were (and still are) questions over its accuracy (The Economist 2014). This (ongoing) saga serves to highlight both the lack of respect, and the lack of development of key institutions of the state which are needed to enhance its capacity to facilitate and manage the development process in Argentina.

A series of new regional institutions emerged across Latin America in the early years of the 21st century. This is partially a reflection of the rise of a number of pink tide states across the region, and a collective desire to move away from regional institutions that reflected globally hegemonic principles of World Order. Therefore, bodies such as MERCOSUR stalled in terms of expanding free trade in the region—although free trade was not rolled back at all. Instead, new bodies such as the ALBA or UNASUR were created, which sought to expand regionalism into areas not traditionally associated with either old or new regionalism literature (see Chap. 4). For example, regional healthcare initiatives (ALBA, UNASUR), or regional infrastructure initiatives (UNASUR) represent post-hegemonic manifestations beyond a more traditional lexicon of more free and open trade.

This analysis can be expanded through interpreting these initiatives as partly a reflection of a changing balance of social forces at the level of the state, which then influence the regional spatial level of analysis through the process of structuration (see Chap. 3). Therefore, changing social relations domestically are reflected and refracted through the lens of the state into regional spatial analysis. However, it must not be forgotten that this is a mutually reconstitutive relationship. Existing regional institutions—such as MERCOSUR—whilst not expanded, were not dismantled either. Post-hegemonic regionalism captures the processes of sedimentation of complex social relations across multiple levels of spatial analysis, and the mutually (re)constitutive manner in which social relations and institutions shape state capacity and autonomy.

Conclusions

Argentina's development trajectory underwent clear shifts away from both *Peronismo* and *Menemismo*. From a shift in the link between citizenship and welfare to the renegotiation of Argentina's relationship with international capital *Kirchnerismo* represented a different model of capital accumulation. This renegotiation was not to hold, however. Many of the CFK administration's policies served to unravel core aspects of the socio-economic relations that underpinned *Kirchnerismo* in the immediate post-crisis period. By abandoning fiscal and current account surpluses, by allowing inflation to erode the SCRER, and by using export restrictions to limit the amount of foreign exchange in the domestic economy, Cristina's extension of the post-neoliberal Developmental Regime in Argentina became incoherent and unsustainable. In other words, whilst the suite of unorthodox economic policies worked in correcting a number of adverse trends and pressures on the Argentine economy (but not others), these policies served to undermine the constellation of social relations that underpinned the post-crisis development model; a constellation that was always vulnerable given the lack of institutionalisation of these newly forged post-crisis relationships. As a result, they often ended up resulting in policies designed to buy certain groups support in a clientelist manner, rather than foster long-term support that could be institutionalised in an enduring way.

It is through the application of a Developmental Regime framework that the full and changing nature of Argentina's post-crisis contours of capital accumulation can be traced. Argentine state capacity and autonomy can be illuminated through an analysis of the regime tripod. The mutual interaction of institutions and institutionalisation, combined with analysis of social relations understood through the manifestations of state power in the form of public policy profiles has revealed a nuanced understanding of 21st-century developmentalism in an emerging market such as Argentina.

This analysis has also helped map the contours of power at the different levels of structuration. The interests of World Order have clearly shaped the limits of the possible in Argentine post-crisis development; although perhaps demonstrating that this room for manoeuvre can change over time and is a function not only of the relative power of global capital vis-à-vis more domestically grounded interests, but also fundamentally shaped by the strategic terrain of the state understood as a condensation of previous models of capital accumulation. Furthermore, through application of the lens of post-hegemonic regionalism, the changing nature of state responses to their own national commitments and to new region building shows a series of projects (such as UNASUR) that contest the politics and policies of established neoliberal architecture. These new capacities and associated transformations in regional cooperation must be seen in terms of new spaces for action driven by new aspirations for autonomous development and socio-economic inclusion (Riggirozzi 2012: 19).

References

Beccaria, L., Esquivel, V., & Maurizio, R. (2007). *Crisis y recuperación: Efectos sobre el mercado de trabajo y la distribución del ingreso*. Argentina: Universidad Nacional de General Sarmiento.

Bezchinsky, G., Dinenzon, M., Guissani, L., & Caino, O. (2007). *Inversion extranjera directa en la Argentina. Crisis, reestructuracion y nuevas tendencias despues de la convertibilidad. Documento de Proyecto*. Santiago: CEPAL.

Blanksten, G. I. (1969). *Peron's Argentina*. New York: Russell and Russell.

Castañeda, J. (2006). Latin America's left turn. *Foreign Affairs, 85*(3), 28–43.

CEPAL. (2010). *Economic survey of Latin America and the caribbean: 2010–2011*. Santiago de Chile: CEPAL.

Chudnovsky, D. (2007). *The elusive quest for growth in Argentina*. London: Routledge.

Cohen, M. A. (2012). *Argentina's economic growth and recovery: The economy in a time of default*. London: Routledge.

Cortes, R. (2009). Social Policy in Latin America in the Post-neoliberal Era. In J. Grugel & P. Riggirozzi (Eds.), *Governance after Neoliberalism in Latin America*, 49–67. New York: Palgrave Macmillan.

Di Tella, G. (1983). *Argentina under Peron: 1973–1976: The Nation's Experience with a Labour-Based Government*. Hong Kong: Macmillan Press.

Dinerstein, A. (2002). The battle of buenos aires. *Historical Materialism, 10*(4), 5–38.

Etchemendy, S., & Collier, R. B. (2007). Down but not out: union resurgence and segmented Neocorporatism in Argentina (2003–2007). *Politics and Society, 35*(3), 363–401.

Ferrer, A. (2005). *La economía Argentina*. Buenos Aires: Fondo.

Ferrero, J. P. (2014). *Democracy against neoliberalism in Argentina and Brazil: A move to the left*. Basingstoke: Palgrave Macmillan.

Ffrench-Davis, R., & Reisen, H. (1998). *Capital Flows and investment performance: Lessons from Latin America*. Paris: ECLAC.

Frenkel, R., & Rapetti, M. (2008). Five years of competitive and state real exchange rate in Argentina 2002–2007. *International Review of Applied Economics, 22*(2), 215–226.

Gambini, H. (2007). *Historia del peronismo: El poder total (1943–1951)*. Buenos Aires: Vergara.

Gerchunoff, P., & Aguirre, H. (2004). La política economía de Kirchner en la Argentina: Varios estilos, una sola agenda. DT No. 35/200, Madrid: Real Instituto Elcano.

Gervasoni, C., & Peruzotti, E. (2015). Continuidades y discontinuidades del período kirchnerista. In C. Gervasoni & E. Peruzotti (Eds.), *Década ganada? Evaluando el legado del kirchnerismo*. Buenos Aires: Debate.

Godio, J. (2006). *El tiempo de Kirchner: El devenir de una 'revolucion arriba'*. Buenos Aires: Letra Grifa.

Grugel, J. (2009). Basta de Realidades, Queremos Promesas: Democracy After the Washington Consensus. In J. Grugel & P. Riggirozzi (Eds.) *Governance After Neoliberalism in Latin America* (pp. 25–49). New York: Palgrave Macmillan.

Grugel, J., & Riggirozzi, P. (2007). The return of the state in Argentina. *International Affairs, 83*(1), 87–107.

Grugel, J., & Riggirozzi, P. (2012). Post-neoliberalism in Latin America: Rebuilding and reclaiming the State after crisis. *Development and Change, 43*(1), 1–21.

Heidrich, P. (2005). Argentina buscando una salida: Kirchner, el FMI y la renegociacio´n de la deuda externa. *Chronique des Ameriques, 21*, 1–8.

INDEC. (2010). *Anuario Estadístico de la República Argentina*. Buenos Aires: INDEC.

Lievesley, G. A., & Ludlam, S. (2009). *Reclaiming Latin America: Experiments in radical social democracy*. London: Zed.

MacDonald, L., & Ruckert, A. (Eds.). (2009). *Post-Neoliberalism in the Americas*. Basingstoke: Palgrave Macmillan.

Ministry of Economy and Production (2008) *Argentine economic indicators*. www.mecon.gov.ar. Accessed 3 Nov 2008.

Ministry of Economy and Production (2010) *Argentine economic indicators*. www.mecon.gov.ar. Accessed 12 Sept 2010.

Munck, R. (2003). *Contemporary Latin America*. Hampshire: Palgrave Macmillan.

O'Donnell, G. (1973). *Modernisation and bureaucratic authoritarianism*. Berkeley: Institute of International Studies.

Panizza, F. (2005). Unarmed utopia revisited: The resurgence of left of centre politics in Latin America. *Political Studies, 53*(4), 716–734.

Petras, J. (2006). Centre-left regimes in Latin America: History repeating itself as farce? *Journal of Peasant Studies, 33*(2), 278–303.

Portantiero, J. C. (1989). Political and economic crisis in Argentina. In G. Di Tella & R. Dornbusch (Eds.), *The Political Economy of Argentina, 1946–1983* (pp. 16–31). Hampshire: Macmillan.
Repetto, F. (2015). Institucionalidad estatal para una mejor política social: Asignaturas pendientes de una década. In C. Gervasoni & E. Peruzotti (Eds.), *¿Década ganada?: Evaluando el legado del kirchnerismo*. Buenos Aires: Debate.
Riggirozzi, P. (2009). After neoliberalism in Argentina: Reasserting nationalism in an open economy. In J. Grugeland & P. Riggirozzi (Eds.), *Governance After Neoliberalism in Latin America* (pp. 89–113). New York: Palgrave Macmillan.
Riggirozzi, P. (2012). Reconstructing regionalism: what does development have to do with it? In P. Riggirozzi & D. Tussie (Eds.), *The rise of post-hegemonic regionalism: The case of Latin America* (pp. 17–41). New York: Springer.
Roberts, K. (2007). Latin America's populist Revival. *SAIS Review, 27*(1), 3–15.
Rock, D. (2002). Racking Argentina. *New Left Review, 17*, 55–86.
Sader, E. (2011). *The new mole: Paths of the Latin American Left*. London: Verso.
Smith, W. C. (1991). State, market, and neoliberalism in post-transition Argentina: The menem experiment. *Journal of Interamerican Studies and World Affairs, 33*(4), 45–82.
Smith, M. (2009). *Power and the state*. Basingstoke: Palgrave Macmillan.
Stiglitz, J. (2002). *Globalisation and its discontents*. London: Penguin Books.
Stokes, S. C. (2001). *Mandates and democracy: Neoliberalism by surprise in Latin America*. Cambridge: Cambridge University Press.
Svampa, M. (2008). The end of Kirchnerism. *New Left Review, 53*, 79–95.
Svampa, M. (2014). Revisiting Argentina 2001-13: From "¡Que se vayan todos!" to the Peronist Decade. In C. Levey, D. Ozarow, & C. Wylde (Eds.), *Argentina since the 2001 Crisis: Recovering the past, reclaiming the future* (pp. 155–175). New York: Palgrave Macmillan.
Tedesco, L. (2002). Argentina's turmoil: The politics of informality and the roots of economic meltdown. *Cambridge Review of International Affairs, 15*(3), 469–481.
The Economist. (2012, September 29) *The President and the Potbangers*.
The Economist. (2013a, January 19) *Sparks in the Dark*.
The Economist. (2013b, February 9) *Motion of Censure*.
The Economist. (2014) *New data, old qualms*, February 14.
Torre, J. C., & Riz, L. (1991). Argentina since 1946. In L. Bethell (Ed.), *The Cambridge History of Latin America, Vol. VIII* (pp. 73–195). Cambridge: Cambridge University Press.
Vellacott, C. (2006). Institutions and economic stabilisations in Argentina and Spain 1958–1959: The political economy of reform in crony capitalist systems. Unpublished paper delivered at Economic History Society Annual Conference, University of Reading.

World Bank. (2001). *WDR 2000/2001—Attacking poverty: Opportunity, empowerment and security*. Oxford: World Bank.

Wylde, C. (2011). State, society, and markets in Argentina: The political economy of *Neodesarrollismo* under nestor Kirchner, 2003–2007. *Bulletin of Latin American Research, 30*(4), 436–452.

CHAPTER 7

Malaysian Development Since Independence

Introduction

Since independence in 1957, Malaysia has been ruled by the same coalition government. In its contemporary form it is known as the BN (*Barisan Nasional*) and consists of the three largest religion and ethnic-based political parties—the United Malays National Organisation (UMNO), the Malaysian Chinese Association (MCA), and the Malaysian Indian Congress (MIC)—as well as a number of smaller parties. The key platform of this coalition has been the maintenance of ethnic harmony through the promotion of a Malay positive rights agenda (Ming 2015).

In the period from independence to the first major development plan in 1970, Malaysia pursued a broad development policy of laissez-faire, exporting the same primary commodities that they had done under British colonialism: rubber and tin. However, Felker (2015: 135) argues that even during this period there were a number of significant moves on the part of the UMNO to foster some proto-*Bumiputera* (Malay)-focused policies. After violent uprisings grounded in ethnic tensions on 13 May 1969 there was a significant shift in Malaysia's development trajectory, extending and formalising *Bumiputera*-centred state largesse. Laissez-faire was to quickly change. The nature of that change is a subject of debate in the literature, splitting into a dichotomous opinion; one side suggesting reform along neoclassical lines (see, e.g., Little 1979, 1981, 1982; Rodrik 1992) and the other postulating the concept of the Developmental State (see, e.g., Johnson 1987; Wade 1988; Amsden 1989; Haggard 1990;

C. Wylde, *Emerging Markets and the State*, International Political Economy Series, DOI 10.1057/978-1-137-55655-4_7

Wade 1990; Chowdry and Islam 1996; Jomo 1997). A third set of literature emerged from this debate offering a synthesis to this dichotomy; suggesting that, '[t]he state could be an engine of growth, and combined it with the market orientated ethos of conventional economics' (World Bank 1993: 22; see also ADB 1997: 24; Hill 1997).

In the period 1971–1990, the New Economic Policy (NEP) was implemented in Malaysia. The NEP had two core stated objectives, reducing poverty and the restructuring of society so that identification of ethnicity with economic function would be reduced and ultimately eliminated (Andaya and Andaya 2001: 303–304; see also Case 2002: 106–109). In the 1990–2010 period this was replaced with the New Development Policy (NDP), which focused on four areas of balanced development, stable growth, ethnic harmony, and the removal of social and economic inequality (Andaya and Andaya 2001: 218). In 2010 the New Economic Model (NEM) was introduced: essentially a development blueprint grounded in a desire to foster the capacities for more effective state interventions—through reforming the public sector and liberalising selectively—in order to realise Mahathir's (Malaysian Prime Minister from 1981 to 2003) 'Vision2020' plan, where Malaysia would become a high-income economy.

It is the purpose of this chapter to analyse the policies and subsequent impacts of these various development strategies, seeking to understand the impact of that change on Malaysian development through analysis of both quantitative data and more qualitative analysis of interview data and secondary literature. This analysis will demonstrate a largely successful development trajectory understood in terms of GDP per capita growth; albeit within a context of 'pseudo-democracy' (Case 2002). Analysis will proceed with four sections. The first will look at the first stages of the NDP, the second will analyse the impacts of the 1985 recession and subsequent shift in development focus, with a third section analysing the impact of the Asian financial crisis in 1997 and its aftermath. A final section will bring the analysis into the post-2010 period. Chapter 8 will then contextualise this analysis in terms of the Developmental Regime tripod, facilitating a more complete understanding of Malaysia's development trajectory through the concepts of capacity and autonomy.

The Construction of Malay Hegemony

The NEP focused on positive discrimination towards the *Bumiputera* (ethnic Malay) population. Such positive discrimination was justified as a result of the 'Malay Dilemma', a belief that the *Bumiputera* were somehow disabled as a race due to largely hereditary factors, 'poor educational facilities, inbreeding, chronic endemic diseases like malaria and tuberculosis, [and] colonial government policies and practices' (Mahathir 2011: 230). Since this original prescription, Mahathir has modified his analysis, and rather than blaming external factors, he has come to blame the Malays themselves, referring to a 'disabling dilemma' (Mahathir 2011: 233), eerily echoing Sir Thomas Stamford Raffles' conclusion that Malays did not achieve a high intellectual stage of development (Raffles 1835: 30, cited in Alatas 1977: 38).

This positive discrimination has in reality led to the capture of the state and big business by 'Super-Bumis', facilitating superior access to economic rents based on ethnic lines (see, e.g., Gomez and Jomo 1999; Andaya and Andaya 2001; Hilley 2001). Monopoly and transfer rents manifested themselves in various forms. '... discounted privatisations, overpriced contracts, permits and licences, special loans and credit facilities, as well as subsidised education and training opportunities' (Gomez and Jomo 1999: 177). Furthermore, such ethnocentric goals manifested in policies such as the requirement that all enterprises have at least 30% Malay participation (World Bank 1993: 185). Monopoly and transfer rents also manifested themselves in other ways. Malaysian political economy has been described as an example of 'Ersatz Capitalism' (Yoshihara 1988), leading to a discourse of 'Crony Capitalism' (see, e.g., MacIntryre 1994; Gomez and Jomo 1999; Andaya and Andaya 2001; Stiglitz 2001).

Such rent-seeking behaviour is not a priori a drag on economic growth and development as '[t]he rent-seeking welfare losses may well be more than offset by the dynamic gains of productivity growth which the rent facilitates... so while rent seeking activities may be "directly unproductive", they may well constitute transaction costs which indirectly facilitate productivity gains' (Chang 1994; see also Khan and Jomo 2000). This argument was presented in Chap. 2 when examining the Developmental State literature more broadly. In the case of Malaysia, Chang et al. seem to be proved correct. Examination of a number of key data reveals this. Table 7.1 shows impressive and sustained annual GDP growth across the period of both the NEP and the NDP up to the Asian financial crisis in 1997. This was accompanied by a healthy balance of trade profile, although a growing current account deficit began to appear in the run-up to the Asian financial crisis. Exports were clearly a significant driver of GDP growth and attendant Malaysian development during this period, with sustained investment from the global political economy in the form of FDI helping to sustain this alongside domestic savings.

Table 7.1 Select economic indicators for Malaysia, 1975–1997

	GDP per capita (current US$)	*GDP (annual percentage change)*	*FDI (percentage of GDP)*	*External debt (percentage of GDP)*	*Inflation (CPI percentage)*	*Federal government overall surplus (RM millions)*	*Poverty (percentage)*	*Unemployment rate (percentage)*
1975	755.3	0.8	3.8	21.9	4.5	−1901	–	–
1976	877.0	11.5	3.5	23.9	2.6	−1705	37.7	–
1977	1019.2	7.8	3.1	25.4	4.8	−2476	–	–
1978	1240.1	6.7	3.1	26.1	4.9	−2249	–	–
1979	1570.9	9.3	2.7	23.9	3.7	−1535	37.4	–
1980	1770.2	7.4	3.8	27.5	6.7	−3704	–	–
1981	1763.4	6.9	5.1	37.3	9.7	−9015	–	–
1982	1843.0	5.9	5.2	51.3	5.8	−10,421	–	3.4
1983	2033.0	6.3	4.1	61.0	3.7	−6933	–	3.8
1984	2213.7	7.8	2.3	58.1	3.9	−4775	20.7	5.0
1985	1979.2	−0.9	2.2	68.6	0.3	−4407	–	5.6
1986	1709.7	1.2	1.8	82.9	0.7	−7506	–	7.4
1987	1926.6	5.4	1.3	75.6	0.3	−6153	19.4	7.3
1988	2050.4	9.9	2.0	55.7	2.6	−3290	–	7.2
1989	2193.9	9.1	4.3	44.4	2.8	−3410	16.5	5.7
1990	2417.4	9.0	5.3	36.4	2.6	−3437	–	4.5
1991	2626.6	9.5	8.1	36.6	4.4	−2640	–	–
1992	3080.9	8.9	8.8	35.7	4.8	−1243	12.4	3.7
1993	3395.5	9.9	7.5	41.1	3.5	354	–	4.1
1994	3685.9	9.2	5.8	42.8	3.7	4408	–	–
1995	4280.0	9.8	4.7	40.5	3.5	1861	8.7	3.1
1996	4743.7	10.0	5.0	41.3	3.5	1815	–	2.5
1997	4585.7	7.3	5.1	49.8	2.7	6626	6.1	2.4

Source Columns 1–6: World Bank (2016); column 7: EPU (2016); column 8: Malaysian Statistics Agency (2016)

The NEP ostensibly intended to eliminate poverty and interethnic economic inequalities in order to establish the socio-economic basis for national unity. The aim of the NEP was to increase the economic stake of the poor Malays through affirmative action including quotas for education and the civil service and acquiring '30% of equity in private business' (Montesino 2011: 6). The NEP was largely successful; poverty fell from 64.8 to 23.8% from 1970 to 1988, whilst in the same period Malay corporate ownership rose to about 24% (Singh 2001: 52; see also Table 7.1). By 1999, only 5.5% of the entire population and 10.2% of Malays lived in poverty. To a considerable degree, social harmony and stability was ensured through sustained economic growth that averaged 8% from 1970–1990 (Ibid; see also Tables 7.1 and 7.2). In exchange for this social harmony, the ethnic Chinese seemed to be willing to give up some economic dominance (Montesino 2011: 6).

State policies reflected many of these principles. In comparison with the immediate period after independence, there was a change in emphasis away from a balanced budget and towards expanding the economy. This is reflected in the fiscal figures of the state (see Table 7.1). Operating expenditures were required to not exceed current revenues, leading to a surplus most years. However, as a result of development expenditures and 'off-budget activities' (She 2015: 149) the overall surplus was negative almost throughout the period. As Table 7.1 shows, the overall federal budget deficit grew throughout the late 1970s and peaked at 10,421 million RM. This would have been much larger were it not for significant influxes of petroleum rents during this period (Meesook 2001). The deficit was largely the result of spending on policy thrusts associated with the NEP, with wider fiscal policy used to create incentives and disincentives that guided private behaviour (She 2015: 150). This was to facilitate the overall objectives of the NEP as analysed earlier.

Table 7.2 Structure of Malaysian merchandise exports (percentage), select years

	1970	*1975*	*1980*	*1985*	*1990*
Agricultural raw materials	50.1	34.1	31.0	18.4	13.8
Food	12.6	23.2	15.1	17.4	11.7
Fuel	7.3	10.9	24.7	31.5	18.3
Manufactures	6.5	17.3	18.8	27.2	53.8
Ores and metals	22.6	13.9	10.2	5.3	2.1

Source World Bank (2016)

Monetary policy complemented this fiscal stance. Bank Negara Malaysia (BNM)—the central bank of Malaysia—is the institution responsible for price stability, economic growth, and financial stability. As Table 7.1 shows, this commitment to price stability was maintained throughout the late 1970 and early 1980s; with the only significant challenge in this period coming in 1974 when CPI inflation hit 17.3% as a result of the global oil shock (She 2015: 152). A stable currency was the second plank to monetary policy during this period. This was in order to complement broader NEP development strategies focused on FDI induced export-oriented industrialisation.

There was a change from an implicit urban emphasis towards an explicit rural development focus—where many of the ethnic Malay's were situated. Also, social services and welfare were significantly expanded—with extra benefits channelled to the Malay majority (Ness 1967: 90). This helps account for the significant reductions in poverty during this period (see Table 7.1). A significant number of new state institutions focused on the control and distribution of NEP funds were created in order to enhance state capacities. This was also reflected in the proliferation of public and state-owned enterprises in strategic sectors of the economy.

The twin goals of alleviating absolute poverty and eliminating the identification of socio-economic status and occupation with ethnicity and race were to be realised through the fostering of an expanding economy, with state redistribution of the proceeds of that growth. Growth policy itself shifted from the agriculturally focused programmes of the immediate post-independence era—notably the World Bank sponsored primary sector ISI programme in 1957—to the manufacturing and commercial sectors. This began with the Investment Incentives Act 1968 where, through the government agencies and institutions associated with the NEP, export-oriented industrialisation strategies were pursued. By 1971 and the Free Trade Zone (FTZ) Act there was a significant inflow of FDI (see Table 7.1), in particular in labour-intensive industries such as textiles and semiconductor assembly (Felker 2015: 137). The results were significant: not only in terms of GDP and GDP per capita growth (see Table 7.1) but also in terms of the overall structure of the economy. Agriculture as a percentage of the economy shrank precipitously, with attendant rises in manufactures and extractive commodity industrial complexes (see Table 7.2).

Manufacturing grew swiftly at rates of around 25% a year throughout the 1970s (Felker 2015: 136). Whilst agriculture represented a declining proportion of the economy, it nevertheless remained a significant component of the economy (see Table 7.2). Rising global commodity prices and diversification away from rubber and tin into palm oil as well as increasing petroleum discoveries generated significant expansion in primary exports, representing over 30% by 1980 (Felker 2015: 136; see also Table 7.2). Petroleum in particular was an increasingly important aspect of Malaysia's rising export profile, and was to become of increasing importance over the course of the century (see later sections). Rising to 25% of Malaysian exports by 1980 (see Table 7.2) the state realised the importance of this dynamic early and passed the Petroleum Development Act 1974. This Act facilitated partial foreign divestment of Royal Dutch Shell exploration and extraction assets in Borneo and those of Esso on the peninsula. The company that was created—Petronas (*Petroliam Nasional Berhad* or Malaysian National Oil Company Inc.)—was modelled on the Indonesian state oil company founded in 1971 and renegotiated production-sharing contracts as well as implementing joint venture agreements.

The rise in manufactures, to around 20% by 1980 (see Table 7.2), was grounded in the expansion of a network of state-owned enterprises (SOEs). The largest plantation and mining corporations were nationalised, along with a host of strategic clusters developed—with long-term successors in areas such as semiconductors, computer components, and textiles. These were complemented with crown jewels such as MAS (Malaysian Airline Systems) and Petronas. These state-owned enterprises were also used to aid the state in its NEP goals associated with eliminating the identification of socio-economic status and occupation with ethnicity and race. This helped alleviate rising ethnic tensions increasingly present throughout the 1950 and 1960s. Rising rural to urban migration, predominantly from ethnic Malay's who as a group were rurally ensconced at the time of independence, led to increasing urban (Malay) unemployment (see Table 7.1). Through the *Perbadanan Nasional* (Pernas) and, subsequently, *Permodalan Nasional* (PNB) investment capital was pooled for Malay enterprises to be supported (Felker 2015: 136). This was complemented with a series of government-owned banks and finance companies that facilitated general and favourable support of the financial sector for *Bumiputera* capital.

Significant changes and reform occurred in public administration in order to generate the capacity required by the state to enact the development-focused programmes of the NEP. The strategy of development through industrialisation, urbanisation, and primary commodity diversification, combined with the spread of education in particular, all lent added momentum to the new functions of the government (Mansor and Ariffin 2015: 105). The role of the administration changed from that of an administrator model taken from the former colonial power to one of a change agent. As a result, many existing institutions were strengthened. For example, the Development Administration Unit (DAU) in the Prime Minister's Department that had been started as a result of the Montgomery-Esman report of 1965 saw its role expand as it was reformed into the Implementation Coordination and Development Administration Unit (ICDAU) in 1972. five years after that, in 1977, became the Malaysian Administrative and Modernisation and Manpower Planning (MAMPU). In addition, several new institutions were added, designed to improve development planning and implementation. A series of 5-year development plans that came under the envelope of the NEP were coordinated by the National Development Planning Committee (NDPC), which stood at the heart of the government through being chaired by the chief secretary to the government (Mansor and Ariffin 2015: 107).

In summary, during this period Malaysia pursued a state coordinated development programme. This was very successful in its stated goals. First, poverty was significantly reduced. At the start of the NEP in 1970 Malaysian poverty stood at 49.3%, with 64.8% among the *Bumiputera* population (Malaysian Statistics Agency 2016). 10 years into the NEP poverty had been reduced to 37.4% (see Table 7.1), with 46.4% among ethnic Malays. The second was the goal of eliminating the identification of socio-economic status and occupation with ethnicity and race. A series of *Bumiputera*-focused policies and institutions facilitated significant urban manufacturing employment, both in SOEs and private firms given loans and financial services on favourable terms. These firms were further fostered through a macroeconomic policy conductive towards selective and strategic free trade and broad price stability (see Table 7.1). Primary commodity exports remained a significant component of Malaysian exports, although in the context of state promotion of manufactured exports a declining percentage of that total export profile.

The Recession of 1985 and Mahathir's Response

Elected Prime Minister at the beginning of the 1980s, Mahathir launched a series of new programmes. Essentially, they were a package of measures designed to promote a secondary import substituting industrialisation programme (Felker 2015: 137). Under the banner 'Look East', these policies were designed to push the Malaysian economy beyond import dependent, low value-added production. A state-owned Heavy Industries Corporation of Malaysia (HICOM) was formed, which launched large, capital-intensive projects. For example, in the automobile sector the Proton was launched in a joint venture with Mitsubishi, who supplied much of the technology—in particular in the more high-value-added elements of production. This pattern was repeated in other industries such as cement, fertiliser, steel, and petrochemicals (Jomo 1994).

These investments were expensive, and led to a significant deterioration in the federal government's budget balance. In 1980, the budget deficit was 3704 million RM, which increased to 10,421 million RM by 1982, although in subsequent years this improved, falling to 4407 million RM by 1985. This was compounded by the development of a current account deficit, collapsing to a low of 13.4% of GDP by 1982, which rebounded to an 8% surplus by 1986 (World Bank 2016). Arguably these were the product of large government investments in heavy industry, partially financed through external borrowing and resulting in the import of significant amounts of intermediate capital goods.

Combined with a global cyclical downturn in both commodity prices and in the electronics industry, an area in which Malaysia had invested heavily, recession seemed inevitable. In 1985 Malaysia experienced just that (Ariff 1998: 2), reflected in a drop in GDP growth into negative territory (see Table 7.1). Average per capita income fell for 3 years and official unemployment doubled from 4.6% in 1982 to 9.1% in 1987 (EPU 2016). GDP contracted by 0.9% in 1985, having grown at a fair clip of 7.8% the year before (see Table 7.1). Debt to GDP grew from 68.6% in 1985 to 82.9% in 1986, and the federal government deficit grew from 4407 million RM in 1985–7506 million RM in 1986 (see Table 7.1).

Mahathir and the Malaysian state's response to these recessionary pressures was to (re)encourage investment in existing assembly-based export industries. The Promotions of Investment Act 1986 enhanced earlier reforms associated with EPZs. *Bumiputera* provisions were even relaxed, with the Act initially providing for 100% foreign ownership in projects exporting more than 80% of their output. This was a shift in emphasis away from the higher value-added secondary EOI reforms that Mahathir had initiated at the beginning of his tenure in 1981. The strategy that emerged has been termed 'embedded mercantilism' (Jayasuriya 2003). The relaxing of the NEPs objectives through reducing the *Bumiputera* requirements associated with its laws and institutions led to an attendant rise in FDI. As Table 7.1 shows, FDI represented 8.8% of GDP by 1992. This facilitated a foreign-dominated, internationally competitive export sector. This existed simultaneously with a 'domestic political economy in which non-tradable sectors—finance, construction, infrastructure, property development—were shaped by quasi-corporatist or clientelist interventions' (Felker 2015: 138; see also Gomez and Jomo 1999). The significant increase in FDI was the product of TNCs investing in technology upgrades in order to take advantage of increasing demand in global markets.

Fiscal and monetary policy during this period complemented Mahathir's objectives. Fiscal incentives were shifted to reflect the new priorities, and significant infrastructural investment undertaken by the Federal government. This was partially offset by rising income from petroleum sales and expanding exports from foreign TNCs (Ritchie 2004). These lucrative revenue streams actually pushed the Malaysian federal budget into surplus in 1993 for the first time since before 1970. This surplus reached 6626 million RM by 1997. In monetary policy terms, the 1985 recession saw the BNM manage a depreciation of the ringgit as monetary policy was loosened in the face of declining international commodity prices. This served to help stimulate the recovery as it complemented Mahathir's policies of liberalisation and privatisation in strategic export sectors to stimulate his EPZ policy.

There was also significant administrative reform in the post-1985 recession period, reform that broadly followed the principles of New Public Management (NPM). Influenced by neoclassical and neoliberal thought, NPM entails the adoption of private sector principles in public bureaucracy. Reform was thus geared towards 'the development of an efficient and professional managerial administration' (Mansor and Ariffin 2015: 108). Initiatives included the introduction of manuals of work procedures and desk files which aimed to improve work systems and procedures, and Quality Control Circles (QCCs), which had a remit to improve the quality of public services. Furthermore, 'the Malaysia Incorporated Policy and the Look East Policy were to change the orientation of the British legacy of a detached civil service (the regulator) from the private sector (the regulatee)' (Mansor and Ariffin 2015: 109). However, it is important to stress that this did not represent a comprehensive and complete overhaul of Malaysia's various layers of administration. Many procedures, permits, and licences that stemmed from the NEP were not reviewed; the Malaysian Civil Service remained de jure open to all applicants, independent of ethnic origin, but de facto became Malay dominated as ethnic Chinese and Indian Malaysian's in particular went into the private sector in the context of a dynamic economy and relatively high remuneration (Mansor and Ariffin 2015: 112).

This transition away from *Bumiputera*-focused imperatives led to significant political opposition to Mahathir and his post-recession policies. Following the turmoil, the ruling political party, the UMNO, split into two factions in early 1987. Both rival factions stirred ethnic tensions in order to gain Malay support. During this period of UMNO weakness, Malaysian Chinese politicians were also fuelling communal tensions. They were increasingly animated over issues such as: a mandatory loyalty pledge in school which had heavy Islamic overtones; the University of Malaya's decision that all optional courses be taught in Malay; and the appointment of 200 ethnic Chinese who spoke Malay and lacked Mandarin, as senior officials in government-run Chinese-medium primary schools (Montesino 2011). The Chinese community demanded appeasement on these issues. In response, in mid-October 1987, the UMNO Youth called a rally urging the government to keep the Chinese schools' policy (Montesino 2011). The rally denounced the Chinese objections and raised the threat of racial mobilisation. Furthermore, the Chinese were branded as disloyal because many of their investments were in sectors that offered quick returns (Gomez 1998 in Tan 2010: 963).

In response to the growing ethnic tensions, Mahathir banned all public rallies and authorised the arrest of 119 people. He attributed primary responsibility for the escalation of racial tensions to the leading opposition—the Chinese-based DAP. According to Mahathir, the DAP sought political support by championing communal issues, with the resultant political mobilisation of the Chinese community in turn forcing the UMNO and the Malays to resist (Montesino 2011). Whilst not altogether denying Malay responsibility, Mahathir argued that the Malays were forced to react to growing Chinese provocation, and hence were not the primary cause for the deteriorating ethnic situation. As Malaysia's economy came out of the economic doldrums tensions subsided, but the fragile peace had been re-exposed, like it had been so violently in 1969. Nevertheless, the rapid expansion of GDP in the wake of the 1985 recession was very impressive (see Table 7.1), averaging over 9%. In the context of this success, Mahathir codified his post-1985 reforms into a new development plan. The National Development Plan (NDP) ran from 1990–2010 and provided a framework for fostering growth in the unexpectedly dynamic low value-added manufactured export sector. 'Finding Malaysia a conducive site in which to produce for global markets, multinationals upgraded their technology through process automation, invested selectively in deepening production of components and subassemblies, and engaged in limited production-related design' (Felker 2015: 138).

The Asian Financial Crisis of 1997 in Malaysia and the Post-crisis Period

This was to come to a dramatic end with the advent of the Asian Financial Crisis late in 1997. The desire to stimulate high and sustained levels of FDI in Malaysia in the aftermath of the 1985 recession had the consequence of a highly liberalised capital account. However, in the context of a stated policy of maintaining low inflation, and a quasi-fixed Nominal Exchange Rate (NER) in order to stimulate EOI, the Mundell-Fleming (Mundell 1963; Fleming 1962) 'impossible trinity' came into force: a country cannot simultaneously maintain an open capital account, an exchange rate target, and a monetary policy that is geared to domestic stabilisation needs and is independent from the exchange rate target (Islam and Chowdhury 2000: 96). Therefore, Malaysia experienced an incremental increase in its Real Effective Exchange Rate (REER) throughout the 1990s (IMF 2009), resulting in declining exports and a subsequent current account deficit throughout the 1990s up until the crisis in 1997–1998 (UNCTAD 2009).

Arguably, such dynamics helped precipitate the crisis of 1997-1998 when combined with Malaysia's fiscal situation. Whilst the government itself had returned to surplus at the turn of the 1990s (see Table 7.1), major corporations had taken on significant debt levels, partially to help finance federal government mega-projects in infrastructure. The financial system was highly leveraged due to the liberalised stock market and capital account in general. Although the crisis started as a currency run in Thailand, it soon spread throughout the region's economies. Here is not the place to go into the causes of the Asian financial crisis, a number of book-length treatments have already done this (see, e.g., Beeson et al. 2003). Rather, the impacts of the crisis will be outlined, before some analysis of the post-crisis Malaysian political economy will sketch out patterns of continuity and change in its development trajectory.

Mahathir and Malaysia's initial response to the Asian financial crisis was a series of austerity measures, very much in line with the neo-classically influenced orthodoxy of IMF advice. These austerity measures were aimed at producing counter inflationary pressures designed to counteract the depreciation of the ringgit (She 2015: 155). However, this policy was soon to be replaced, in a volte-face by Mahathir, by a 7 billion RM stimulus package in 1998, with an overarching focus on public investment. This led to a significant and sustained increase in the federal government's fiscal deficit, reaching over 20,000 million RM by 2001 (see Table 7.3). This only began to shrink by 2003, with the period 1999–2003 representing a counter-cyclical fiscal stance. The prolonged fiscal expansion after 1997 suggests that the Asian financial crisis represented a turning point in Malaysian fiscal policy: a shift from modest deficits or surpluses to significant and sustained deficits (see Table 7.3).

Table 7.3 Post-crisis economic indicators in Malaysia 1998–2010

	GDP (annual percentage change)	*Federal government overall surplus (RM millions)*	*Poverty (percentage)*	*Gini coefficient*	*FDI (percentage of GDP)*
1998	−7.4	−5003	–	–	3.0
1999	6.1	−9487	8.5	0.443	4.9
2000	8.9	−19,715	–	–	4.0
2001	0.5	−20,253	–	–	0.6
2002	5.4	−20,928	6.0	0.461	3.2
2003	5.8	−19,419	–	–	2.9
2004	6.8	−18,724	5.7	0.462	3.5
2005	5.3	−19,109	–	–	2.7
2006	5.6	−20,658	–	–	4.7
2007	6.3	−35,594	3.6	0.441	4.7
2008	4.8	−47,424	–	–	3.3
2009	−1.5	−43,275	3.8	0.441	0.1
2010	7.4	−42,509	–	–	4.3

Source Columns 1 and 5: World Bank (2016); column 2: MOF (2016); columns 3 and 4: EPU (2016)

However, Narayaman (1996) suggests that unsustainably high government expenditures, periodically and inconsistently counterbalanced by unstable petroleum levies, actually predated the crisis. In the crucible of the financial crisis and its attendant reductions in federal government revenues, the long-run non-sustainability of this situation began to reveal itself.

This sustained expansionary fiscal stance was complemented by a monetary policy that also ran against the grain of IMF orthodoxy. A currency crisis where the Ringgit depreciated by 40% soon became a full-blown financial crisis; rapid contagion the result of high levels of short-term debt in the domestic private sector (She 2015: 155). The stock market collapsed, and GDP growth dropped by 7.4% in 1998 (see Table 7.3). Mahathir responded with capital controls and a fixing of the exchange rate—with associated selective exchange rate controls. Highly volatile short-term capital flows and exchange rate volatility had undermined the Central Bank's ability to affect domestic interest rates. These capital controls were designed to deal with the crisis through managing liquidity to control interest rates so as to promote economic activity in the wake of the Asian Financial Crisis (BNM 1999).

In the aftermath of the crisis, a number of prominent businesses owned by Malay capital were bailed out, arguably due to preferential state access, which was the result of ethnocentric government policies. It is possible to argue that bailouts may be necessary and even desirable to mitigate the adverse consequences of systemic crises on the financial system, corporate viability, growth and employment (Jomo 2005: 260). However, for this to be the case they must be constructed in such a way so as to minimise abuse and cronyism. Jomo (2005: 260) argues that in Malaysia this was not the case, as the Malaysian government deployed its resources to save the national economy by propping up and bailing out the financial system and some larger—usually politically connected—enterprises; thus demonstrating a clear bias in favour of politically influential business interest. However, he goes on to argue that 'one should not throw out the baby of such state interventions with the bathwater of abuses which have undoubtedly tainted the Malaysian experience' (Jomo 2005: 261).

High levels of Non-Performing Loans (NPLs) to failed Malay entrepreneurs combined with capital flight during the crisis led to Bank *Bumiputera* Bhd. and *Sime* Bank Bhd. declaring huge losses in 1998. Bank Bumiputera received a capital injection of RM1.1Billion from the government, combined with state purchase of 65% of its NPLs. This was the third time the government had had to bail out Bank *Bumiputera*, with similar bailouts implemented in 1984 and 1989 (Gomez and Jomo 1999: 193). *Sime* Bank Bhd. was sold to Rashid Hussain Bhd. (RHB) Group, controlled by Rashid Hussain, a Super-Bumi with close personal ties to Mahathir. *Sime* Bank was 30% owned by the UMNO cooperative KUB Bhd. and therefore its sale was widely seen as a bailout for the UMNO cooperative (Gomez and Jomo 1999: 194).

Other controversial bailouts included the shipping concern *Konsortium Perkapalan Bhd.* (KPB), owned by Mahathir's son Mirzan Mahathir, and KTM Railway Services. The government therefore nationalised some private debts and liabilities, whilst allowing politically well-connected private interests to retain profitable privatised assets (Gomez and Jomo 1999: 196). Also, the RM1.792Billion government bailout of MAS (Malaysia Airline System Bhd.) was subject to much criticism. As Ching (2005: 180) suggests, '... the cost to the government of the MAS bailout has been well beyond what would be considered necessary. To make matters worse, it was partly responsible for MAS's mismanagement and failure who was generously rescued without reprimand'. Indeed, Lim (2011) characterised the MAS bailout as a 'double government bailout', as it involved paying the principle shareholder Tajudin Ramli, thus bailing out both the company and its principal shareholder. Therefore, Ching (2005: 182) concludes, '[t]axpayers are not only bearing the costs of bailing out MAS but also personally bailing out Tajudin' by paying well above the market price of his holdings.

In summary, Mahathir and Malaysia's post-Asian financial crisis policies sought not to withdraw Malaysia from its engagement with global investors, but to restructure the domestic economy whilst selectively recalibrating its international linkages (Felker 2015: 139). Khoo (2006: 187) termed this a more inward focused, 'semi-autarchic' development strategy. FDI-led export-oriented industrialisation remained the broad development model across the period. Fiscal and monetary policy closely shadowed the needs of this model in the context of changing international circumstances. Domestically, significant sums went into the network of *Bumiputera* policies that sustained many SOEs, including those mega-bailouts outlined above. Overall poverty increased from 6.1% in 1997 to 8.5% in 1999 (see Table 7.3). Among ethnic Malay's the figures were 9% and 12.3%, respectively. This represented the first official increase in poverty in Malaysia since the time series began in 1970. Sustained spending by the Federal government in the wake of the crisis eventually took effect, with poverty subsiding to 6% by 2002 and falling to below 4% by 2010 (EPU 2016). Similar trends can be seen in the Gini coefficient, although with a longer lag effect on its recovery as inequality was still increasing until 2004 (see Table 7.3).

The Challenge to Malay Hegemony

Following Mahathir's retirement in 2003 the subsequent Abdullah and Najib administrations sought to maintain and extend the contemporary development model through nurturing new growth sectors. As a result, significant state-led investment was witnessed in information technology industries such as software, media production, and business process outsourcing. In addition, biotechnology and green technology that could add value to old primary sector output were encouraged. Also, services such as Islamic banking, international education, healthcare, and tourism were fostered (Felker 2015: 139).

The Global financial crisis of 2007–2009 had a significant short-term impact on the Malaysian economy. By mid-2009 GDP had contracted by 6.2%, although was to quickly rebound so that by the end of 2009 GDP had only contracted by 1.5% from 2008 (see Table 7.3). This was mostly the impact of declining exports through the trade channel, the result of collapsing demand in the developed world and the Advanced Capitalist Countries (ACCs). Whilst significant, this impact was much lower than the Asian financial crisis around 10 years earlier (see the previous section). As Tables 7.3 and 7.4 show, GDP growth returned to relatively robust levels, clocking up 7.4% in 2010 before settling into a trend of around 5% since.

Table 7.4 Select economic indicators for contemporary Malaysia

	GDP (annual percentage change)	*FDI (percentage of GDP)*	*Federal government overall surplus (RM millions)*
2011	5.3	5.1	−42,509
2012	5.5	2.8	−41,951
2013	4.7	3.5	−38,584
2014	6.0	3.1	−37,414
2015	4.9	3.7	−37,249

Source Columns 1 and 2: World Bank (2016); column 3: MOF (2016)

Monetary and fiscal policy were both used to garner this rebounding. In terms of fiscal policy, counter-cyclical spending focused much more on private sector recovery and development compared to those policies that emerged after the Asian financial crisis—which were much more about public sector investment (see the previous section). Furthermore, the fiscal taps were largely turned off by 2010—much more swiftly than had been the case in the aftermath of the Asian financial crisis (She 2015: 156). In terms of monetary policy, there was a much more conservative response when compared to 1997. Unorthodox policies such as capital and exchange rate controls were not introduced. Instead, more mainstream tools such as interest rates and other monetary operations were implemented, whilst preserving previous liberalisation measures on foreign exchange administration (She 2015: 157). These relatively limited measures were the product of the fact that at the time of the Global financial crisis Malaysia had a fairly robust financial system. Reforms in the wake of the Asian financial crisis such as improvements to financial risk management and the Central Bank's use of forward guidance to help manage expectations in the market better served to cushion Malaysia from the most egregious impacts of the financial crisis.

In the wake of the global financial crisis, on 3 April 2009, Najib Tun Razak assumed the office of Prime Minister of Malaysia. Najib stepped into political centre stage at a time when the country was facing political and economic challenges and when his party, UMNO, faced unprecedented demands to reform and redefine itself. UMNO has been characterised by undemocratic practices, money politics, nepotism, and cronyism. The party has faced challenges from other smaller parties and has even suffered defeat in several states in the 2008 general election, as well as by-elections in *Permatang Pauh* on 26 August 2008, *Kuala Terengganu* on 17 January 2009, *Bukit Gantang* together with *Bukit Selambau* on 7 April 2009, and *Manek Urai* on 14 July 2009. Furthermore, UMNO nor any other party in the BN contested the *Penanti* by-election on 31 May 2009 (Azizuddin 2011).

In 2010 the New Economic Model (NEM) was introduced, replacing the NDP. This aimed to transform Malaysia into a high-income economy, in line with Mahathir's original Vision 2020. Official publications highlight four key pillars of 'national transformation' as part of the NEM (NEAC 2012). The first pillar is the Economic Transformation Programme (ETP). This aims to boost growth through stimulating private investment, 'enabling the private sector to step up and make a full contribution to growth' (NEAC 2012: 4). Commitments to broad economic ethnic equality were maintained. The second pillar is the *1Malaysia* ('Satu Malaysia') policy, designed to 'unite all Malaysians to face the challenges ahead' (NEAC 2012: 3). This is essentially a suite of policies associated with 'transparent and market-friendly affirmative action' (NEAC 2012: 24): an attempt to reduce levels of rent-seeking and market distortions traditionally associated with *Bumiputera* policies of the past. The third pillar is the Government Transformation Programme (GTP). This seeks to reform the different organs of government to be more professionalised, meritocratic, and efficient in delivering the capacities necessary to implement the other pillars. This came in the form of the introduction of Key Performance Indicators (KPIs) and increasing inclusivity in decision-making processes (Mansor and Ariffin 2015: 111). The fourth and final pillar is the 10th Malaysia Plan: a series of macroeconomic targets and fiscal measures aimed at realising the vision of the first two pillars.

The impact—successful or not—of the NEM cannot yet be understood. However, there are several important trends that can be highlighted here. First, has been the evolution of the fiscal situation. As Table 7.4 shows, despite commitments to its reduction, the Federal government overall surplus has barely moved—although it is on a downward trend. This has been despite key institutions like the Economic Planning Unit (EPU) expressing concern over investor attitudes towards unsustainable sovereign debt levels (EPU 2013; She 2015: 156). This has been exacerbated by the second trend, which is one of increasing reliance on petroleum revenues to fund federal government expenditure (see, e.g., Varkkey 2015). This is not a new trend. Since the mid-1980s, more than 25% of government revenue has come from activities related to oil and gas. However, in the wake of sustained expenditures and an inability to widen the tax base through the introduction of a Value Added Tax (a Goods and Sales Tax or GST in Malaysian parlance) for example have rendered an increasingly precarious fiscal situation. A third issue has been the changing political landscape, and a stronger and more organised opposition. The official opposition has been in the form of the *Pakatan Rakyat* and its current leader Anwar Ibrahim. This body consists of a number of opposition political parties: the People's Justice Party (PKR), Democratic Action Party (DAP), and Pan-Malaysian Islamic Party (PAS). This opposition coalition established a broad reformist platform that centred on a crackdown of semi-official corruption conducted mostly by Super-Bumis, dismantling many aspects of the *Bumiputera* agenda, and introducing electoral and constitutional reform to enhance Malaysia's stalled process of democratisation.

These policies earned the opposition in Malaysia the support of civil society. Civil society activism in challenging the government policy (in general but concerning democracy in particular) has become increasingly vociferous in post-Asian financial crisis Malaysia. The year 2007 saw several large protests against the government and its policies—protests that have continued and intensified in the wake of the Arab Spring that began in 2011. For example, the 2007 *Bersih* (which means 'clean' in Malay and represents a coalition of NGOs and civil-rights organisations) rally held in Kuala Lumpur and attended by approximately 40,000 people. This non-violent and peaceful rally organised by the opposition parties and civil society movements to campaign for electoral reform was denied a permit by the police and was marred by the confrontation between the police and the rally participants near Masjid Jamek. Police used chemical-laced water bombs and tear gas in a violent crackdown. The police arrested 34 people, released a night later, and injured several more. In a separate demonstration, two people suffered bullet wounds from Police actions during a *Bersih* information rally held in September in Batu Burok, Terengganu. In addition, nine people were arrested for their participation in the International Human Rights Day and twelve more were arrested for organising or participating separate rallies calling for government reform (Azizuddin 2011).

This pattern of demonstration and repressive police crackdown has continued to the present day. The *Bersih* rallies, for example, have established themselves as a cornerstone of Malaysian civil society protest in recent years. In 2011, the rally in Kuala Lumpur witnessed a repressive police crackdown on this 'illegal' activity (freedom of association is not something Malaysian's enjoy as rallies and protests are controlled through a permit system) that saw police brutality and sanctioned state violence towards unarmed, peaceful protesters, culminating in over 1600 arrests. In 2012 the '*Bersih 3.0*' rally attracted as many as 80,000 people and once again saw repressive police action involving water cannon, tear gas, and over 400 arrests. Several local reporters were beaten by police, forcing an official apology from Prime Minister Najib. More recently, in mid-2015 50–80,000 protestors peacefully protested against the 1MDB scandal, involving payments to the personal bank account of Najib himself.

This intolerant, authoritarian attitude has been exemplified by the trials of Anwar Ibrahim, the leader of the opposition coalition *Pakatan Rakyat*. Jailed for 6 years in 1998 for sodomy (a crime in Malaysia even if between two consenting adults) after he mounted a successful challenge to the ruling coalition party he was freed in 2004 only after it was ruled that testimony against him had been coerced. In 2008, as his party made major gains against an increasingly weak government, another accusation surfaced, dubbed 'Sodomy II' or 'Sodomy, the sequel' (The Economist 2010). As the Economist suggests, '[p]utting an opposition leader on trial inevitable carries a whiff of politics. When that leader is Anwar Ibrahim… the whiff becomes a stink' (The Economist 2010). Indeed, the saga was to continue as despite acquittal by the High Court in 2012 the Appeals Court overturned this in 2014 and Anwar was sentenced to 5 years in prison—which he is currently serving. The fact that this occurred in the wake of significant electoral losses by the UMNO in the 2013 general election at the expense largely to Ibrahim's *Pakatan Rakyat* coalition has led to a number of domestic and international organisations to condemn the trials as politically motivated.

Increasing civil society expressions combined with increasingly heavy-handed government responses have occurred in the context of relative economic torpor. Najib came into office inheriting the weakest economic situation since the Asian financial crisis in the late 1990s, and in a longer context of economic growth having never recovered to its pre-1997 crisis levels (see Tables 7.3 and 7.4). He faced the prospect of FDI being halved and the country going through a severe recession, with the economy contracting by 4–5%. As finance minister (prior to becoming prime minister), Najib announced two economic stimulus packages: the first in November 2008 totalling RM7 billion and an additional package in March 2009 totalling RM60 billion. Complementing this fiscal stimulus was a stress on the necessity of coming up with a new economic model for the country, which breaks away from the Multimedia Super Corridor (MSC) initiative that only focused on Information and Communication Technology (ICT). Najib announced on 22 April 2009 the immediate dismantling of a rule that required companies in 27 service subsectors to set aside 30% of their company for Malay investors. Later, he announced new measures to boost the country's financial services sector, allowing greater foreign stakes in investment banks and both Islamic and commercial insurers from 49 to 70%.

On 30 June 2009, Najib announced a slew of changes, most notably the removal of *Bumiputera* equity requirements for public listings and the effective dismantling of the all-powerful Foreign Investment Committee (FIC), long the bane of the business community and foreign investors. The new rule removed the 30% requirement but also stipulated that half of the free-float shares be offered to *Bumiputeras*. This effectively sets the minimum allocation for *Bumiputeras* at 12.5%. However, even this condition was to be waived if there are no *Bumiputeras* willing or able to take up the allocation. Najib also cut the powers of the FIC, repealing its guidelines covering the acquisition of equity stakes, mergers and takeovers. He also liberalised ownership in the wholesale segment of the fund management industry, allowing total ownership for qualified and leading fund management companies seeking to set up shop in Malaysia.

To contain a potential *Bumiputera* backlash, Najib announced the creation of a private equity fund, called *Ekuiti Nasional Berhad* (Ekuinas), which had an initial capital of RM500 million but would eventually grow to RM10 billion. The initial fund came from the budget and Ekuinas reported to the prime minister, with the Economic Planning Unit (EPU) playing a supervisory role. It is owned by the government and focuses on nurturing *Bumiputera* businessmen in sectors considered to be high growth such as education, tourism, oil and gas, and ICT. To date, it seems Najib has been able to contain the *Bumiputera* elements of the UMNO, which is reflective of how much groundwork he and his team did to assure the UMNO base that Malay special rights would not be jeopardised (Montesino 2011: 6). However, recent interventions by Mahathir himself (The Economist 2016) at the time of writing this book mean this conclusion is highly contingent.

In summary, the global financial crisis did not impact Malaysia as bad as the Asian financial crisis had. Monetary policy was more orthodox, in the context of a more robust and reformed financial sector in the wake of the Asian financial crisis. Fiscal policy was initially counter-cyclical, but stimulus was reigned back much sooner than had been the case in 1997–1998. The post-crisis period has been dominated by the NEM. This has sought to generate a greater role for the private sector in future Malaysian growth trajectory. Whilst it is too soon to evaluate the impact of these reforms, the rise of a credible opposition and the nature of Malaysian politics post-2008 suggests a (albeit limited) shift towards a post-ethnic dimension of political competition (Ming 2015: 27).

Conclusions

Post-colonial Malaysian political economy has been dominated by the state-led plans of the NEP, NDP, and currently the NEM. These plans have institutionalised ethnic privilege and preferential treatment, and in practice facilitated widespread officially sanctioned corruption—leading to a characterisation of Malaysia's political economy as one of crony capitalism. As a result, Malaysian state-society relationships can be seen as being fundamentally shaped by an ethnic contract, where stability and racial harmony is achieved through an ethnic agenda. The political opposition in Malaysia that emerged in the post-Asian financial crisis era and has grown in strength ever since has challenged the hegemony of the BN and its ethnocentric agenda.

One manifestation of this form of political economy has been the monopoly rent-seeking behaviour of well-connected business elites. In the case of Malaysia, '[a]lthough yielding handsome pecuniary returns, substantial profits and capital gains, the business operations of most Bumiputeras—and some non-Bumiputeras—benefiting from government allocated rents are mostly non-entrepreneurial, unless one stretches the definition of entrepreneurship beyond recognition' (Gomez and Jomo 1999: 179). Thus, '... continued dependence on the state for protection, their subsidy mentality, and their lack of business focus [means that] their minds are confused' (Gomez and Jomo 1999: 179). Such factors have led Gomez and Jomo to conclude that '... the government's preoccupation with inter-ethnic economic redistribution and related abuses of state policies and the public sector have compromised the purpose, nature, and quality of state intervention' (Gomez and Jomo 1999: 191).

The Malaysian state has been characterised as authoritarian (Gomez and Jomo 1999), semi-authoritarian (Crouch 1992, 1993), semi-democratic (Case 1993) or semi-democratic with strain points (Case 2002: 99), quasi-democratic (Zakaria 1989), or pseudo-democratic (Sing 2001). Whatever the specificities of the nature of Malaysian democracy, the fact remains that '... fair elections, adequate opportunities for independent political opinion making and political organisation, and minimal protection for the individual from arbitrary state power, hardly exist in Malaysia' (Gomez and Jomo 1999: 2; Case 2002: 120). Such authoritarian tendencies were largely the responsibility of the Mahathir years with incremental executive encroachment on the other branches of government. Such creeping authoritarianism is also present beyond the formal political institutions of democracy (Case 2002: 116). For example, 'the government controlled media have been used by the BN to promote and legitimise itself as well as to discredit political opposition and dissent more generally' (Gomez and Jomo 1999: 3). Furthermore, there has been '... an intolerant official attitude towards opposition, dissent and independent criticism by largely ignoring and even discrediting public interest groups, NGOs, and Trade Unions, which have been gradually emasculated through repression, legislation, regulation, and manipulation' (Gomez and Jomo 1999: 3). This has been most exemplified through analysis of the case of Anwar Ibrahim (see the previous section).

The next chapter will develop an understanding of Malaysian state-led development within the Developmental Regime approach. The overwhelmingly ethnic nature of Malaysian politics represents a challenge to mainstream development thinking, as well as representing a different model of development and associated political economy as witnessed in Argentina. In demonstrating the continued efficacy of the Developmental Regime in this context, the exercise will reveal how a common framework can be established to understand the nature of contemporary developmentalism in emerging markets across the globe.

References

Alatas, S. (1977). *The myth of the lazy native*. New York: Routledge.

Amsden, A. H. (1989). *Asia's next giant: South Korea and late industrialisation*. New York: Oxford University Press.

Andaya, B., & Andaya, L. (2001). *A history of Malaysia* (2nd ed.). Hampshire: Palgrave

Ariff, M. (1998). The Malaysian economic experience and its relevance for the OIC member countries. *Islamic Economic Studies, 6*(1), 1–41.

Azizuddin, M. (2011) Governance and politics in Malaysia: New wine in a new bottle? Paper presented at PSU-USM international conference on humanities and social sciences, Penang, Malaysia.

Beeson, M., Jayasuriya, K., Kim, H. R., & Robison, R. (2003). *Politics and markets in the wake of the Asian crisis*. London: Routledge.

BNM. (1999). *Annual report 1998*. Kuala Lumpur: BNM.

Case, W. (1993). Semi-Democracy in Malaysia: Withstanding the pressures for regime change. *Pacific Affairs, 66*(2), 183–205.

Case, W. (2002). *Politics in South East Asia: Democracy or less*. Oxford: RoutledgeCurzon.

Chang, H.-J. (1994). *The political economy of industrial policy*. London: MacMillan.

Ching, W. (2005). Corporate Restructuring: Case Studies. In W. Ching, K. S. Jomo, & C. Fay (Eds.). *Malaysian "Bail Outs"? Capital controls, restructuring, and recovery*. Singapore: Singapore University Press.

Chowdry, I., & Islam, A. (1996). The institutional and political framework of growth in an ethnically diverse society: The case of Malaysia. *Canadian Journal of Development Studies, 17*(3), 487–512.

Crouch, H. (1992). Authoritarian trends, the UMNO split and the limits to state power. In J. Kahn & F. Wah (Eds.), *Fragmented vision: Culture and politics in contemporary Malaysia*. Sydney: Allen and Unwin.

Crouch, H. (1993). Malaysia: Neither authoritarian or democratic. In K. Hewison, R. Robinson, & G. Rodan (Eds.), *South Asia in the 1990s: Authoritarianism, democracy, and capitalism*. Sydney: Allen and Unwin.

EPU. (2013). *Eighth Malaysia plan 2001–2005*. Kuala Lumpur: Economic Planning Unit.

EPU (2016) *Malaysian economic indicators*. http://www.epu.gov.my. Accessed 4 Aug 2016,

Felker, G. (2015). Malaysia's development strategies: Governing distribution-through-growth. In M. L. Weiss (Ed.), *Routledge handbook of contemporary Malaysia*. London: Routledge.

Fleming, M. J. (1962). Domestic financial policies under fixed and floating exchange rates. *IMF Staff Papers, 9*, 369–379.

Gomez, E., & Jomo, K. S. (1999). *Malaysia's political economy: Politics, patronage, and profits*. Cambridge: Cambridge University Press.

Haggard, S. (1990). *Pathways from the periphery: The politics of growth in the newly industrialising countries*. Ithaca: Cornell University Press.

Hill, H. (1997). Towards a political economy explanation of rapid growth in Southeast Asia. In H. Soesastro (Ed.), *Southeast Asia in a new regional and international setting*. Jakarta: Centre for Strategic and International Studies.

Hilley, J. (2001). *Malaysia: Mahathirism, hegemony, and the new opposition*. London: Zed.

Islam, A., & Chowdhury, I. (2000). *The political economy of East Asia: Post-crisis debates*. Oxford University Press: Oxford.

IMF. (2009). World economic outlook database. http://www.imf.org. Acccessed 3 Feb 2016,

Jayasuriya, K. (2003). Embedded mercantilism and open regionalism: the crisis of a regional political project. *Third World Quarterly, 24*(2), 339–355.

Johnson, C. (1987). Political institutions and economic performance: The government-business relationship in Japan, South Korea, and Taiwan. In F. C. Deyo (Ed.). *The political economy of New Asian industrialism* (pp. 165–79). Ithaca: Cornell University Press.

Jomo, K. S. (1994). The PROTON saga: Malaysian car, Mitsubishi gain. In K. S. Jomo (Ed.), *Japan and Malaysian development: In the shadow of the rising sun* (pp. 263–290). London: Routledge.

Jomo, K. S. (1997). *South East Asia's misunderstood miracle: Industrial policy and economic development in Thailand, Malaysia, and Indonesia*. New York: Westview Press.

Jomo, K. S. (2005). Conclusion: From financial crises to economic recovery. In W. Ching, K. S. Jomo, & C. Fay (Eds.), *Malaysian "Bail Outs"? Capital controls, restructuring and recovery*. Singapore: Singapore University Press.

Khan, M. H., & Jomo, K. S. (Eds.). (2000). *Rents, rent-seeking and economic development: Theory and evidence in Asia*. Cambridge: Cambridge University Press.

Khoo, B. T. (2006). Malaysia: Balancing development and power. In G. Rodan, K. Hewison, & R. Robinson (Eds.), *Policy regimes and the political economy of poverty reduction in Malaysia*. New York: Palgrave Macmillan.

Lim, D. (2011). Economic development: A historical survey. In Institution of Strategic and International Strategies (Ed.), *Malaysia: Policies and issues in economic development*. Kuala Lumpur: Institution of Strategic and International Strategies.

Little, I. M. D. (1979). An economic reconnaissance. In Galenson (Ed.), *Economic growth and structural change in Taiwan: The post-war experience of the Republic of China*. Ithaca: Cornell University Press.

Little, I. M. D. (1981). The experiences and causes of rapid, labour intensive development in Korea, Taiwan Province, Hong Kong and Singapore and the possibilities of emulation. In Lee (Ed.), *Export processing zones and industrial employment in Asia*. Geneva: ILO/ARTEP.

Little, I. M. D. (1982). *Economic development: Theory, policy and international relations*. New York: Basic Books.

MacIntryre, A. (1994). *Business and government in industrialising Asia*. Ithaca: Cornell University Press.

Mahathir, M. (2011). *A doctor in the house: The memoirs of Tun Dr Mahathir Mohamad*. Petaling Jaya: MPH Group Publishing.

Malaysian Statistics Agency (2016). *Time series data*. http://www.statistics.gov.my. Accessed 12 Aug 2016,

Mansor, N., & Ariffin, N. R. (2015). Public administration in Malaysia: Origins, influence, and assessment. In M. L. Weiss (Ed.), *Routledge handbook of contemporary Malaysia* (pp. 103–115). London: Routledge.

Meesook, K. (2001). *Malaysia: From crisis to recovery*. Washington, DC: IMF.

Ming O. K. (2015). Malaysian political parties and coalitions. In M. L. Weiss (Ed.), *Routledge handbook of contemporary Malaysia* (22–35). London: Routledge.

MOF (2016). *Key economic indicators*. http://www.treasury.gov.my. Accessed 21 Aug 2016.

Montesino, M. U. (2011). Cross-cultural conflict and affirmative action: Inter- and intra-ethnic dilemmas of Malaysia's heterogeneous workplace. *International Journal of Cross Cultural Management, 12*(1), 115–132.

Mundell, R. A. (1963). Capital mobility and stabilization policy under fixed and flexible exchange rates. *Canadian Journal of Economic and Political Science, 29*(4), 475–485.

Narayaman, S. (1996). Fiscal reform in Malaysia: Behind a successful experience. *Asian Survey, 36*(9), 869–881.
NEAC. (2012). *New economic model for Malaysia*. Kuala Lumpur: NEAC.
Ness, G. D. (1967). *Bureaucracy and rural development in Malaysia*. Berkeley: University of California Press.
Ritchie, B. K. (2004). *Politics and economic reform in Malaysia*. William Davidson Institute Working Paper No. 655.
Rodrik, D. (1992). The limits of trade policy reform in developing countries. *Journal of Economic Perspectives, 6*(1), 87–105.
She, X. (2015). Fiscal and monetary policy in Malaysia: Juggling economic imperatives and political reality. In M. L. Weiss (Ed.), *Routledge handbook of contemporary Malaysia* (pp. 148–161). London: Routledge.
Singh, H. (2001). Ethnic conflict in Malaysia revisited. *Commonwealth and Comparative Politics, 39*(1), 42–65.
Stiglitz, J. (2001). *Globalisation and its discontents*. London: Penguin.
Tan, L. O. (2010). The emergence of a virtual civil society: Transcending ethnic politics? In F. K. W. Loh (Ed.) *Building bridges, crossing boundaries: Everyday forms of inter-ethnic peace building in Malaysia* (273–296). Kuala Lumpur: The Ford Foundation.
The Economist (2010, May 13). *Sodomy, the sequel: Another tawdry court case for Anwar.*
The Economist (2016, September 17). *Can a Leopard change its spots.*
UNCTAD (2009). *UNCTADStat*,. http://unctadstat.unctad.org. Accessed 25 Jan 25.
Varkkey, H. (2015). Natural resource extraction and political dependency: Malaysia as a rentier state. In M. L. Weiss (Ed.), *Routledge handbook of contemporary Malaysia*. London: Routledge.
Wade, R. (1988). The role of government in overcoming market failure: Taiwan, Republic of Korea and Japan. In Hughes (Ed.), *Achieving industrialisation in Asia*. Cambridge: Cambridge University Press.
Wade, R. H. (1990). *Governing the market: Economic theory and the role of government in East Asian industrialization*. Princeton: Princeton University Press.
World Bank. (1993). *The East Asian miracle: Economic growth and public policy*. New York: World Bank.
World Bank (2016). World development indicators. http://www.worldbank.org. Accessed 5 August 5.
Yoshihara, K. (1988). *The rise of Ersatz capitalism in South-East Asia*. Oxford University Press: Singapore.
Zakaria, A. (1989). Malaysia: Quasi-democracy in a divided society. In L. Diamong, J. Linz, & S. Lipset (Eds.), *Democracy in developing countries* (Vol. III). Boulder: Lynne Rienner.

CHAPTER 8

Malaysia's Developmental Regime

Malaysian developmentalism has experienced both continuity and change in its trajectory since independence from the British. The previous chapter mapped the contours of those changes in the historical record, culminating in an outline of Malaysia's development path in the 21st century. This forms the empirical bedrock from which an extended analysis of Malaysian developmentalism can be constructed. Not only will this serve to render a clearer account of Malaysian developmental trajectories, but also engender an opportunity to make some ad hoc comparative observations. By no means are these intended in terms of a formal comparative method (see introductory chapter); they represent observations that emerge organically from the analysis of both Malaysia and Argentina through the lens of the Developmental Regime approach.

This analysis will reveal that Malaysian developmentalism has oscillated in focus over the decades since independence between growth focused trajectories and those with a more ethno-nationalist focus. However, these shifts have been incremental, and sometimes somewhat ephemeral in the face of an understanding that its trajectories of changing state capacity and autonomy continued to fall under the broad aegis of state-led developmentalism. Analysis in this chapter will further reveal the robustness of a Developmental Regime approach in embracing *sui generis* understandings of different discrete emerging markets and their rich and unique historical trajectories and attendant processes of institutionalisation. At the same time, such an approach will offer a common framework and language for facilitating better understandings of

C. Wylde, *Emerging Markets and the State*, International Political Economy Series, DOI 10.1057/978-1-137-55655-4_8

common threads of developmentalism in emerging markets in the 21st century.

Malaysia is clearly different to Argentina. Socio-economic relations are aligned along a fundamentally ethnic split, shot through with a powerful discourse around 'Asian Values' (see later section). Different actors operate on very different strategic terrains and their concomitant processes of institutionalisation. The literature has often tried to interpret Malaysia's development trajectory through the lens of elite power (see, e.g., Magaloni 2006: 18). However, more nuanced understandings have been developed grounded in a more institutional analysis (see, e.g., Brownlee 2007) which reveal underlying fractions in Malaysian elites (Case 2015), leaving gaps in our understanding regarding the projection of political power in Malaysia. These gaps are filled through an understanding of other broad factors at play: the mediating capacity of the Malaysian state, the sense of community aroused through the Malay agenda, or legacies and institutional residues of struggle and ethnic solidarity (Brownlee 2007: 203).

This shows the importance of an understanding of power as domination, and how it manifests in different ways across different spatial-temporal horizons. Whilst elite power has clearly influenced the nature of the Malaysian state and the attendant trajectory of Malaysia's development, other forms of power have been expressed that must be mapped and understood in order to reveal the full picture of Malaysian development; simultaneously sharpening our focus of the Developmental Regime approach. It further, and once again, reveals the importance of the Strategic-Relational Approach: not only must the underlying power relationships behind the agency of agents be revealed, but the strategic terrain upon which those agents operate must be understood through associated processes of institutionalisation. This of course operates across multiple levels of structuration.

Once again, the chapter will be structured around the three legs of the tripod for any Developmental Regime: public policy profiles, socio-economic relations, and institutions. Analysis of each leg and their inter-relationships will draw a complete map of Malaysia's political economy of development, as an emerging market in the 21st century. This analysis will inevitably draw on the same theoretical principles and forms as were used in Chap. 6 when outlining Argentina's Developmental Regime, designed to reveal the common framework that can be used to understand very different experiences of 21st century developmentalism in the contemporary global south.

Public Policy Profile

The public policy profile of Malaysia has experienced a continuous broad developmental trajectory since the introduction of the NEP, and perhaps even before this according to William Case (2015). However, there have been important shifts in emphasis that must be accurately mapped in order to establish a sense of Malaysia's post-independence development trajectory. Indeed, Malaysia's development features a pattern in which recurrent political and economic crises have prompted sudden shifts in development priorities. For Felker (2015: 139) this means that the Malaysian development record is 'hard to portray in terms of a coherent strategic sequence, much less as a singular development model'. However, states don't stand 'above' society and direct it towards predetermined policy goals. Instead, the state must be understood as a social relation, and the exercise of power mapped along multiple axes of domination. Therefore, manifestations and expressions of that power—public policies—morph and evolve in relation to the changing contours of social relationships in Malaysian society. In other words, the relative autonomy of the state is not a static phenomenon and requires understanding of actors and the ways in which they exercise their agency, the structures (or strategic terrain) upon which they operate, and the ways in which these interact and mutually influence one another.

The accurate mapping of these changing relationships begins with an examination of the first leg of the Developmental Regime tripod. Public policy profiles are tangible manifestations of any Regimes power, and in a Developmental Regime necessarily are of a consistently developmental persuasion. Furthermore, in an era characterised by globalisation, the influences of different levels of structuration must be recognised as not only helping shape the strategic terrain upon which actors exercise agency, but also facilitating new actors and institutions that themselves act and interact with the state. Therefore, the rest of this section will outline the evolution and interaction of four key areas of the Malaysian (developmental) public policy profile: industrial policy, anti-poverty policy, monetary policy, and fiscal policy.

Malaysian industrial policy has centred on maintaining relative international openness, whilst strategically intervening in key elements of the economy. Developmental strategies in the form of the NEP, NDP, and NEM have provided the policy and political conditions for FDI-led export-oriented industrialisation to flourish. As the previous chapter outlined, this has involved policy shifts in the face of changing priorities, as well as changing national and international conditions. This 'adaptive capacity' (Rahman 2008) has been the result of 'political factors' more than the discipline of market forces, whether external or domestic. In other words, the Malaysian state has engaged in an active industrial policy aimed at attracting FDI in key strategic sectors through subsidies, promotion of SOEs, and a variety of other incentives through wielding its relative autonomy rather than as a simple function of the needs of (different fractions of) capital.

This is further reinforced through an understanding of Malaysia's anti-poverty policies. Fundamentally tied with ethnicity, the vast array of *Bumiputera*-focused policies served simultaneously to reduce poverty and promote development. With poverty overwhelmingly to be found in the rural Malay communities, the Malaysian state fostered significant and sustained poverty reduction through targeting those groups. This was partially administered through industrial policy. Large SOEs could easily be cajoled into affirmative action employment, and even foreign firms had *Bumiputera* hiring requirements. As the state's relative autonomy shifted—for example in the context of crisis—this policy would shift in the face of competing goals of development (targeted by the Malaysian state as GDP growth) and (re)distribution. It is important to note that this strategy should not be seen as a simple balance between growth and distribution. Rather, these goals were simultaneously pursued as they were intertwined. This 'distribution-through-growth' (Felker 2015: 140–143) strategy was essentially achieved through the ethno-nationalism of the development plans (NEP, NDP, and NEM) combined with patronage and rent-seeking (Hasli and Jomo 2007).

In the face of historical conjectures—both domestic and international—Malaysian development strategy can be seen as a selective layering of new policies onto old ones, rather than clean breaks with past strategies. The broad trajectory in Malaysian development must therefore be understood in terms of sedimentation rather than metamorphosis. The oscillation of public policy profile between growth and distributional goals was in order to maintain both and therefore sustain its development strategy. The historical trajectory as outlined in the previous chapter can be re-interpreted in this light. Post-independence liberalism was replaced in 1970 with the NEP and its redistributive emphasis through the edifice of *Bumiputera* policies. This rise in ethno-nationalist policies can be understood in the context of contemporary increases in racial tensions: shifting relative autonomy as a result of the expression of power through ethnic domination. In the context of the 1985 recession, Mahathir facilitated a second shift in the mid-1980s. As sustained GDP growth came under threat, the state was able to shift towards an industrial policy more traditionally associated with the NICs (see Chap. 2), rather than further liberalisation and integration into the global economy.

In 1997 with the onset of the Asian Financial crisis there was a third shift in the Malaysian public policy profile—this time designed to protect the distributive element of its development trajectory. As detailed in the previous chapter, the crisis precipitated a number of bailouts of large, strategic corporations. Given the nature of the NEP and NDP, these corporations were dominated by *Bumiputera* capital and associated 'Super-Bumis'. The systematic bailing-out of these corporations can be interpreted as the state seeking to maintain its ethnic-centred redistributive development goal through selective patronage. Many have pointed out the costly nature of these bailouts, as well as making the point that many of those corporations that went to the wall did so due to poor management practices and corporate governance; there was no real underlying economic rationale for these decisions (Gomez and Jomo 1999). However, in the context of concerns over distribution, the Malaysian state acted.

A number of commentators (see, e.g., Felker 2015; Weiss 2015) have suggested that a fourth shift may be occurring under the premiership of Najib. The NEM and associated suite of policies suggested a pivot towards liberalisation once again. As the previous chapter detailed, some of the *Bumiputera* edifices of positive-discrimination policies began to be dismantled, with the Najib administration seeking to reignite GDP growth to levels seen before the Asian financial crisis (see Tables 7.3 and 7.4). More effective state intervention has been pursued through reforming the public sector and liberalising selectively, whilst continuing to assert the state's central role in guiding development through new strategic investments. Najib has faced an interesting dilemma, however. On the one hand, the more hard-line elements of the UMNO have pushed back against even partial dismantling of *Bumiputera* rights, leading to some important climbdowns on policies such as *Bumiputera* thresholds for employment. On the other, the *Bersih* movement and associated rise in civil society activism (see the previous chapter) have worked as a powerful and growing counter to these traditional policies of redistribution.

Monetary policy has complemented these shifts. Commitment to price stability and exchange rate stability in the NEP era was linked to the FDI-led EOI trajectory of the Malaysian economy; encouraging investment and allowing growth of key strategic sectors. In the face of the 1985 recession monetary policy was eased, in line with Mahathir's broader objective of re-stimulating economic growth in the wake of declining global commodity prices. Managed depreciation of the Ringgit was combined with select liberalisation and privatisation to stimulate a desired economic recovery.

In the wake of the Asian financial crisis monetary policy embraced 'unorthodox' (at least in the eyes of the IMF) capital controls combined with a (temporary) fixed exchange rate. This offers important insight into the influence of World Order at higher levels of structuration (see Chap. 3). The IMFs role in the Asian financial crisis has been much criticised *ex post facto*, not least by the former Chief Economist to the World Bank and Nobel laureate Stigltz (2002). The iconic photo of Camdessus (then Managing Director of the IMF) leaning over Suharto (the Indonesian dictator) who is signing Indonesia's bailout agreement represent a powerful image of the power of the IMF, and World Order more broadly over states. However, the contingent nature of this power and its characterisation as more limiting the room for manoeuvre rather than absolute control can be seen in Malaysia's response. At that time capital controls were not considered by the IMF to be appropriate, but could not prevent Malaysia from implementing them, along with the associated fixing of the Ringgit exchange rate.

In contrast, the monetary response to the global financial crisis was more conservative, although rather than a product of international factors such as IMF (or other agents of World Order) power, this can be seen as a more state-initiated policy. As a result of wider reforms in the wake of the Asian financial crisis, Malaysia's financial sector was much more robust in 2007 than it was in 1997. The led to a much more muted impact on Malaysia's economy, and therefore did not require such a stringent response in order to maintain the twin goals of economic growth and redistribution.

Malaysian fiscal policy also complemented the oscillations between economic growth and redistribution. Whilst adherence to fiscal conservatism led to tight budgetary control over operating expenditures—with operating expenditure rarely exceeding revenue—development expenditures and 'off-budget activities' expanded significantly under the

NEP (Meesook 2001). This fiscal stance injected tax and other sources of revenue into fuelling policy thrusts associated with economic expansion through state support of strategic sectors and positive discrimination policies towards ethnic Malay's. As concerns rose over attracting international capital in the wake of the 1985 recession fiscal policy tightened, with surpluses maintained between 1993 and 1997 (see Table 7.2). This was in order to maintain economic growth through gaining the confidence of international capital markets, thus helping ensure a continued flow of FDI.

In the wake of the Asian financial crisis there was a prolonged fiscal expansion (see Table 7.3). In order to protect the redistributive element of the development strategy, large bailouts were funded. Simultaneously, counter-cyclical spending helped GDP growth recover, although never to pre-crisis levels (see Table 7.4). A similar pattern was seen after the global financial crisis, although with the key differences of that stimulus being more focused on the private sector (rather than SOE bailouts), and withdrawn much earlier. This was in the context of the NEM, which itself had led to the pendulum swinging once again back to focus on GDP growth after the prolonged post-(Asian financial) crisis focus on shoring-up redistribution.

In summary, Malaysia's development trajectory has been fundamentally driven by the state. Several pivots or oscillations can be discerned between growth and distributional goals. The common thread that underpins this political economy is that it has been the state that has promoted development (and then claimed the credit), 'rather than either the demands of market competition or the rise of liberalising social conditions' (Felker 2015: 144). This reveals that the state's development goals of economic growth and redistribution have not been mutually contradictory; they have been pursued simultaneously. Furthermore, these pivots identified above have led to a 'selective layering of new policies onto old ones, rather than clean breaks with prior strategies' (Felker 2015: 141). Finally, it must also be noted that changes in economic strategy have not been matched with deep changes in governance. The BN, with UMNO leading, has been in power every year since independence.

Public policy profiles offer an understanding of how power is being exercised in any given Developmental Regime. In order to develop a more complete understanding, it must also be explored why these policies are being pursued. Examining the nature of those policies themselves and who benefits, as this section has outlined, offers a starting point; clearer insight into understanding the nature of Malaysia's relative autonomy over time can be generated through examination of the socio-economic relations that underpin Malaysia's Developmental Regime, as well as attendant institutions and processes of institutionalisation. It is to this task that the rest of the chapter now turns.

Socio-Economic Relations

Malaysian political economy has been fundamentally shaped by an ethnocentric agenda. The strength of an understanding of power that goes beyond overly agent-centric or structural conceptualisations, as well as recognising that domination emerges from a number of factors, is demonstrated. Due to the historic specificity of Malaysia's development trajectory, power has manifested and expressed itself overwhelmingly through an ethnic lens. This stands in contrast to Argentina, where a very different colonial experience led to domination being expressed through alternative structures. The Developmental Regime approach is capable of mapping out the contours of power and concomitant strategically selective terrain that is (re)constituted through actor's expressions of agency. That agency is necessarily expressed through various lenses of power, or domination. In the context of Malaysia, its state project of developmentalism can only be understood in the context of ethnocentric expressions of power as domination. Malaysia can therefore be characterised as pursuing a social contract based on development defined as economic growth. This must be further qualified by the understanding that the largest portion of the proceeds of this new growth would go to the *Bumiputera* sections of Malaysian society, rather than being split along other socio-economic lines such as poverty and unemployment.

In the Malaysian context, the role of the state in the economy cannot be disaggregated from the centrality of the ethnic agenda in Malaysian political economy. The institutional reflections of *Bumiputera* policies as outlined in previous sections generate systemic intervention in the market by the state. The principles upon which such intervention is based are grounded in an ethnic agenda, not a social one. Characterisation of this intervention within an understanding of power restricted to class dimensions is therefore inappropriate. Furthermore, the opposition's desire to dismantle these institutions is not only as a result of a policy grounded in principles of social domination. Rather, it is a necessary part of the process of removing ethnic Malay privilege and special rights. This in turn could be interpreted as a desire to foster equality of opportunity. However, the desire to dismantle *Bumiputera* privileges by opposition is not directly part of a broader political pursuit of equality of opportunity in social terms; instead, it should be seen once again as part of the broader suite of policy proposals designed to foster ethnic equality.

This conclusion is further justified when the gap between the rhetoric of the NEP and NDP and the reality on the ground is taken into account. As previous sections demonstrated, the reality of almost 40 years of *Bumiputera* policies has been the fostering of ethnocentric development, where well-connected elites are given special access to restricted markets. Crony Capitalist elements of this model reached a peak in the aftermath of the 1997–1998 Asian financial crisis, with multiple controversial 'bailouts' of Malaysian companies owned and run by influential Malay elites (Wong et al. 2005). Therefore, the reality on the ground in Malaysia of the promotion of an ethnic agenda has been strong economic growth and poverty reduction, but simultaneously the creation of an Ersatz Capitalism whose main beneficiaries have been the 'Super-Bumis' (see the previous sections).

Such an agenda cannot be encapsulated by attempting to frame these dynamics within an understanding of power solely situated in class domination. The political debate is not that of a large state to help facilitate material equality versus a small state that restricts itself to provision of an equality of opportunity through establishing the rule of law and the principle of private property. Instead, the large state sector in Malaysia is the product of a need to institutionalise the governing party's *Bumiputera* agenda. Subsequent opposition to this emerges from and is framed in the same context, i.e. a desire to dismantle ethnic privilege.

Malaysian political economy since the introduction of the NEP has been dominated by a developmentalist agenda. This here is defined as 'the existence of a dominant developmental discourse and on the necessity of industrialisation and of state-intervention to promote it' (Woo-Cumings 1999: 13). The pursuit of such an agenda once again cannot be disaggregated from the ethnic agenda of the Malaysian state. The ethnic contract that has dominated Malaysian politics to the present day has been one where pre-existing colonial wealth structures have not been attacked—through, for example, redistributive taxation—but where the proceeds from new post-colonial growth have been overwhelmingly channelled to the *Bumiputera* sections of Malaysian society.

This is key to understanding the basis of Malaysia's ethnic contract. Proceeds of new growth were redistributed overwhelmingly to ethnic Malay elements of Malaysian society. Existing wealth and capital distribution were left largely untouched, and was dominated by ethnic Chinese elements of Malaysian society (Islam and Chowdhury 2000). This facilitated their acquiescence. Chinese elements (and also the smaller ethnic South Asian groups in Malaysian society) were in possession of most Malaysian capital immediately after de-colonisation. Radical redistribution of this capital was not pursued by the Malay dominated state—a policy that has been maintained by subsequent Malaysian government's in exchange for which they pursued a *Bumiputera*-focused suite of positive discrimination policies—funded by state-led developmentalism. In order for such an ethnic contract to work the level of economic growth has to be relatively high, and maintained over time. Thus the wealth generated by this growth in economic activity was sufficient to lift vast swathes of the Malay population out of poverty and into a middle class who owe their position to the state and its associated suite of *Bumiputera* policies (Tyson et al. 2011: 177).

The legitimacy of the Malaysian state is therefore grounded in a developmentalist paradigm. Lack of substantive democracy (see the previous chapter) means that legitimacy cannot be derived from a popular mandate. Instead, it is derived from an ability to deliver economic growth, and through *Bumiputera* policies stimulate the formation of a Malay middle class that has a stake in the maintenance of existing state institutions and therefore in the maintenance of stability. In order to generate sustained economic growth over time in the context of a lack of democratic legitimacy, whilst at the same time ensuring the proceeds from this development are channelled to the Malay elements of society, the Malaysian state has pursued a very specific strategy. This strategy has led to a highly dualistic economy: an export sector that is dynamic, competitive, operates in a liberal trading regime and is dominated by foreign capital; combined with a more domestic orientated sector, dominated by ethnic Malay's, highly protected, and beneficiary of state largesse in the form of subsidies and bailouts (Wong et al. 2005).

Interpreting these dynamics from within a mono-causal framework of power is problematic. Liberalisation of large parts of the export sector has not been driven by a desire to roll back the state but as a way of funding other parts of the economy that are used to pursue the state's ethnic agenda. The political opposition's desire to dismantle the domestic protection present throughout large swathes of Malaysia's economy is not out of a desire to realise a principle of equality of opportunity, rather it is seen as a necessary part of removing the ethnic agenda of the state. Therefore, ethnic politics dominates the motivations and aspirations of politicians, politics, and Malaysian society—not a more traditional, perhaps Western-centric, focus on other sources of domination in politics such as class.

The interweaving of a strategy of developmentalism, the pursuit of an ethnic agenda, and the subsequent implications for Malaysian democracy demands further investigation of the role of civil society in Malaysia. Generally, the government, including the Prime Minister, does not set a high priority on expressions of agency outside of the ethnic framework in Malaysian democracy. Indeed, the government is of the view that opposition parties and civil society's activists, often encouraged by foreign countries and organisations, are a hindrance to the country's economic development and jeopardise its stability (Milne and Mauzy 1999). Former Prime Minister Mahathir Mohamad has argued that the activities of movements in civil society that tend to meddle in politics should be curbed as they clearly aim to weaken government authority and do not contribute to the public good. The government is of the opinion that opposition parties and Non-Governmental Organisations (NGOs) should be closely monitored as they have the ability to influence public opinion, endanger public order and even obstruct well-planned, national development. The state has labelled advocacy-oriented NGOs together with the organised left, dissident student movements, labour groups, and opposition political parties an 'internal other' against whom society must struggle to remain peaceful, unified, and secure. Before, NGOs and other dissident groups were labelled 'communist'; now, they are lambasted as 'Western' or 'non-national'. For instance, former Federal Territory Minister Abu Hassan Omar declared in December 1986 that 7 groups—2 opposition parties and 5 NGOs—were out to destroy 'the country's political and social fabric' (Tan and Singh 1994). Thus, the role of this group in politics is so essential to ensure the smoothness of democratic system in Malaysia, credibility of the judiciary, effectiveness of the police institution, and media. The political organisation is likely to be seen as the group that will maintain effectiveness and efficiency of all those political institutions for the public good, although they will probably face a risk of government's sanctions.

As analysed in the previous chapter, this official state attitude towards elements of Malaysian society has led to many of these organisations and movements to gravitate towards the opposition coalition, led by Anwar Ibrahim. The opposition movement, defined as the coalition of opposition political parties combined with much of Malaysia's nascent civil society organisations, is therefore associated with pressure for greater democratisation. Democratisation here is not just in terms of formal electoral reform such as ending the extreme gerrymandering practices of the state to ensure continued Malay political hegemony (The Economist 2012a) but also in broader terms of deliberative democracy and civil society involvement in the decision-making processes of the state. In other words, democratisation is understood as a fundamentally contested, ongoing process with particular resonance for democratic institutions and their development in Malaysian society. This factor will be explored more in the following section on institutions.

This alliance between political parties and civil society movements in other parts of the world in order to promote deeper democratisation such as Latin America is very much associated with a more class-based politics, with pink tide governments across the continent responding to pressures from civil society and translating into constellations of public policy profiles associated with pro-poor growth, indigenous rights, reformed corporatist practices, and macroeconomic policy (Cannon and Kirby 2012). In the context of contemporary Malaysia, such dynamics cannot be discerned. The demand for greater democratisation from opposition political parties and their civil society allies is seen as synonymous with the dismantling of the *Bumiputera* regime. Therefore, once again, the whole agenda and process is linked to the debate around a Malaysian ethnic contract, rather than a social contract. Facilitating an invigorated process of democratisation in Malaysia is not the result of societal pressures concerned with equality of opportunity versus material equality in any socio-economic sense, as in contemporary Latin America, for example (Ferrero 2014). Rather, it is concerned with a desire to incorporate social movement demands for a dismantling of an ethnically driven agenda. The subsequent fostering of any social contract post-*Bumiputera* could facilitate a transition of Malaysian relative autonomy that would in turn allow an examination of Malaysia's development trajectory from alternative patterns of power and domination. However, whilst Malaysian state–society relations are grounded in an ethnic contract rather than a social contract, this exercise is not appropriate.

Institutions

Mainstream analysis of Malaysian political economy stresses the broad continuity of competent macroeconomic management and relative international openness; with the development strategies (see the previous chapter) providing the policy and political conditions under which such a model could flourish (see, e.g., Hill 2012). This has been critiqued, particularly in the post-crisis period, as being more about favourable international circumstances rather than capacity, particularly in the context of the many costly failures and bailouts in the aftermath of the Asian financial crisis (Gomez and Jomo 1999; see also the previous chapter). As analysis from the previous chapter shows, the evolution of Malaysian state capacities under the aegis of developmentalism have facilitated significant and sustained economic growth and poverty reduction—particularly among the ethnic Malay elements of the Malaysian population. Therefore, an account of those institutions, and how they have been forged through the agency of different actors operating on strategically selective terrain, becomes imperative.

In order to understand the changing nature of Malaysian state capacities, and how they influence and are influenced by underlying relations of power understood as domination, this final section will analyse Malaysian institutions. Consideration of state-level institutions will engage not only in the myriad developmental initiatives and their attendant institutional forms, but also how democratisation and the associated discourse of Asian Values in Malaysia have facilitated specific developmental capacities in the Malaysian context. This analysis will then be complemented with a focus on regional institutions—namely the Association of South-East Asian Nations (ASEAN)—and the nature of regional governance that emerges from such forms. Finally, global level institutions will be discussed, with a focus on the evolving relationship with International Financial Institutions (IFIs) such as the IMF.

State-Level Institutions

As previously analysed the state acts as the institution that is primus inter pares in terms of analytical focus. It is the site where social conflicts are played out, and concomitant processes of institutionalisation help reveal the outcome of those conflicts through analysing the power relations present and understanding the institutional contours that emerge as part of agent's strategic selectivity. In the Malaysian case, the key institutional variable has been the changing nature of democracy and processes of democratisation within the state. Furthermore, other institutional arrangements—chiefly those concerning the capacity to implement developmental imperatives—represent an important opportunity to further develop an understanding of 21st century developmentalism in that country.

Institutionalisation of Malaysian Developmentalism

As the previous chapter argued, the fostering of key state capacities through institutionalisation of developmentalist visions has been key to sustained economic growth in the Malaysian context. From the NEP onwards each new developmentalist drive by the state has been matched by an attendant reformulation of key institutions. The evolution of the DAU to the ICDAU and then the MAMPU is a case in point. The DAU saw its powers and role expand significantly when it became the ICDAU in order to help facilitate the ambitious goals of the NEP. As the ethnocentric timbre of the NEP came to fruition, the ICDAU was transformed into the MAMPU in order to help maintain the significant gains made in terms of developing Malaysia's capacities to sustain FDI-led EOI development.

The NDPC and its place in the state apparatus was also key. In a similar vein to MITI in Japan or the EPB in South Korea, the NDPC stood at the heart of government, was chaired by the chief secretary to the government, and was responsible for central coordination of Malaysia's NEP. This command and control function facilitated a strong steering capacity on the part of central government, that gave it the institutional capacity to direct developmental imperatives and ensure the processes of reforms throughout the period were constantly and consistently directed towards its overarching FDI-led EOI developmentalist strategy.

The Malaysian state was also adept at changing and reforming its key institutions, and therefore its developmental capacity, in the face of changing circumstances—both at home and abroad. Declining FDI abroad combined with declining revenues at home led Mahathir to shift policy focus away from ethnic redistribution towards (re)stimulating economic growth. This changing public policy profile (see the previous section as well as the previous chapter) was underpinned and facilitated by a changing institutional matrix. The desire to stimulate growth through FDI—particularly in the export sector—was matched with a series of administrative reforms under to umbrella of NPM. However, this reform was not sweeping and complete, with significant elements of the *Bumiputera* edifice remaining intact. What this facilitates is a representation of the agency of the state being restricted by the strategically relational terrain upon which it was operating. In other words, an understanding of the form and function of Malaysian institutions can only be realised through an understanding of how state agents react to changing events, yet those reactions and their nature are fundamentally shaped by the character and form of existing institutions and the concomitant capacities that they underpin.

Similar dynamics can be observed in the post-Asian financial crisis period. Ethnic Malay concerns came to the fore in the wake of the Asian financial crisis, with fiscal and monetary policy designed to help alleviate the worst impacts of the crisis on those groups in particular. The Central Bank underwent institutional reform to help it conduct its remit in the face of these changing priorities—such as better financial risk management and the use of forward guidance—as well as a series of state-led reforms to the plethora of SOEs in the Malaysian economy. Whilst controversial, these bailouts helped stabilise the Malaysian economy, as well as stabilising the social relations within Malaysia as ethnic Malay elements were once again prioritised.

The introduction of the NEM in 2010 also represents another swing of the Malaysian developmental pendulum, with a concomitant shift in its underlying institutional structures. With the NEM shifting focus to a more technologically sophisticated development model, the institutions of the state that would generate the capacity to implement this changing public policy profile once again were reformed. The GTP and the ETP were monitored by the EPU, which adopted the role of central coordinator of the NEM efforts to realise Mahathir's original Vision 2020. However, and once again, the agency of these institutions was limited by the strategically selective terrain that represented the institutional residue of former efforts and state-led development. Therefore, whilst the EPU EPU stressed the need to have more sustainable fiscal policies (given steadily rising debt to GDP ratios—see the previous chapter) in the context of attracting foreign capital, this was never realised in the context of a need to maintain spending levels in order to help maintain significant poverty reduction successes, in particular within the Malay community. Or, the creation of Ekuinas: a private equity fund for Malay capital that was supervised directly by the EPU. This can be interpreted as an attempt to forge ahead with broader NEM reforms, whilst maintaining elements of the *Bumiputera*-focused development model through such favourable practices.

A final area for analysis in the context of state-level institutions associated with Malaysian developmentalism is concerning the official political opposition in the form of Anwar Ibrahim and the *Pakatan Rakyat*. The broadly intolerant attitude to political opposition in Malaysia—as detailed in the previous chapter—has led to a series of institutional reforms at the political party level. Whilst there has been extraordinary continuity in the institutional make-up of the ruling coalition the BN, the rise of the *Pakatan Rakyat* and its stressing of a discourse of democratisation and engagement with civil society represent a challenge to the hegemony of the BN. These developments deserve close attention and are clearly tied to the role of democracy and democratisation in Malaysia. These important dynamics will be considered in the next section.

The Role of 'Asian Values'

The maintenance of authoritarianism in Malaysia has been justified and legitimised through reference to 'the threat of ethnic conflict and the necessity of making such political sacrifices in the interests of political stability, ethnic harmony, economic redistribution, economic growth and accelerated modernisation, especially industrialisation' (Gomez and Jomo 1999: 3). Such arguments conform to the developmental state literature more broadly. For example, Johnson (1982, 1987) has argued that whilst there is no necessary connection between the developmental state and authoritarianism there is an 'elective affinity' between the two, echoing the work of O'Donnell (1973) and his analysis of the connection between bureaucratic-authoritarian regimes in Latin America and their emphasis on heavy industrialisation. This elective affinity that Johnson (1982, 1987) refers to is based on a belief that developmental imperatives can often contradict the interests of powerful sections of society who benefit from the status quo, and therefore a system in which the government is insulated from these interests allows for the stable, long-term economic policies required for sustained economic development to be realised. In other words, due to the lack of perfect mobility of factors of production, development leads to obsolescence, unemployment, and changes in income differentials (Chang 1999: 196–198). This makes the development process potentially very conflictual and authoritarian government allows the state to stand separate from or above society and therefore be able to direct the development process.

These arguments have also been complemented with the use of an 'Asian Values' discourse. 'Invoking different values for Malaysians in particular and Asians more generally, Prime Minister Mahathir has dismissed the assumption that the Malaysian political system should aspire to and evolve in the direction of a Western model of liberal democracy' (Gomez and Jomo 1999: 3; see also Case 2004: 125). Therefore, '"Asian Values"... invoked as a form of developmentalism... until prosperity is achieved, democracy remains an unaffordable luxury... This Protestant-ethic-like form of "Asian Values" attributed high growth rates to hard work, frugality, discipline, and teamwork which only a "disciplined" (i.e. authoritarian) regime could provide during the early stages of development' (Thompson 2004: 1086).

In Malaysia, such an Asian Values discourse was also used to justify authoritarianism after developmental goals had been substantially achieved (Thompson 2004: 1092). Mahathir has argued that '... since "Asian political culture" emphasises loyalty to the collectivity over individual freedom and needs, shuns adversarial relations and favours order over conflict, the Western understanding and practice of liberal democracy is inappropriate in the Asian context' (Pye 1985; see also Mahathir 2011: 598). However, such arguments ignore the historical fact of suppression of political rights over time in the post-colonial era; suppression that has gradually socialised Malaysian's to accept and even appreciate authoritarian rule, norms, and institutions (Gomez and Jomo 1999: 4). 'Subservience and community' have thus been used by the state in Malaysia as a weapon of political control (Islam and Chowdhury 2000: 65).

Since the Mahathir era, there has certainly been a shift in emphasis and rhetoric away from an antagonistic attitude to the global human rights agenda that the Asian Values discourse is designed to undermine; although not necessarily an attendant shift in policy. For example, Prime Minister Abdullah (2003–2009) commissioned a review of human rights (a Royal Commission to Enhance the Operation and Management of the Royal Malaysian Police), but failed to implement many of its recommendations—in particular the establishment of an Independent Police Complaints and Misconduct Commission (IPCMC), largely as a result of internal pressures from the UMNO (Liu 2015: 294–295). Indeed, this (lack of) institutional reform conforms to the 'BNs modus operandi during times of political crisis—invoking the ISA [Internal Security Act] to censor discussions deemed "too sensitive" in a multi-ethnic society and raising the "spectre of racial conflict" as a form of regime maintenance' (Liu 2015: 296).

Under the administration of Najib (2009–present) there was again an initial commitment to human rights reform. In 2011, it was announced that the ISA and Sedition Act would be repealed, which were in April 2012. However, the ISA was replaced with the Security Offences (Special Measures) Act (SOSMA) 2012. Whilst this new Act introduced improvements in some areas, it also imposed more restrictions in others. For example, whilst imprisonment without charge or trial was arrested (from over 2 years under the ISA to 28 days under the new Act), but this was combined with a broadening of police apprehension and surveillance powers (Spiegel 2012). Therefore, whilst Mahathir's successors have not been as outspoken as him in their defence of 'Asian Values', successive administrations have continued to invoke the argument that 'collective' and 'community' rights should be prioritised over civil liberties (Liu 2015: 298).

Constructions of an imaginary Asian political culture through political discourse have facilitated a number of important characteristics of Malaysian political economy important to the analysis of Malaysian institutions and an associated developmental mode of political economy. For Islam and Chowdhury (2000: 78–79) '... [in] adhering to the unsubstantiated view that there are distinctive Asian values that promote economic growth, political leaders expose their polities to the risk that ideas and human ingenuity—the wellsprings of innovation-driven growth—are insufficiently recognised and rewarded. Ideas and human ingenuity are not simply market-driven outcomes. They require a conducive institutional context characterised by a robust civil society, free-flowing information, debate, and dissent'. Therefore, due to the authoritarian governments need to push an agenda based on promoting a subservient Asian Values discourse in order to perpetuate its own power, economic growth through productivity gains in Malaysia were suppressed thus affecting the long-run growth trajectory of the country as input-driven growth without concurrent improvements in productivity led to long-term diminishing returns.

This represents an interesting dilemma for the Malaysian state. Progress towards a more appropriate human rights agenda, and associated processes of democratisation, has been very slow in the context of the government's continuing rhetoric of the need to curtail some liberties on the grounds of economic development, national security, and public stability. Yet, transition towards a high-value-added model of development—as well as seeking to understand development as not solely about economic growth—is arrested by such attitudes. With the Malaysian development agenda underpinned by its particular ethnic relations, the patterns of previous modes of political economy and associated development trajectories have created strategically selective limits for subsequent administrations. These strategically selective limits seem particularly entrenched in the context of the above analysis, and largely explain the general understanding of Malaysia's human rights and democratisation agenda as a case of progress and retrogression.

Regional Institutions

Regional institutions and attendant processes of institutionalisation in Malaysia and the South-East Asian region in general have been relatively nascent in comparison with the Argentine and Latin American experience. Whereas Latin America in general, and Argentina specifically, is ensconced in a number of regional enterprises and concomitant processes of regionalisation and regionalism, Malaysian regionalisation and regionalism has been largely restricted to the activities of ASEAN. Two developments in this area are of relevance to the current analysis, and will be investigated in this section: namely, the role of ASEAN in the development of Malaysia's human rights agenda as discussed in the previous section, and the role of ASEAN in facilitating Malaysia's broader developmentalist agenda in terms of trade and investment.

In 2009 ASEAN established the ASEAN Intergovernmental Commission on Human Rights (AICHR). The commission reaffirmed the 'ASEAN Way' of non-interference in other member's internal affairs, decision-making by consensus rather than some form of qualified majority voting, and respect of principles of cultural and regional particularities in relation to human rights. However, its very existence signals that developments in ASEAN in this form represent some form of shift in state's acceptance of human rights discourse in the region—albeit with a view to steer rather than direct. This is a similar dynamic to the creation of the Human Rights Commission of Malaysia (SUHAKAM). This Commission was set up in 1999 in the wake of human rights abuses during the *reformasi* era. The independence and effectiveness of the Commission has been questioned as the state has largely ignored many of its recommendations, but its establishment can be understood as a response to external pressures and influences, especially when linked with local struggles (López 2001).

The second area of concern for understanding the role of regional institutions in Malaysia's development trajectory is in the area of trade and investment. Two recent landmark ASEAN undertakings have come during the (rotating) chairmanship of ASEAN by Malaysia (Koon 2015: 411). First, the ASEAN Economic Community (AEC). The vision of the AEC is to develop a regional trading bloc that is 'highly integrated and cohesive; competitive, innovative and dynamic; with enhanced connectivity and sectoral cooperation; and a more resilient, inclusive, and people-oriented, people-centred community, integrated with the global economy' (AEC 2015). The second undertaking was the ASEAN-led Regional Comprehensive Economic Partnership (RCEP). This is a proposed free-trade agreement (FTA) between the existing members of ASEAN and the six states that ASEAN has an existing FTA with (Australia, China, India, Japan, South Korea, and New Zealand).

The relationship between Malaysia and regional institutions aids understanding of the relationship between regional- and state-level governance. Malaysian policy in this area has been to shape regional institutions such as ASEAN and its different constituent parts towards complementing its developmentalist agenda: a focus on free trade and international investment as key drivers of its GDP growth. This has led to the AEC and RCEP initiatives as analysed above, which are clearly designed to burnish the free-trade credentials of ASEAN. This shows the mutually reconstitutive relationship between the regional and state levels as understood through the theory of structuration. Malaysia is clearly able to influence the agenda of ASEAN and has sought to do so in terms of its own developmental imperatives associated with export of its manufactures and FDI in its key industries. The non-presence of the kind of post-hegemonic regional institutions that have been witnessed in Latin America (see the previous chapters on Argentina) can also be understood in these terms. Hegemonic regionalism in South-East Asia is weak, as neoliberal principles of free trade have yet to take hold in the same manner as say MERCOSUR or the North American Free Trade Association (NAFTA). Therefore, Malaysia specifically, and South-East Asia in general, had historically been absent from regional trends towards greater free trade. Malaysia has been able to use its regional status to shape the nascent regional agenda in South-East Asia towards its developmental imperatives. The construction of the regional infrastructure in relation to Malaysian imperatives has elided the need to construct post-hegemonic regional structures in the same vein as those institutions that have emerged in contemporary Latin America.

Global Institutions

Malaysia's relationship with global institutions has oscillated between engagement and resistance. The relationship between Malaysia and the IMF in the wake of the Asian financial crisis is an important case in point. Mahathir blamed the crisis on the West and took stances that were decidedly anti-Western: most notably in his attitude towards the IMF. In ignoring IMF policy advice relating to capital controls in the wake of the Asian financial crisis Malaysia clearly rejected the IMF drive towards an orthodox response. Initially conforming to IMF policy advice Malaysia experienced significant outflows of capital and attendant destabilisation of its core mode of political economy, only to then execute a *volte-face* and install significant (although only temporary) capital controls—in a similar vein to Chile's capital controls in the wake of regional crisis in Latin America in the preceding decade.

That Malaysia was able to resist the IMF and instead install a series of (temporary) capital controls not only facilitated a cushioning of the most egregious effects of the crisis, but also demonstrate the limiting but not absolutely constraining nature of global institutions on contemporary emerging markets. This conclusion of globalisation presenting room for manoeuvre rather than absolute constraints runs against a more general narrative in the development literature that the IFIs and associated SAPs prevented the evolution of appropriate state capacities in the context of broader societal opposition to IFI induced reforms (Van de Walle 2001: 20).

Whilst Malaysia was not able to use its agency to change the fundamental nature of the IMF—such a task falls to the global hegemon (see Chap. 3)—it was able to create some policy space using its state autonomy to ensure developmentalist principles were not sacrificed on the altar of neoliberal hegemony. Therefore, broader Malaysian policies in this area sought to engage with its own national developmental priorities: demonstrating the appropriateness of the theory of structuration in understanding the evolution of global processes and their impact on national development agendas. Those priorities can be clearly identified as maximising FDI in the midst of both stiff regional competition and somewhat contradictory *Bumiputera* policies; minimising capital flight in the context of regional crisis and competition; improving competitiveness through both internal reform and engagement with the IFIs; and accelerating Malaysia's globalisation process through broader engagement with other institutions such as the WTO and World Bank (Dhillon 2015: 380).

Conclusion: Developmentalism and Malaysia's 'Ethnic Contract'

Malaysia's development trajectory and the political economy that underpins it is dominated by an ethnic agenda associated with state-driven *Bumiputera* policies, substantively present since the introduction of the NEP. This has generated an oscillation between promoting economic growth and promotion of Malay positive discrimination. In reality, both have been pursued simultaneously as the post-independence developmentalist ethnic contract of Malaysia has been centred on redistributing the proceeds of economic growth to the ethnic Malay sections of society, whilst leaving largely intact the ethnic Chinese dominance of existing wealth structures present at the time of independence.

Political and social opposition in Malaysia is framed completely from within this ethnic agenda. Therefore, issues of equality are not debated from a framework of equality of opportunity versus material equality on a social level but on an ethnic level. The appropriate role of the state in the economy is therefore more concerned with the ways in which state intervention helps facilitate an ethnic agenda grounded in consolidation of Malay ethnic political and economic power. Processes of democratisation as understood in terms of state–(civil) society interaction are not grounded in a desire to foster any kind of social agenda that can be linked to political concepts of the Left and Right but as a desire to produce change in the contemporary ethnic agenda.

Due to the lack of Schumpeterian democratic legitimacy in Malaysia, the social contract instead was based on developmentalism. As long as the government could continue to produce strong macroeconomic performance and sustained economic growth, the pressures for democratic reform could be resisted. However, despite very high domestic savings rates, such investment could not be achieved domestically alone. This resulted in a specific characteristic of Malaysian development, the use and encouragement of high levels of FDI. Such (over) reliance on FDI as a source for investment and growth has problems. For example, as Gomez and Jomo (1999: 171) point out '[t]he export oriented industrial sector's reliance on foreign investments, technology, and market access, and Malaysia's limited success in developing its own industrial and technological capacity as well as moving into greater value-added manufacturing renders industrialisation vulnerable and constrains its potential contribution'. Indeed, 'there is a growing consensus that accepting a package of finance, technology, managerial skills, and other capabilities offered by TNCs may not be as good for long-term industrial development as encouraging national firms to construct their own packages using their own managerial skills—with some necessary outsourcing' (Chang 2003: 256). Long-term productive enhancement may be better achieved by an industrialisation strategy that puts emphasis on building local managerial and technological capabilities and uses TNCs in a selective, strategic manner to accelerate that process (Chang 2003: 260).

References

AEC. (2015). *ASEAN economic community blueprint 2025*. http://www.asean.org. Accessed 9 Aug 2016.

Brownlee, J. (2007). *Authoritarianism in an age of democratisation*. Cambridge: Cambridge University Press.

Cannon, B., & Kirby, P. (Eds.). (2012). *Civil society and the state in left-led Latin America: Challenges and limitations to democratization*. London: Zed.

Case, W. (2004). *Politics in South East Asia*. Oxford: RoutledgeCurzon.

Case, W. (2015). Malaysia's unexceptionalism: Like elsewhere, elites are fractious. In M. L. Weiss (Ed.), *Routledge handbook of contemporary Malaysia* (pp. 36–49). London: Routledge.

Chang, H.-J. (1999). The economic theory of the developmental state. In M. Woo-Cummings (Ed.), *The developmental state* (pp. 182–199). New York: Cornell University Press.

Chang, H.-J. (2003). *Globalisation, economic development, and the role of the state*. London: Zed Books.

Dhillon, K. S. (2015). Foreign policy priorities. In M. L. Weiss (Ed.), *Routledge handbook of contemporary Malaysia* (pp. 379–390). London: Routledge.

Felker, G. (2015). Malaysia's development strategies: Governing distribution-through-growth. In M. L. Weiss (Ed.), *Routledge handbook of contemporary Malaysia*. London: Routledge.

Ferrero, J. P. (2014). *Democracy against neoliberalism in Argentina and Brazil: A move to the left*. Basingstoke: Palgrave Macmillan.

Gomez, E., & Jomo, K. S. (1999). *Malaysia's political economy: Politics, patronage, and profits.* Cambridge: Cambridge University Press.

Hasli, H., & Jomo, K. S. (2007). Rent-seeking and industrial policy in Malaysia. In K. S. Jomo (Ed.), *Malaysian industrial policy* (pp. 157–178). Singapore: Singapore University Press.

Hill, H. (2012). Malaysian economic development: looking backward and forward. In H. Hill, T. Sieq Yean & R. Zin (Eds.), *Malaysia's Development Challenges: Graduating from the Middle* (pp. 1–42). New York: Routledge.

Islam, A., & Chowdhury, I. (2000). *The political economy of East Asia: Post-crisis debates.* Oxford: Oxford University Press.

Johnson, C. (1982). *MITI and the Japanese miracle.* Stanford: Stanford University Press.

Johnson, C. (1987). Political institutions and economic performance: The government-business relationship in Japan, South Korea, and Taiwan. In F. C. Deyo (Ed.), *The political economy of new Asian industrialism* (pp. 165–179). Ithaca: Cornell University Press.

Koon, H. P. (2015). A maturing partnership. In L. Weiss (Ed.), *Routledge Handbook of Contemporary Malaysia*, Routledge: London.

Liu, J. (2015). Civil liberties in contemporary Malaysia. In M. L. Weiss (Ed.), *Routledge handbook of contemporary Malaysia* (pp. 290–301). London: Routledge.

López, C. C. (2001). Ideological-structural analysis of external influences on current human rights discourses in Malaysia. *Akademika, 59*(July), 53–73.

Magaloni, B. (2006). *Voting for autocracy: Hegemonic party survival and its demise in Mexico.* Cambridge: Cambridge University Press.

Mahathir, M. (2011). *A doctor in the house: The memoirs of Tun Dr Mahathir Mohamad.* Petaling Jaya: MPH Group Publishing.

Meesook, K. (2001). *Malaysia: From crisis to recovery.* Washington, DC: IMF.

Milne, R. S., & Mauzy, D. K. (1999). *Politics under mahathir.* Selangor: Perdana University Press.

O'Donnell, G. (1973). *Modernisation and bureaucratic authoritarianism.* Berkeley: Institute of International Studies.

Pye, L. (1985). *Asian power and politics: The cultural dimensions of authority.* Cambridge: Harvard University Press.

Rahman, A. (2008). Developmentalist state in Malaysia: its origins, nature, and contemporary transformation. In J. M. Nelson & A. Rahman (Eds.), *Globalization and National Autonomy: The Experience of Malaysia* (pp. 27–58). Bangi: Institute of Malaysian and International Studies, Univesiti Kebangsaan Malaysia.

Spiegel, M. (2012). Smoke and mirrors: Malaysia's "new" internal security act. *Asia Pacific Bulletin* (Vol. 167). Washington: East-West Center.

Stiglitz, J. (2002). *Globalisation and its discontents.* London: Penguin Books.

Tan, B. K., & Singh, B. (1994). *Uneasy relations: The state and NGOs in Malaysia* (Vol. 1). Gender and Development Programme, Asian and Pacific Development Centre.

The Economist. (2012a, June 9). *Cracking open the fixed deposits.*

Thompson, M. (2004). Pacific Asia after "Asian Values": Authoritarianism, democracy, and "Good Governance". *Third World Quarterly, 25*(6), 1079–1095.

Tyson, A. D., Jeram, D., Sivapragasam, V., & Azlan, H. N. (2011). Ethnicity, education and the economics of brain drain in Malaysia: Youth perspectives. *Malaysian Journal of Economic Studies, 48*(2), 175–184.

van der Walle, N. (2001). *African economies and the politics of permanent crisis.* Cambridge: Cambridge University Press.

Weiss, M. (2015). *Routledge handbook of contemporary Malaysia.* London: Routledge.

Wong, S. C., Jomo, K. S., & Chin, K. F. (2005). *Malaysian "Bail Outs"? Capital controls, restructuring, and recovery.* Singapore: Singapore University Press.

Woo-Cumings, M. (1999). *The developmental state.* Cornell: Cornell University Press.

CHAPTER 9

Developmental Regimes and Emerging Markets

Introduction

The challenges of state-led development in the 21st century present both an opportunity and a threat to emerging markets. The plethora cases of development torpor or failure demonstrate the need to meet these challenges with reinvigorated understandings of developmentalism in the 21st century. This book has suggested that analysis needs to move away from understandings of development that are grounded in a linear model as envisioned by the Modernisation school; challenging the mainstream use of the term emerging markets in the process. Through an examination of the development experience in both Argentina and Malaysia this book has attempted to show that whilst development paths of individual countries differ—and are clearly grounded in sui generis understandings of that experience in the context of a rich tapestry of history, geopolitics, and experiences of (de)colonisation—common threads can still be highlighted that form the basis of a common framework for understanding developmentalism in the 21st century.

These common threads are best captured using the Developmental Regime framework. This framework seeks to understand 21st century developmentalism through a tripod image; an image that captures the (re)shaping of a state's capacity and (relative) autonomy. Therefore, analysis of socio-economic relations, institutions, and public policy profiles becomes essential. Socio-economic relations are to be understood as expressions of domination. In other words, power becomes a heuristic for

C. Wylde, *Emerging Markets and the State*, International Political Economy Series, DOI 10.1057/978-1-137-55655-4_9

understanding social relations (Smith 2009). Power, and its use, is understood to manifest across a number of spheres: class, ethnicity, religion, status, party, gender, etc. As such, this approach conforms to a (neo) pluralist view. However, unlike (neo) pluralism sections of society understood in these terms are not assumed to have equal access to expressing their domination across time and space. In other words, different agents are able to articulate their interests, and ultimately manifest them in public policy profiles, to different degrees depending upon the nature of the terrain upon which they operate and strategically exercise their agency.

Understanding the shaping of the strategic terrain within which different agents operate requires examination of institutions. The complex and mutually reconstitutive relationship between agency and structure is borne out through such an analysis. Agents are able to express their agency only within the confines of the strategically selective terrain that represents the state structures that they are operating within. Whilst agents clearly are responsible for shaping that terrain, their agency is also restricted by it. This is the source of a stratified social ontology that characterises any understanding of the state as a social relation. Institutionalism and the attendant study of processes of institutionalisation become important in this context. Studies of how social forces make history in specific institutional contexts are clearly necessary to form appropriate analysis of contemporary developmentalism. It facilitates focus on 'complex actors rather than individuals; on actor's interests, identities, action orientations, and resources in specific actor constellations rather than in generic, context-free terms; and on different forms of interaction' (Jessop 2016: 9). Furthermore, it focuses on the emergent logics and dynamics of different institutional orders or functional sub-systems and on the associated asymmetrical opportunities they grant different actors.

Institutionalism represents a necessary yet insufficient analysis. Completion requires an analysis of other substantive aspects of the state: its social bases, state projects, and national-popular objectives. This facilitates an understanding of state power as a contingent expression of a changing balance of forces that seek to advance their respective interests inside, through, and against the state system. This changing balance of forces is mediated institutionally and discursively; i.e. it is conditioned by the specific institutional structures and procedures of the state apparatus as embedded in the wider political system and social relations. Therefore, actors act because of the relational nature of structure and agency—a conclusion grounded in Bob Jessop's Strategic-Relational Approach.

Public policy profiles emerge from this complex and strategic interaction of actor's agency, and the strategically selective terrain upon which they operate. Specific policy thus becomes the condensation of class (and other) forces and how they are able (or not) to express their power within the institutional structures that have also been formed through previous expressions of agency. Public policy tends to coalesce around specific state projects, or hegemonic visions. These elaborate the nature and purposes of the state for the wider social formation and offer general guidelines for conducting state policy. A state project therefore denotes the political imaginaries, projects, and practices that define and regulate the boundaries of the state system vis-à-vis wider society; it seeks to provide the state apparatus thus demarcated with sufficient substantive internal operational unity for it to be able to perform its inherited or redefined socially accepted tasks (Jessop 2016: 86).

This complex understanding of agency and structure must also be contextualised within multiple spatial levels of analysis. In an era of globalisation, there are clearly degrees of interdependence hitherto unknown in global political economy. Yet interdependence is hardly likely to prove politically neutral, in the sense that relations which are interdependent are likely to be far less tractable and amenable to political intervention than those which are more clearly characterised by dependence (Hay 2014: 33). As a result, regional and global forces clearly play a role in shaping state power. Whilst the theory of structuration offers a powerful heuristic for understanding this complex set of interactions, it must be supplemented with an understanding of what happens at the highest level due to the global level being understood as an object without a subject. This book has suggested Robert Cox's concept of World Order is best placed to complete this task. This concept reveals that whilst globalisation clearly imposes structural limits on developing countries, these countries still retain a certain margin of autonomy (Cardoso 2008: 25–26), or what Jose Santiso (2006) has called a 'political economy of the possible'. Globalisation constrains political choices of states, but they do not fully determine them.

On Capacity and (Relative) Autonomy

State capacity and (relative) autonomy are a supplementary tool for understanding the dynamics of a Developmental Regime approach. These are the key variables that distinguish between successful (i.e. developmental) outcomes and unsuccessful (i.e. clientelistic, populist, and neo-patrimonial) outcomes of state intervention in the development process. State autonomy is best defined as the formulation and pursuit of goals that are not simply reflective of the demands or interests of social groups, classes, or society; and state capacity is best defined as the ability to implement goals, especially over the actual or potential opposition of powerful social groups or in the face of recalcitrant socio-economic circumstances (Evans et al. 1985: 9).

Developmental States have historically been viewed as configurations of organisation and action that influence the meanings and methods of politics for all groups and classes in society. In other words (Evans et al. 1985: 21): '...states matter not simply because of the goal orientated activities of state officials. They matter because their organisational configurations, along with overall patterns of activity, affect political culture, encourage some kinds of group formation and collective political actions (but not others) and make possible the raising of certain political issues (but not others)'. Cardoso echoes this concept well when he says that 'one cannot see the state just as an expression of class interests, without recognising that such an expression requires an organisation which, since it cannot be other than a social network of people, exists in its own right and possesses interests of its own' (Cardoso 1979: 51).

Developmentalism and the Developmental State literature that emerged from the study of East Asian experiences generated particular understandings of state capacity and autonomy. Capacity came to be understood in terms of Weberian-style bureaucracies: grounded in meritocratic principles combined with insulation from politics through independent paths for career progression. Organisationally 'pilot agencies' were seen as key, guiding and cajoling different elements of the state apparatus to conform to a singular logic of a strategic mode of capital accumulation. MITI was such an institution in Japan, or the EPB (Economic Planning Board) in the South Korean context. For Ha-Joon Chang these institutional characteristics facilitated the necessary state capacities to generate distinct industrial policies that were able to transcend the issues of crony capitalism and clientelism that plagued the development experiences of so many Latin American countries in the mid-twentieth century.

These capacities were combined with a particular understanding of autonomy. Peter Evan's concept of embedded autonomy departed from Weber by suggesting that whilst the bureaucracies were insulated from specific interests they were simultaneously, and somewhat paradoxically, embedded within specific forms of bureaucratic–business relations. This two-way information flow generated public policy profiles that were the product of business imperatives refracted through the lens of the national interest, as articulated by the state bureaucracy. This was further reinforced through authoritarianism, distilled into Chalmers Johnson's famous dictum about the 'elective affinity' between a Developmental State and dictatorship. The reasoning was that an authoritarian state stood above from and separate to societies and was thus able to direct a development process that, by definition, would be disruptive to the existing social order and would therefore be resisted by the contemporary parvenus. In other words, the authoritarian state possessed the necessary autonomy from the interests of specific class fractions so as to be able to direct state apparatus to forge specific capacities associated with rapid catch-up development.

The central critique of such a view that has emerged is concerning the source of the national interest. Whilst bureaucrats may exercise their power in order to facilitate a national interest synonymous with rapid catch-up development, there is no a priori reason that this must be the case. Or, in the words of Bruce Cumings, the state ends up being seen as a web with no spider. As a result, bureaucratic competence (capacity) combined with authoritarianism and ties with business groups (autonomy) emerge as rather thin reeds to grasp for a comprehensive understanding of successful state-led development. Furthermore, they remain rather reductionist accounts of what could theoretically be represented through myriad different constellations of social relations and institutions.

A national interest that is focused on rapid catch-up development can be articulated by different patterns of social relations, which forge concomitant patterns of autonomy and capacity. From this starting point, a very different understanding of the state can be realised. The study of state capacities becomes the study of institutions and processes of institutionalisation. In understanding the relationship between agency and structure as mutually reinforcing, it can be seen that different agents are able to exercise their agency in the context of a stratified social ontology. Different actors have differing abilities to shape the strategic terrain upon which they are operating, as well as being influenced by that very terrain.

This complex set of relationships is in turn shaped and forged by state autonomy. The reductive nature of Peter Evans' concept of embedded autonomy can be overcome through replacing it with the concept of relative autonomy. Not only does this draw attention to social relations (rather than simply the relations of different social groups with the state), but also to the need for a robust understanding of power. As such, analysing the contours of a state's relative autonomy represents an explanandum, not an explanans. The explanans comes from understanding power, and how domination is expressed across a number of spheres: class, ethnicity, religion, gender, nationalism. Through mapping out the distinct form of power relations across multiple and crosscutting spheres in any given institutional context, the function of attendant institutions becomes clearer. In addition, those institutions and attendant processes of institutionalisation further shape the nature of social domination, due to the mutually (re)constitutive relationship between capacity and autonomy.

Integrating the role of different spatial levels of governance represents the final piece of the puzzle. The theory of structuration represents a powerful heuristic for understanding the complex relationships between different levels of spatial analysis of governance. As a result, state capacities and autonomy are further shaped by agency at governance levels above and below the state. Regional and global institutions influence the 'political economy of the possible' in any given development context. Nevertheless, the state remains primus inter pares in analytical focus. In other words, mapping the contours of state autonomy and capacity remains the central concern; although with the realisation that an accurate map can only be drawn in the context of detailed understandings of how those patterns of domination and expressions of power at spatial levels other than the state influence and shape state capacities and the nature of its relative autonomy.

Developmental Regimes in Argentina and Malaysia

In the context of understanding the state as a social relation it follows that there can be no one theory of the state as such; rather, analysis can only generate a theory of a state in any given time and space. In other words, understanding the state as a form determined condensation of social relationships reveals the constantly changing nature of the state and its inherent institutional flux. Different agents exercise agency through asymmetrical power whilst strategically navigating the terrain (institutions) that has been laid by previous social formations.

A dialectic between agency and structure characterised as mutually reconstitutive is at the heart of this analysis, leading to the need for empirically rich accounts of how states operate in any given spatial and temporal context. The Developmental Regime approach as developed in the first half of this book offers a common framework for understanding states at early stages of capitalist development, one that is grounded in an analysis of social relations of domination. This helps reveal why these states follow certain (non-)developmental paths over others. This successfully combines strong sui generis accounts of state-led capitalist development with the analytical and theoretical rigour of a robust framework for contextualising such state projects.

The two cases that this book analysed were those of Argentina and Malaysia. Whilst both states are at similar levels of capitalist development in broad terms, they are very different states with very different histories, experiences of (de)colonisation, politics, and local geopolitical concerns. Whilst they both represent emblematic cases of developmentalism in the global south, they do so on the basis of very different contemporary insertions into the global political economy. This represents a robust empirical challenge to the efficacy of the Developmental Regime approach. In analysing these two cases through the lens of the Developmental Regime, the changing contours of the state and its concomitant mode of developmentalism can be best understood.

Argentina

Argentina at the turn of the 21st century was emerging from a deep and structural crisis of its dominant mode of capital accumulation: neoliberalism. The *Kirchnerismo* model that was to emerge from this crisis has been characterised as neo-developmental (or *neodesarrollismo*). This represented a bending and moulding of previous modes of capital accumulation present in the Argentine record: namely Peronism and neoliberalism. Peronism broadly conformed to principles of developmentalism as understood during the middle of the twentieth century and were therefore grounded in ISI; the neoliberalism of Carlos Menem (*Menemismo*) in the 1990s was grounded in sound money (taming of hyperinflation experienced at the end of the 1980s), privatisation, trade liberalisation, and attracting foreign capital—particularly FDI.

In the post-crisis period prioritisation of economic growth by the federal government was the central concern, and was realised through the maintenance of twin surpluses in the current account and in the fiscal account. Through an SCRER policy, exports were stimulated to aid in the generation and maintenance of a current account surplus. Whilst agricultural commodities remained the dominant factor in Argentina's export profile, the most dynamic sector of growth up to 2007 were exports of a manufactured origin. This meant that significant portions of that economic growth were independent of the rising terms of trade for agricultural commodities experienced in the global economy at that time. This combined with an industrial policy that used the power of the state to help stimulate key sectors through infrastructure investment and fiscal pump priming. The export taxes generated from these activities, combined with fiscal conservatism on the part of Nestor Kirchner, led to a sustained fiscal surplus up to 2007. Whilst significant anti-poverty policies were maintained or extended (*Plan Jefes y Jefas de Hogar* as well as a series of other *Planes*), and the minimum wage was increased several times, the majority of the reduction in poverty under this administration were more the result of expanding employment in the context of a growing economy.

After 2008, economics in Argentina began to stall. The impact of the global financial crisis was felt primarily through the trade channel and helped facilitate a decline in economic growth in 2009. Counter-cyclical spending by the state helped revive economic growth in 2010, but at the cost of a loss of the fiscal surplus. The current account surplus was eroded significantly as demand for Argentine exports collapsed (in the wake of the global financial crisis), and the surplus became deficit by 2012. This was further exacerbated by a steady appreciation of the Real Exchange Rate in the context of sustained domestic inflation. A series of heterodox economic policies were pursued by the CFK administration that did serve to arrest the declining current account surplus, but this came at the cost of political resistance and an unravelling of the post-crisis Argentine social contract. This was reflected in the breakdown of its meticulously constructed social alliances and slowdown in growth alongside persistently high inflation. This led to the end of the Kirchner project with the election of Mauricio Macri in 2016.

Use of the Developmental Regime framework to contextualise and analyse the precise nature of the series of socio-economic relations and alliances that characterised the Kirchner era, and how those relations formed a mutually reconstitutive relationship with state institutions, represents an original contribution of this book. The linked concepts of capacity and autonomy were used to help reveal the nature of Argentine capacity and autonomy during this period, facilitating an understanding Argentine development as one of *neodesarrollismo*. The complex relationships between Argentina's public policy profile, its institutions, and its socio-economic relations were mapped across multiple levels of spatial analysis in order to trace the contours of Argentina's Developmental Regime.

Malaysia

Malaysia's engagement with broad principles of developmentalism has lasted much longer, and been much more consistently applied than in Argentina. From the post-colonial policies associated with the NEP through to the current NEM, via the NDP, the Malaysian state has applied state-led development plans that have institutionalised ethnic privilege and preferential treatment. This has facilitated a developmentalist model with a distinctive ethnic focus, seeking to redistribute the proceeds of post-colonial state-led development to different sections of the Malaysian population along ethnic lines. Interestingly, whilst the proceeds of new growth have been disproportionately redistributed to ethnic Malays, the existing wealth structures of the ethnic Chinese in particular (who dominated ownership of capital in the colonial period) have not been reformed by the state. This has been the essence of the post-independence Malaysian ethnic contract.

Malaysian political economy in the post-independence era can be seen to oscillate between the twin developmental goals of state-led economic growth through FDI-led EOI, and redistribution of the proceeds of that growth to ethnically Malay elements of Malaysian society. The introduction of the NEP in 1971 can be read as a response to the ethnic tensions that spilt over into riots in 1969. The core stated objectives of reducing poverty and restructuring society so that identification of ethnicity with economic function would be eliminated were clearly in line with this ethnocentric agenda. In the wake of the 1985 recession, Mahathir rebalanced Malaysia's development strategy towards stimulating economic growth; sacrificing a number of *Bumiputera*-focused policies along the way. In 1990, the NDP was introduced, which saw a further swing of the pendulum back towards a focus on redistribution of the proceeds of economic growth along ethnic lines. By 2010, in the context of a global financial crisis and relative stalling of Malaysian progress towards its Vision 2020, the NEM was introduced. This can be seen in terms of another broad swing of the pendulum: away from *Bumiputera*-focused policies once again and towards more economic growth focused policies.

The application of this oscillating policy between a focus on economic growth and a focus on ethno-based redistribution has always occurred under the aegis of state-led developmentalism. Whilst monetary policy and fiscal policy have shifted according to the swings of the pendulum and changing state priorities, those priorities have unerringly been grounded in economic growth and ethnic-based redistribution, with the state as a key actor and institution in this process. As the previous chapter demonstrated, the Malaysian state's institutional matrix has been realigned to suit its oscillation between growth and redistribution in terms of its public policy profile. Furthermore, its ethnocentric development goals and the concomitant social relations that underpin such a model have facilitated the autonomy necessary to drive these state capacities in the same direction. The autonomy to carry out these policies has also stemmed from the non-democratic nature of Malaysian politics, granting the Malaysian state significant room for manoeuvre in terms of its political economy of development. Maintenance of a pseudo-democracy in the face of significant societal developments (particularly in the post-Asian financial crisis context and the rise of the *reformasi* movement) has been achieved partially through a discourse that centres on Asian Values.

The Developmental Regime framework is simultaneously flexible enough to incorporate the ethnic nature of Malaysia's social relations as well as provide useful insights into that model. Despite the fact that Malaysia represents a very different application of developmentalist principles in the discipline of the political economy of development, the Developmental Regime has been able to provide a robust framework for contextualising its social relations, its institutions, and its public policy profile through the related concepts of autonomy and capacity. Such analysis has facilitated an understanding of the Malaysian development experience as one grounded in FDI-led EOI, where the proceeds of this new growth stimulated by coordinated state action has been redistributed to the ethnically Malay elements of the population.

Avenues of Further Research

There is a clear need to continue to refresh our understandings of the specific empirical contexts and experiences of development as we move through the 21st century. In Argentina, the election of Mauricio Macri is a fascinating development. Whether this represents a change in the flavour of Argentine developmentalism (Wylde 2017), or a more significant (re)embrace of neoliberalism (Cantamutto 2017) is a debate that will develop as *Macrismo* becomes increasingly articulated (see also EDI 2016). As this empirical context evolves, the continued efficacy of a Developmental Regime approach will be challenged, facilitating induced theoretical confrontations.

In Malaysia, the recent machinations of Mohamad Mahathir could spell the beginning of the end for Najib, who has also been embroiled in the 1MDB scandal. The implications of this cannot yet be understood, but events and shifting loci of power will always facilitate a changing state autonomy that will need to be contextualised and understood through theoretical lenses. The robustness of the Developmental Regime concept must be tested in the context of these evolving empirical realities, ensuring not only a continually refreshed understanding of development trajectories in emerging markets but also enhance the theoretical sophistication of the model itself.

There are many other emerging markets in the world today. Understanding the unique shape of their specific blend of autonomy and capacity represents an important challenge for academics and researchers to ensure the continued efficacy of the discipline. One way in which this could occur is through systemic application of the Developmental Regime approach to these empirical challenges. Can Brazilian developmentalism from Lula to Rousseff to Temer be understood at a deeper level as a result of application of a Developmental Regime framework? Could Indonesia? Such a research agenda would offer the opportunity for sophisticated analyses of contemporary states that are able to capture the empirical nuances of unique historical structures in national contexts, without descending into sui generis arguments and interpretations. As such, a unifying theoretical framework that is able to capture both the breadth and depth of different development experiences in emerging markets is a valuable agenda to work towards.

References

Cantamutto, F. (2017). *Después del Kirchnerismo: Desafíos del programa de Cambiemos*. Paper presented in panel entitled 'The Cambiemos government in Argentina: A return to 1990s neoliberalism, a break with Kirchnerismo or somewhere in between?' SLAS Annual Conference 2017, Glasgow.

Cardoso, F. H. (1979). On the characterisation of Authoritarian Regimes in Latin America. In D. Collier (Ed.), *The New Authoritarianism in Latin America*, Princeton: Princeton University Press.

Cardoso, F. H. (2008). New paths: Globalisation in a historical perspective. *International Journal of Communication, 2*, 379–395.

EDI. (2016). A dónde va la economía del gobierno Macri? *Anuario EDI.*

Evans, P. B., Rueschemeyer, D., & Skocpol, T. (Eds.). (1985). *Bringing the state back in.* Cambridge: Cambridge University Press.

Hay, C. (2014). Levels of governance and their interaction. In A. Payne & N. Phillips (Eds.), *The handbook of the international political economy of governance.* Cheltenham: Edward Elgar.

Jessop, B. (2016). *The state: Past, present, and future.* London: Polity.

Santiso, J. (2006). *Latin America's political economy of the possible.* Massachusetts: MIT Press.

Smith, M. (2009). *Power and the state.* Basingstoke: Palgrave Macmillan.

Wylde, C. (2017). *The end of neodesarrollismo? The political economy of Argentina under Mauricio Macri.* Paper presented in panel entitled 'The Cambiemos government in Argentina: A return to 1990s neoliberalism, a break with Kirchnerismo or somewhere in between?' SLAS Annual Conference 2017, Glasgow.

Bibliography

Evans, P. B. (2008, December). In search of the twenty-first century developmental state. *CGPE Working Paper Series*, No. 4.

Grugel, J., & Bishop, M. (1991). *Democratization: A critical introduction*. Basingstoke: Palgrave Macmillan.

IMF (2009). World economic outlook database. http://www.imf.org. Accessed 3 Feb 2016.

Koon, H. P. (2014). Malaysia and the United States: A maturing partnership. In M. L. Weiss (Eds.), *Routledge handbook of contemporary Malaysia* (pp. 403–416). London: Routledge.

Ministry of Economy and Production (2008). *Argentine economic indicators*. http://www.mecon.gov.ar. Accessed 16 August 2016.

Ministry of Economy and Production (2015). *Argentine economic indicators*. http://www.mecon.gov.ar. Accessed 16 August 2016.

Panizza, F. (2009). *Contemporary Latin America: Development and democracy beyond the Washington consensus*. London: Zed.

Przeworski, A., & Limongi, F. (1997). Modernization: Theories and facts. *World Politics, 49*(2), 155–183.

Riggirozzi, P. (2012). Reconstructing regionalism: What does development have to do with it? In P. Riggirozzi & D. Tussie (Eds.), *The rise of post-hegemonic regionalism: The case of Latin America* (pp. 17–41). New York: Springer.

UNCTAD (2009). *UNCTADStat*. http://unctadstat.unctad.org. Accessed 25 January 2016.

White, G. (2002). Constructing a democratic developmental state. In M. Robinson & G. White (Eds.), *The democratic developmental state*. Oxford: Oxford University Press.

C. Wylde, *Emerging Markets and the State*, International Political Economy Series, DOI 10.1057/978-1-137-55655-4

Index

A
AEC, 204
AFIP, 152
AICHR, 203
ALBA, 153
Althusser, 74
Amsden, 22, 159
Andaya, 160, 161
ANSES, 152
ASEAN, 89, 197, 203, 204
Autonomy, 1, 5–7, 10–12, 18, 19, 28, 44, 52, 72, 75, 76, 91, 211
  In Argentina, 108, 110, 112, 115, 117, 118, 120, 122, 130, 136, 142, 149, 150, 152–154, 218
  Embedded, 10, 24, 26, 36, 71, 72, 80
  In Malaysia, 7, 172, 173, 177–179, 190, 192, 193
  Relative, 5, 10, 29, 34–38, 52, 60, 64, 71, 72, 75–77, 79–83, 85, 86, 213, 216, 219
Azizuddin, 175, 177

B
BCRA, 100
Beccaria, 100, 112, 113, 131, 140, 141
Bezchinsky, 99, 104, 107, 108, 133
BN, 159, 175, 180, 191, 200, 201
BNM, 164, 168, 172
Bonefeld, 29
Braudel, 78
BRIC(S), 51

C
CAP, 90
Capacity
  In Argentina, 105, 112, 140, 145, 146
  In Malaysia, 159, 160, 170, 171, 180, 186, 193
  theory of, 1, 5, 6, 10, 15, 18, 22–24, 29, 30, 32–34, 38, 46, 52, 54, 55, 71, 72, 77, 79–81, 83, 84, 86, 89–91, 211
Cardoso, 213, 214
Case, 160, 180, 181, 186, 187, 201
Castañeda, 129, 130
Castells, 88
CCT, 91

C. Wylde, *Emerging Markets and the State*, International Political Economy Series, DOI 10.1057/978-1-137-55655-4

CEPAL, 100, 104, 106–110, 117, 118, 131, 132
Cerny, 4, 44, 53, 63, 76
CFK, 11, 97, 116–122, 131, 134–136, 140, 141, 144, 145, 147, 148, 152, 154, 218
CGT, 148, 149
Chang, D., 20, 28
Chang, H.J., 21, 79, 161, 207, 214
Chudnovsky, 49, 98, 99, 101, 106, 142
CONICET, 152
Cox, 5, 11, 53, 55–62, 65, 85
CPI, 111, 162
CPINu, 153

D
DAP, 169, 176
DAU, 166, 198
Democratisation, 2, 59, 84, 151, 152, 177
Dependency, 8, 9, 47, 48
Dos Santos, 9, 48

E
Economist, The, 120, 134, 153, 178, 179, 196
EIU, 105, 109, 132
Emerging markets
  In context of globalisation, 11, 52, 54, 55, 85, 166, 169, 187, 205
  Definition of, 3, 4, 6
  Development trajectories of, 6, 43, 44, 85, 93, 181, 221
EOI, 168, 170, 190, 198
EPB, 198
EPU, 162, 167, 171, 174, 176, 179, 199
ETP, 175, 199
EU, 44, 90
Evans, 10, 18, 22, 24–28, 36, 71, 80, 81, 214, 215

F
FDI, 161, 162, 164, 168, 170, 171, 173, 174, 178
FIC, 179
Fine, 19, 20
Fiscal policy
  In Argentina, 71, 72, 80, 136, 142, 149, 150, 152–154, 218
  In Malaysia, 172, 173, 195–197, 199, 200, 206, 221
  In theory, 50, 91
Foucault, 53, 64
FPV, 102
Frenkel, 106, 107, 110–112, 117, 118, 121, 133. *See also* Rapetti
FTA, 204
FTZ, 164
Fukayama, 58, 62, 83

G
Galbraith, 20, 76
Gamble, 51, 52, 55, 62, 63, 87
GATT, 44, 46, 48, 60
GDP, 1–3, 9, 10, 12, 98, 103, 106–112, 115, 121, 131–133, 135, 136, 160–162, 164, 167, 168, 170–172, 174, 188, 189, 191, 199, 204
GFCF, 104
Gill, 51, 62, 85
Gramsci, 31, 33, 35, 36, 44, 56, 61, 62, 64
Grugel, 2, 49–51, 84, 100, 101, 129–131, 136–144, 146
GST, 176
GTP, 176, 199

H
Haggard, 86, 159
Harvey, 46, 51, 56, 82, 90
Hay, 5, 11, 16, 31, 38, 44, 53, 54, 62, 80, 90
HICOM, 167

I
ICDAU, 166, 198
ICT, 178
IFI, 50, 205
IMF, 44, 46, 50, 59, 60, 65, 145, 146, 150, 153
INDEC
  Corruption in, 119
  Statistics, 104, 112, 115, 117, 120
Inflation. *See* Monetary Policy Investment
Investment, 21, 46, 48, 51, 77, 83, 91, 98, 104, 108, 117, 119, 122, 134, 146, 161, 164, 171
IPCMC, 201
IPE, 52, 116
ISA, 201
ISI, 22, 24, 49, 129, 139, 141, 142, 164, 217

J
Jessop, 5, 16–18, 28–34, 36–38, 53, 55, 64, 74, 75, 81
Jomo, 9, 160, 161, 167, 168, 172, 173, 180, 181, 188, 189, 197, 200, 201, 207

K
Kirby, 196
Kohli, 19, 21, 78
KPI, 176

L
Leftwich, 1, 15, 79, 83, 84

M
Mahathir, 160, 161, 167–175, 179, 189, 190, 195, 198, 199, 201, 202, 205
MAMPU, 166, 198
Marx, 34, 35
MAS, 165, 173
MCA, 159
MERCOSUR, 89, 142, 153, 204
MIC, 159
MITI, 21, 23, 198
MOF, 171, 174
Monetary policy
  In Argentina, 108, 110, 112, 115, 117, 118, 120
  In Malaysia, 172, 173, 177–179, 190, 192, 193
  In theory, 47, 48, 59, 61
MSC, 178

N
NAFTA, 204
NDP, 160, 161, 170, 175, 180, 187–189, 193
NDPC, 166, 198
NEAC, 175
NEM, 160, 175, 176, 179, 187–189, 191, 199, 200, 219
NEP, 160, 161, 163–166, 168, 169, 180, 187–191, 193, 198, 206, 219
NER, 170
NGO, 195
NIE, 50
NPM, 168, 199
NTB, 141

O

O'Donnell, 23, 143
OECD, 2, 3

P

Panizza, 104, 140
PAS, 176
PASO, 148
PJ, 139, 148
PKR, 176
Polanyi, 45, 78
Poulantzas, 28, 29, 31, 35, 38, 82
PPP, 131, 132
PRSP, 50

Q

QCC, 168

R

Rapetti, 106, 107, 111, 112, 117, 118, 121, 133. *See also* Frenkel
RCEP, 204
REER, 118, 120, 132, 170
RER, 111, 118
Riggirozzi, 87–89, 100, 101, 104, 107, 110, 113, 129–131, 136–144, 146, 147, 155

S

SAP, 49, 50, 205
SCRER, 106, 107, 109, 121, 133, 140, 141, 154
SOE, 165, 166, 173, 188, 191, 199
SOSMA, 202
Stokes, 84
Structuration, 5, 11, 44, 53–56, 63–65, 72, 75, 77, 79, 85, 86, 91, 92, 130, 153, 154, 186, 187, 190, 204, 205
SUHAKAM, 203
Svampa, 7, 11, 97, 117, 135, 148

T

TNC, 20, 65, 76, 85, 117, 134, 137, 146, 168, 207

U

UMNO, 159, 169, 173, 175, 178, 179, 189, 191, 201
UN, 60
UNASUR, 153, 155

W

Washington Consensus, 49–51, 87, 129, 130, 151
WMD, 61
World Bank, 2–4, 9, 10, 44, 46, 50, 59–61, 86, 103, 109, 117, 132, 144, 160–164, 167, 171, 174, 190, 206
World Order, 5, 6, 11, 44, 51–53, 55, 56, 59–65, 73, 75–77, 85, 86, 89, 92, 93, 153, 154, 190, 213
WTO, 44, 46, 59, 60, 65, 86, 90, 206

Y

YPF, 119, 122

The manufacturer's authorised representative in the EU is Springer Nature Customer Service Centre GmbH, Europaplatz 3, 69115 Heidelberg, Germany. If you have any concerns regarding our products, please contact ProductSafety@springernature.com

Printed and bound by CPI Group (UK) Ltd, Croydon, CR0 4YY
14/10/2026
02233140-0001